FAT

FAT

A CULTURAL HISTORY
OF OBESITY

SANDER L. GILMAN

polity

Copyright © Sander Gilman 2008

The right of Sander Gilman to be identified as Author of this Work has been asserted in accordance with the UK Copyright, Designs and Patents Act 1988.

First published in 2008 by Polity Press

Polity Press
65 Bridge Street
Cambridge CB2 1UR, UK.

Polity Press
350 Main Street
Malden, MA 02148, USA

ISBN-13: 978-0-7456-4440-0
ISBN-13: 978-0-7456-4441-7(pb)

A catalogue record for this book is available from the British Library.

Typeset in 10.75 on 14 pt Adobe Janson by
Servis Filmsetting Ltd, Stockport, Cheshire
Printed and bound in Great Britain by Biddles Ltd, Kings Lynn, Norfolk

The publisher has used its best endeavours to ensure that the URLs for external websites referred to in this book are correct and active at the time of going to press. However, the publisher has no responsibility for the websites and can make no guarantee that a site will remain live or that the content is or will remain appropriate.

Every effort has been made to trace all copyright holders, but if any have been inadvertently overlooked the publishers will be pleased to include any necessary credits in any subsequent reprint or edition.

For further information on Polity, visit our website: www.polity.co.uk

给我的中国朋友

CONTENTS

INTRODUCTION

SOME WEIGHTY THOUGHTS ON

DIETING AND EPIDEMICS

In November 2005 George W. Bush, then the President of the United States, evoked the influenza pandemic of 1918 as the reason for a massive preparation for a potential world-wide outbreak of avian 'flu. He noted, 'there is no pandemic influenza in the United States or the world, but if history is our guide there's reason to be concerned'. His fear was of the repetition of the pandemic 'which struck in 1918, killed over half a million Americans and more than 20 million people across the globe. One-third of the U.S. population was infected, and life expectancy in our country was reduced by 13 years.' And the proof of the risk, as we shall see in the course of this book was that in the very recent past 'a previously unknown virus called SARS appeared in rural China. . . . It infected more than 8,000 people and killed nearly 800.'[1] Hardly, one can add, a pandemic but an indicator that an older model of illness could be revivified.

But, as one rather shrill book published in 2006 about the potential public health crisis argues, we stand on the brink of disaster. Not only do all forms of infectious disease, from HIV/AIDS to polio, threaten us but 'what if obesity was caused by a virus?'[2]

The parodic implications of such a view were not lost on American satirists. Based on George W. Bush's evocation of a world-wide avian 'flu disaster, comics had a field day. The United States had already been declared to be in the middle of an obesity epidemic. The jokes mounted quickly:

> In a press conference at the White House today, President George W. Bush announced an ambitious plan to slow the potential spread of avian flu by making birds obese. 'Birds spread the flu by flying', the president told reporters. 'So it stands to reason that if birds are too fat to fly, they can't spread the flu.' The president said that he personally developed the strategy for slowing the spread of the deadly flu after realizing that 'obesity is America's secret weapon in the battle for global health'. Mr Bush said that starting next week, government-issued pamphlets would be distributed at such fast-food outlets as McDonald's, Burger King, and Kentucky Fried Chicken, encouraging customers to buy an additional fat-laden meal and feed it to birds. If all goes according to plan, the president said, the global population of birds will be so badly out of shape and easily winded, 'they will only have enough energy to sit around and watch television'.[3]

As we shall see in the course of this volume the odd pairing of the two also makes some kind of historical sense, if we listen to the recapitulation of concerns about risk and the dangers of certain diseases as well as about the efficacy of certain treatments.

But we must remember that this anxiety about epidemics is a recent phenomenon (even though it mirrors the rhetoric of the nineteenth century). As late as 1969 the then Surgeon General of the United States, William T. Stewart, suggested to Congress that it was now 'time to close the book on infectious disease as a major health threat'.[4] Three decades later, in 1996, Gro Harlem Brundtland, the then Director-General of the World Health Organization, gave a very different prophecy: 'We stand on the brink of a global crisis in infectious diseases. No country is safe from them.'[5] We have moved from a sense of accomplishment to one of foreboding.

Parallel to the seemingly unstoppable spread of obesity as a new epidemic was the development of new, radical cures. From the mid-nineteenth century until today, medical specialists and lay practitioners have tried to claim fat people (however defined) as their patients. Would the 'war against obesity' in the late twentieth century be conquered by surgical means (stomach stapling), genetic intervention ('conquering' of the 'obesity-gene'), or would it be the old, tried and true 'cure' of dieting?

Fat, however, is truly in the eye of the beholder. Each age, culture, and tradition has defined acceptable weight for itself, and yet all have a point beyond which excess weight is unacceptable, unhealthy, ugly, or corrupting. Today we call this 'morbid obesity', and it is always seen as an issue of health. Yet health, as we well know, is a code word for a positive range of qualities that any given society wishes to see in its citizens: from beauty to loyalty to responsibility to fecundity (and the list marches on). This is in no way to minimize the health implications of excess weight, but it is also clear, from the extraordinary explosion of public concern and blame associated with obesity, that fat has taken on a new and rather sinister quality over the past century. Obesity is a national rather than an individual problem and that, not only because of epidemiological evidence, but also because of the meanings now firmly attached to an expansive waistline.

Since the 1860s diet culture dominated the marketplace as the appropriate 'cure' for obesity. Bio-medical science developed the tools to understand the biochemical nature of metabolism after the 1830s, yet the claim that weight gain was the result of endrocrinological imbalance rarely dominated the discussion of cure. More recently, even with the claims about human genetics being the underlying cause of obesity, most people still turn to dieting.

Dieting was the tool of the physician, but it was also the means by which lay practitioners of the modern 'health culture' were able to lay claim to fat people (or those who imagined themselves to be fat) as their clients. Dieting or (more recently) 'lifestyle change' became a way to halt the obesity epidemic, to intervene so as to improve the private life of the individual and thus the health of the nation. These two qualities were regularly linked. There were claims that morbid obesity impacted on the health of the mother and child, and thus weakened the state. Others believed that fat people could not fulfill their civic and military duty and became a drain on the state. The obese, from at least the mid-nineteenth century on, were seen as a danger to themselves as well as to others. The general stigma associated with a potentially unhealthy body which stood out because of its size made it imperative that fat people seek treatment. Thus there were financial incentives to seek this group out and to rehabilitate them. Fat people could be made productive and healthy through the interventions of medical professionals, but also through lay specialists.

In France, the modern food culture, without its sauces and exotic ingredients, was created in the 1820s by Jean Anthelme Brillat-Savarin, whose *Physiology of Taste or, Meditations on Transcendental Gastronomy* was this fat man's confession about how he tried to lose weight. It was a self-help book that created the modern French cult of food and France as the 'food nation' *par excellence*.'Obesity', as Brillat-Savarin states, 'is not actually a disease, it is at least a most unpleasant state of ill health, and one into which we almost always fall because of our own fault.'[6] It was a change in the way one ate that could control one's weight.

The American food faddists of the late nineteenth century, who produced 'modern' machine-made foods such as 'corn flakes', sought to reform the body politic. Healthy citizens are better citizens: closer to God and able better to function in the modern world. In the twenty-first century we hear their heirs advocate 'natural' or 'organic' food with many of the same claims. Today their argument is that unprocessed food is close to nature and thus healthier. In 1894, Dr. Will Keith Kellogg was trying to improve the vegetarian diet of his brother's patients at the Battle Creek Sanatorium when he invented Corn Flakes; one patient, Charles William Post, invented the Postum cereal beverage in 1895. Two years later, Post developed the Grape-Nuts cereal, part of the new health-industrial complex. They followed the lead of those who first canned milk during the Napoleonic wars; they saw in the modern manufacture of food the introduction of the principles of hygiene. And they were right – boiled, condensed milk was certainly healthier than milk from tuberculosis-infected cows, if you discounted the lead that leached into milk in the early containers.

All aimed, and aim, at healthier, better citizens. And all succeed in making a profit as they do it. The cereal manufacturers of the nineteenth century, like Post and Kellogg, moved from fringe food-fad operations in 'Wellville' (read T. Coraghessan Boyle's 1993 novel *The Road to Wellville*) to dominating the food market; 'organic' food today may well rescue the small farm, as it returns much greater profit than 'traditional' food. More than a rhyme links health and wealth.

Dieting aims both at cure and at profit. It is thus very modern. To be sure, fasting as a religious observance was part and parcel of western Christianity beginning with Paul. (It also became part of both rabbinic Judaism and Islam.) But religious fasting is not identical with dieting. It was (and is) a sign of man's relationship with God and God's complex world. Ironically, this is not much different from the conception of the ancient Greeks, who saw food (and food reduction) as part of a complex web that spanned human beings and the gods through the humors. Dieting arose in the post-Copernican world when scientists and lay people from the late seventeenth to the early nineteenth century more and more began to think of the human body as a machine and, later, as a collection of chemical processes. For them, the dieting body was not necessarily an extension of the divine.

That modern notions of health and illness are linked is never in doubt. Yet how they are linked is another question. The philosopher Hans-Georg Gadamer noted, 'we need only reflect that it is quite meaningful to ask someone "Do you feel ill?" but it would be quite absurd to ask someone "Do you feel healthy?" Health is not a condition that one introspectively feels in oneself. Rather, it is a condition of being involved, of being in the world, of being together with one's fellow human beings, of active and rewarding engagement with one's everyday tasks.'[7] Thus, if such an argument is followed, one can be physically ill, yet 'healthy'. Friedrich Nietzsche commented long before Gadamer: 'One must comfort the patient's fantasy as he suffers more from the idea of his illness, than from the illness itself.'[8] We sense our bodies only when we imagine ourselves to be ill, and we subscribe meaning to that sense of disease. It is this historically situated sense of health (and illness) that structures our understanding of the dangers present in the world. It is this that cycles in odd and irregular ways through our recent history.

Dieting has become the means of self-liberation or of self-control and self-limitation. It is a process by which the individual claims control over her body and thus shows her ability to understand her role in society. From the Enlightenment to the present, the healthy body is also the body in control of its own destiny – a basic claim of Enlightenment ideology. The aging philosopher Immanuel Kant actually wrote a study of diet and self-control in response to the appearance of one of the first modern diet books in the 1790s. His essay on 'Overcoming unpleasant sensations by mere reasoning' (1797) argued that you could, as an old man, rationally control your frequent trips to the toilet at night by radically restricting your liquid intake before bed.

Mind over body: the key to 'lifestyle changes' in the twenty first century. But now with a twist: you need the social structure to accomplish this because – and now it is Arthur Schopenhauer's turn – fat is also a sign of another disease process: the lack of will. The will becomes that which is healed by the dieting process and enables the rational mind to control the body. Fat is dangerous because it is now globalized, in complex ways, as our Epilogue will show. Fat is now (as smoking was) a sign of the deleterious effect of the modern (read: the American) influence on the body. Indeed the argument in the twenty-first century is that the gains, among the 'elderly', through changes in lifestyle over the past decades such as the abandonment of smoking, will be 'swamped' by the 'disabilities among the young' grown huge and ill through the pernicious effects of food.[9] We have to restore the healthy mind of the youth and thus heal the unhealthy body of society. McDonald weakens the will through advertising. As we shall discover in Chapter 6, childhood obesity in contemporary China is represented as the result of globalization, that is, of Americanization. It is Ronald McDonald who is at fault. This may certainly be true in the growing urban middle class, but is there a concomitant decrease of body weight among children in the countryside? Is it McDonald or the one-child policy and economic 'liberalization' that are at the root of the 'obesity epidemic' in China? Indeed, the very history of the body in modern China is shaped by images of starving and obese bodies. And this history has a formative influence on the very shaping of the national state.

National identity, at least in the course of the nineteenth century, is framed by images of acceptable and unacceptable bodies. And the 'too fat' body is neither that of a healthy nor that of a good citizen. Here it is not the healthy 'stout' but the unhealthy obese that are at fault, as we can see in Chapter 2. Walt Whitman, in the very first edition of *Leaves of Grass*, already sings of his America as

> A nation announcing itself,
> I myself make the only growth by which I can be
>   appreciated,
> I reject none, accept all, reproduce all in my own
>   forms.

But his America is also thought of through his healthy body, a body neither infected nor obese but beautiful and healthy:

> All comes by the body – only health puts rapport with
>   the universe.
> Produce great persons, the rest follows.
> How dare a sick man, or an obedient man, write
>   poems?
> Which is the theory or book that is not diseased?
> Piety and conformity to them that like!
> Peace, obesity, allegiance, to them that like!
> I am he who tauntingly compels men, women, nations,
>   to leap from their seats and contend for their lives![10]

Whitman's world is one in which 'health' as a badge of

national identity is the antithesis of 'sickness' and 'obesity'. 'Produce great persons, the rest follows', but these great persons are neither a 'sick man, or an obedient man' nor, he adds, someone fat. Such is the world-view of Whitman – the view of a world in which the good citizens of the national state are not fat. The 'moral panic' about 'fat' is one of the major concerns of the nineteenth century. It remains a 'bright line' through the twenty-first.

Obesity presents itself today in the form of a 'moral panic' – that is, an 'episode, condition, person or group of persons' that have in recent times been 'defined as a threat to societal values and interests'.[11] Thus Stanley Cohen in the early 1970s about the public reaction to the 'mods and rockers' who haunted London streets during the 1960s. Obesity is characterized, to continue to quote Cohen on other such manifestations, by its 'stylized and stereotypical' representation, imposed by the mass media, together with a tendency for those 'in power' (politicians, bishops, editors and so on) to man the 'moral barricades' and pronounce moral judgments. Moral panics need not be focused on 'invented' categories such as witches; they can also be associated with real health problems in a way to shape their meanings. They can use 'real' categories of illness to explain such health problems within the ideological focus of the time.

Fat is dangerous, dieting is modern. We can cure ourselves and improve the world, or we are unable to cure ourselves and a cure must be imposed upon us. We know where the weapons of mass destruction are hidden. They are within us, and we can seek to control or even destroy them 'with a little help from our friends' in the dieting culture. But who are our friends? Are they those who are making food cheaper and more accessible, as the critics of the 'famine' culture in China at the close of the nineteenth century believed? One of the claims about the nature of today's obesity is that it is the result of ever cheaper and more easily accessible food. 'The obesity epidemic won't subside until we address the decreasing cost and increasing availability of food options.'[12] Neither the decrease in the energy needed nor poor food choices are at fault – only the lowering of food prices and the increased availability of food as a result of increased urbanization.

How could this be controlled in the twenty-first century? One means of doing it is through the imposition of a 'fat tax' or a 'Twinkie tax'. It was pioneered in the mid-1980s by Kelly D. Brownell, a psychologist at Yale University who proposed that a very small percentage tax be placed on junk and snack foods in order to generate revenue. According to Brownell, the 'toxic environment' of poor food choice is at the heart of the rise in obesity. The federal government should tax foods with little nutritional value. The less healthy the food, the higher the tax. (This principle has been proposed recently in the taxation of the most fuel-inefficient automobiles in the USA and in the UK.) The most highly taxed foods would, it is claimed, quickly become too expensive for consumption, and the revenue generated could be used for 'public exercise facilities – bike paths and running tracks'.[13] This fantasy of the nanny state, providing the 'positive democracy' (to use Isaiah Berlin's term) which may force the ignorant or misled consumers on to the paths of health and longevity through the destruction of the toxic environment in which they live, is seen by many as intrusive and ineffectual.

The 'fat tax' is but the most recent extension of a policy based on the notion that the state, too, has a role in the dieting culture. As Thomas Hobbes observed in the *Leviathan* (1651), the body politic is the subject of the dieting. Hobbes notes that (like human beings) 'Commonwealths can endure no diet: for seeing their expense is not limited by their own appetite but by external accidents, and the appetites of their neighbours, the public riches cannot be limited by other limits than those which the emergent occasions shall require'.[14] Here one has perhaps the best sense of the conflict between the desire for food and the difficulty (if not impossibility) of diet. For, as the diet industry of the modern era shows, its greatest failure would be the elimination of the actual or perceived unhappiness with weight: this success would bring about the end of the dieting industry. For Hobbes, a nation's appetite is actually enhanced by the increase in its consumption of the 'commodities of sea and land'. The more you have, the more you want; so much for a world limited by self-control, and even by the 'fat tax'. Have we come very far from Whitman's anxiety about the politics of a fat America? Will a 'fat tax' 'tauntingly compel men, women, nations, to leap from their seats and contend for their lives?'

The moral implication of a fat tax that would force people to 'eat right' echoes other recent debates about the meanings associated with food. There are, regularly, calls for food bans such as that on the sale of *foie gras*, because of the perception of the widespread success of smoking bans. In the fall of 2007, twelve nations, together with the state of California and the city of Chicago – where a hot dog vender who provided wieners with *foie gras* was the first one fined in March of that year – have banned this delicacy with the mottos: 'Liver let die' or 'This Valentine's Day, have a heart, not a liver'.[15] However, it is not obesity that is in question here, but rather 'humane' treatment of animals and animal rights. As an editorialist notes: 'In the end, Americans work on a sliding scale of sensitivity. The fact breeders keep chickens in tiny pens hasn't created a change in chicken eating. Nor have videos of calves being caught as they are born to be shuttled off and slaughtered for veal hurt the veal industry. And the nation still exports horses to France to be used as food – even a former Kentucky Derby winner'.[16] The question here is not that 'you are what you eat' or that 'bad' food makes you obese, but that some foods are morally bad – and then they, too, will corrupt you.

In his conversations collected as *Table Talk*, the Protestant reformer Martin Luther stated that, '[w]hen it comes to eating, we are the ilk of every tyrannical sort of animal. The wolf eats sheep, so do we; the fox chickens and geese, just like us; hawks and vultures eat birds as we do; pike eat fish, like us. We eat grass, as do oxen, horses, and cows. And, like pigs we eat dung and filth. But internally everything becomes shit'.[17] We are what we eat and in the end, as St Augustine stated, we are at war with our appetite: 'In the midst of these temptations I struggle daily against greed for food and drink. This is not an evil which I can decide once and for all to repudiate and never to embrace again, as I was able to do with fornication'.[18] You are what you must eat!

It is no accident that the phrase 'you are what you eat' was first used in the dieting culture by Jean Anthelme Brillat-Savarin in 1826, in his classic autobiography of a fat man which determined the very notion of 'modern' 'good taste'. It quickly became a bon mot and was repeated in a different context by the German philosopher Ludwig Andreas Feuerbach (1804–72) in his essay of 1863 on 'Spiritualism and materialism'. Friedrich Nietzsche (1844–1900) employed the idea in his cryptic autobiography of 1888, *Ecce Homo* (first published in 1908): 'But as to German cookery in general – what has it not got on its conscience! Soup before the meal (still called alla tedesca in the sixteenth-century Venetian cook-books); meat cooked till the flavor is gone, vegetables cooked with fat and flour; the degeneration of pastries into paperweights! Add to this the utterly bestial postprandial habits of the ancients, not merely of the ancient Germans, and you will begin to understand where German intellect had its origin – in a disordered intestinal tract . . . German intellect is indigestion; it can assimilate nothing'.[19] Such a view is very much in line with Nietzsche's own failure at dieting, to cure his various illnesses.

If you study bad philosophy because you are a German you are, of course, what you eat!

Such a metaphoric use came into practical application with its introduction into English by nutritionist Victor Lindlahr in the 1920s, in a slogan reading: 'Ninety per cent of the diseases known to man are caused by cheap foodstuffs. You are what you eat.'[20] In the 1960s, the meaning of this phrase became much more specific. It was used to convey the message that you would be healthy from eating 'healthy food', often defined as macrobiotic foods. And yet the moral implication of the claim remains clear: 'bad' people (fat people?) eat bad things, *foie gras* included. Good people (meaning thin people) eat humane and kind food and remain healthy.

Are we better people if we avoid becoming fat, or even the temptation offered by immoral (and perhaps highly taxed) foods? It may be too late for these moral tests, not because globesity has overwhelmed the West, but because it may be about to diminish. At least one scholar has argued that obesity, as a western, culture-bound syndrome, has became a global one the less present it actually is in the western cultures of origin.[21] Such illnesses may have diminished simply because of their bad press in the 'West'. Perhaps the tables will turn without us having to make healthy food so expensive that only the wealthy can afford it. Or is it that the healthy, because they are seen to be morally superior, come to wealth more easily? Certainly the moral panic about obesity has reinforced the very notion of excess weight as morally repugnant, unhealthy, and socially irremediable. So diet we must . . . to be saved.

Sander L. Gilman
London / Atlanta

1

EPIDEMIC OBESITY

الإحياء,

Constructing diseases such as obesity does not always mean inventing them. Often real pathological experiences are rethought as part of a new pattern that can be then discerned, diagnosed, and treated. Obesity as a category has been the subject of such a public reconceptualization over the past decades. It has become the target of public health campaigns and spurred a global rethinking of where the sources of danger for the public may lie. Such a rethinking mixes together and stirs many qualities in order to provide a compelling story that defines 'obesity' as the 'new public health epidemic'.[1] This is not to discount the costs, both personal and national, that overweight can accrue, but to understand why, in the twenty-first century, we have suddenly seen the 'moral panic', which was associated in the 1980s with HIV/AIDS as a potentially global disease, being transferred to obesity.

In July 2004 the then American Health and Human Services Secretary Tommy G. Thompson announced that Medicare was abandoning a long-held policy which said obesity was not a disease, opening the way for the government to pay for a whole range of possible treatments, from surgery and diets to psychotherapy.[2] Soon afterwards, a cartoon by Dick Locher of the Tribune Media Services appeared, showing a portly little boy reading a newspaper with the headline 'Obesity now considered a disease'. He then calls his school and says: 'Hello, Principal's office? This is Tommy Frobish . . . I won't be in school today, I got a disease'.

We know what type of disease Tommy Frobish had: scientists at the annual meeting of the American Association for the Advancement of Science in February, 2002 had already warned the government that obesity was now a 'global epidemic' – no longer confined to western, industrialized societies.[3] This reflected a growing consensus in the 1990s that obesity (not smoking) was going to be the major public health issue of the new millennium.[4] By 2005 the 'war against obesity' had replaced the 'war against tobacco', even though world-wide tobacco sales continue to increase. Although the phrase 'war against obesity, sloth, and addiction' appears in the UK in *The Times* as early as 1981,[5] in Canada, as of the summer of 2005,

fat is Ontario's new public health enemy No. 1. Jim Watson, recently appointed by Premier Dalton McGuinty to wage war on our slothful, couch-potato ways, made a first-strike assault against flab this week by warning he intends to get 'aggressive on obesity'. Watson, the province's new health promotion minister, boldly suggested 'fat is the new tobacco. I think obesity is the challenge of the 21st century, just as smoking was the challenge of the 20th century.'[6]

The ironic tone of the news report makes it clear that declaring 'war' against fat is a very much more contentious issue than declaring 'war' against smoking. In the United States at the same moment, military recruiters were dealing with another war – and with an inability to recruit soldiers into the military to fight in Iraq because of their weight.[7] The most innocent victims, children throughout the world, seem to be at greatest risk in this 'war against obesity'.[8]

1 EPIDEMIC OBESITY

Media outlets were (and are) rife with warnings about the 'obesity epidemic'. This was not the first time that the media had used the phrase. The notion of an 'epidemic' of 'obesity' (in cattle) as a 'form that chimes in with a rather artificial idea of animal beauty' was part of the debate between 'contagion-ists and non-contagionists' as early as the 1860s.[9] It is only in the very late twentieth century that obesity becomes an 'epi-demic' in humans.

'Epidemic' was first used in the context of an 'epidemic of heart disease', for which obesity (and smoking) were seen as major causes.[10] By 1987, members of the media began to evoke the specter of 'epidemic obesity' as a problem of its own: '"Childhood obesity is epidemic in the United States," said Dr William H. Dietz Jr of New England Medical Center'.[11] Headlines such as 'Obesity epidemic raises risk of children developing diabetes' grabbed the attention of the reader.[12] Even those reporters who are a bit more attuned to what the term epidemic may imply tend to agree: 'To describe what has happened as an epidemic may seem far-fetched. That word is normally applied to a contagious disease that is rapidly spread-ing. But the population that is obese has grown 400 percent in the last 25 years'.[13] The media saw its goal as being to help fight this new epidemic of obesity.

Even the food industry feels that no one is 'better suited to solve the obesity epidemic' than they are.[14] The 'wellness' industry, too, is aware of the potential of the obesity epidemic: 'According to a new study, Americans consider childhood obesity as serious a problem as smoking or school violence, exceeded only by substance abuse as a health threat to school-age children..[15] For profit-hungry health and nutrition vendors, obesity is a growth industry.

From the USA to Australia, the 'obesity epidemic' has become a 'political issue'.[16] The British Labour government in 2004 admitted that it had removed the tackling of this epidemic from its public health goals and belatedly published a major account of the epidemic, including a horror story about the death of a three-year-old girl from obesity.[17] According to the press, there was no question that 'her death was due to over-feeding and bad parenting'.[18] The story turned out to be a poor indicator of the epidemic, as the child had died of a genetically transmitted disease in which obesity was just one factor. The media stressed the 'fear factor' of children out of control: 'She weighed six stone [84 lbs.], not because her parents stuffed her face with food, but because of a rare genetic condition . . . There can be no license to publish dodgy facts by claiming that they serve a worthy cause'.[19] Even the British afternoon TV hosts Richard and Judy got into the act bemoaning 'the wild-eyed woman on the TV news trying to scare the pants off us all with a vision of hugely overweight children being choked by their own fat, and the committee's warnings that today's children would be "the first generation to die before their parents as a consequence of obesity". It also predicted that large numbers of people would be disfigured by blindness and amputation as a result of diabetes – to which obesity can contribute. I knew it was all cobblers, scare tactics on a lunatic scale'.[20] Yet in spite of these regular revelations of hyperbole and poor science, we remain in the twenty-first century both literally and conceptually in the middle of an obesity epidemic.

What fascinates me is the power of using the term 'epidemic' in the context of obesity as a means of characterizing obesity as a 'disease'. Obesity is not itself a 'disease' but rather a phenomenological category which reflects the visible manifestation of bodily size, which in turn can have multiple (or multifactorial) causes. No one dies from 'obesity'. One dies from those pathologies which may result from extreme overweight. Obesity may be a tertiary cause of morbidity or mortality: it may lead to diabetes, which may lead to vascular disease. Thus the image of an 'epidemic' of obesity demands a single, clearly defined cause for this 'disease', much as we have encountered in other recent epidemics of infectious diseases. It is striking that the assumptions about the monocausality of 'obesity' – the latter's representation as having a single cause – is part of the urban myth of disease.[21]

Yet politicians' use of the term 'epidemic' is in many ways very much in line with that of the medical profession. '. . . Obesity and sedentary lifestyle are escalating national and global epidemics that warrant increased attention by physicians . . . at the pivotal role of physicians and other health care professionals in curbing these dangerous epidemics. . . .'.[22] As early as 2002, the *Lancet* warned against the global 'obesity epidemic' and provided a detailed account of the public health discussions of this new killer.[23] In 2004, E.B.R. Desapriya of the British Columbia Injury Research and Prevention Centre for Community Child Health Research in Vancouver, BC (Canada) warned as follows: 'The obesity epidemic poses a public-health challenge. Obesity has a more pronounced effect on morbidity than on mortality, and an increase in its prevalence will have an important effect on the global incidence of cardiovascular disease, type 2 diabetes mellitus, cancer, osteoarthritis, work disability, and sleep apnoea. A 1% increase in the prevalence of obesity in such countries as India and China leads to 20 million additional cases. The state of childhood obesity in the USA, Canada, and many other countries worldwide has reached epidemic proportions; the

Canadian prevalence tripled between 1981 and 1996'.[24] Yes, everyone agrees, we are in the middle of an obesity 'epidemic'.

Epidemic is a technical term from epidemiology meaning any 'large-scale temporary increase in the occurrence of a disease in a community or region, which is clearly in excess of normal expectancy. Yet it is 'widely used to describe clusters of diseases in general [although it has] traditionally been used when infections strike a population'.[25] 'Epidemic' maintains a powerful metaphoric connection to contagion. It can, of course, be applied to any disease, no matter what its cause, and to all injury, including gun-shot wounds – as the Centers for Disease Control found (to their political embarrassment) a number of years ago – or other health-related event.[26] Epidemics may be global (pandemic), but they are always defined by their rate of increase, not by their universality. But, even here, the model, as given by voluntary contributions to a web site, is that of the spread of an infectious agent: 'When each infected individual is infecting more than one other individual, so that the number of infected individuals is growing exponentially, the disease is in an epidemic state'.[27] Epidemic, as we can see here, has a strong popular use in terms of the spread of infectious diseases. As the *OED* notes, its primary meaning is that of a disease 'prevalent among a people or a community at a special time, and produced by some special causes not generally present in the affected locality'.

'Epidemic' seems to be a creation of the seventeenth century, borrowed from the French at precisely the same time as the term 'obesity'. One of the first uses of the term 'obesity' appears in Tobias Venner's handbook of humoral good diet and health of 1620. Venner notes that 'a fat and grosse habit of body is worse than a leane, for besides that it is more subject to sicknes, it is for all corporall actions farre more unapt. They are more sickly that have grosse and full bodies, not onely because they abound with many crude and superflous humors, but also because they lesse (by reason of the imbicillity of their heat) resist extrinsicall and intrinsicall causes that demolish their health'.[28] 'Obesity' is, according to Venner, a disease process. Thomas Lodge needed to define this new notion of 'Epidemick' for his readership in 1603: 'An Epidemick plague, is a common and popular sicknesse, hapning in some region, or country, at a certaine time, caused by a certaine indisposition of the aire, or waters of the same region, producing in all sorts of people, one and the same sicknesse'.[29] Two decades later Francis Bacon, in his *Historie of the Raigne of King Henry the Seventh* (1622), can speak of the 'sweating-sickness' as 'was conceived not to be an epidemick disease, but to proceed from a malignity in the constitution of the air, gathered by the predispositions of the seasons; and the speedy cessation declared as much'.[30] 'Epidemic' quickly takes on metaphoric meaning, as in John Milton's condemnation of an 'epidemick whordom' in his 1643 treatise on divorce.[31] This movement between illness and metaphor continues in our contemporary anxiety about the epidemic of obesity.

What was seen to cause human 'obesity' has varied over time. Today there seems to be a stress on a plurality of often conflicting causes.[32] Central among them are social and genetic–physiological explanations:

1   A shift in the 'quality of life' and in life expectancy.: we live longer now, have less physically stressful occupations, and have easier access to more food.

2   Our psychological makeup: we depend psychologically on food as a means of manipulating our immediate environment. On this assumption, obesity is simply on a continuum with anorexia nervosa, which has been so labeled by psychologists. Obesity is thus a mental illness.

3 Abundant access to poor food and the absence of structures to engage physical activity: this is the 'obesity of poverty' argument – that is, the argument that poverty is a contributory factor in one's becoming obese.

4 Loss of control over food consumption through addictive behavior: addiction is usually understood on the medical model of some type of genetic pathological predisposition in an individual or group rather than as a 'weakness of will'.[33]

5 A genetic 'normal' predisposition, understood in terms of an evolutionary biological drive to accumulate bodily fat in order to prevent starvation in times of famine: this is the 'ob-gen' argument, first put forth in the classic 1994 paper on the genetics of obesity in mice, which concluded by extrapolating it to human beings.[34]

6 A disruption of normal growth caused by changes in the endocrine system through other, pathological, changes including aging (also understood as pathological).

7 The result of infection, as we shall see below.

What is clear is that any single explanation may be possible for any given individual, but it is the social implications of 'obesity' that have now turned it into an 'epidemic'.

The anxiety about 'epidemics' points out the danger which lies in a 'moral panic' that defines those 'diseases' we openly fear and those 'infected' persons we openly disdain. Obesity is now the central 'danger' to confront all aspects of life or all societies (as it is seen as an epidemic of poverty as well as of affluence). Its spread seems 'like' that of a contagious disease. Yet each discussion of obesity seems to choose some model for its cause and nature – a model which could be the point of intervention to end this plague, be it the danger of fast food, of too much sugar or fat, of too little exercise, of damaged psyche or weak will, of too large portions, of genetic predisposition or of hormonal imbalance. It is not unpredictable that there has been a strong argument for at least some cases of obesity being the result of an infectious agency: this fulfills all of the metaphoric power of the 'moral panic' about fat and limits its locus to a limited and treatable cause. In the United States this is embodied by 'the Center for Science in the Public Interest. That's the advocacy group that periodically issues breathless bulletins ("Food porn!") warning that one food or another (eggs, soda, shellfish, Mexican food, Chinese food, French fries, donuts, beef, salt, etc.) is bad for you'.[35] A magic bullet can be found which is simply more difficult for most of the other imagined biological or social causes postulated for obesity.[36]

2 OBESITY AS AN INFECTIOUS DISEASE

In 1997, researchers at the experimental biology meeting in New Orleans (a city not unknown for its food) argued that obesity could be caused in part by an infectious agent, Adenovirus 36 (Ad–36). Nikhil Dhurandhar (then at Wayne State University, Detroit, MI; now at the Pennington Biomedial Research Center at Louisiana State University in Baton Rouge) and Richard Atkinson (Obetech, Richmond, VA) undertook to show 'this increase [in obesity] is the type of pattern that might occur with a new infectious disease, as has been seen with the AIDS virus'. The moral panic about obesity seems to have filled a gap left by the restructuring of the moral panic about AIDS.[37] Both of these researchers were engaged in obesity research at the moment when obesity came to be the new 'epidemic' disease. Indeed Atkinson had been a founder of the American Obesity Association and an editor of the association's flagship journal. They speculated that Ad–36 makes animals fat by stimulating the growth and reproduction of adipocytes (fat cells) as well as by causing immature adipocytes to mature more quickly. Thus, they claimed, animals infected with Ad–36 may have as much as three times more fat cells than uninfected animals, as well as a vastly decreased metabolism.

In a subsequent paper, Dhurandhar noted that this may well solve the mystery of the rapid spread of

> obesity [which] has been called the number one public health problem in America. The etiology of obesity is considered to be multifactorial. . . . While genetic and behavioral components of obesity have been the focus of intense study, an infection as an etiological factor has received little attention. Although 'infectobesity', a new term to describe obesity of infectious origin, appears to be a new concept, over the past 20 years six different pathogens have been reported to cause obesity in animal models. The relative contribution of these pathogens to human obesity is unknown.[38]

But, of course, no greater 'magic bullet' can be imagined for human obesity than an anti-viral agent that would simply 'cure' obesity, or even a vaccine that could prevent it. 'In 10 years,' Nikhil Dhurandhar stated, 'people may be able to walk into a clinic and be told that their obesity is due to X cause, such as genes, the endocrine system, or pathogens. That may have a more productive outcome than a blanket treatment right now, [which] is not very successful. And because viruses are hard or impossible to treat, prevention through vaccines will be key'.[39]

In the 1970s, Dhurandhar observed that a chicken adenovirus isolated in Bombay caused chickens to accumulate as much as 50 percent more fat than healthy birds. The virus also lowered the animals' cholesterol and triglyceride levels before it killed them. 'Normally, obesity in any species is associated with high levels of cholesterol and triglycerides,' Dhurandhar noted.[40] What interested him at that time was the odd observation that infected chickens ate no more than uninfected ones. Dhurandhar's research group identified the infectious agents as Ad–36. Ad–36 was first isolated in humans in 1978, in the fecal matter of a 7-year-old diabetic girl. Based upon the discovery of Ad–36, Dhurandhar began to theorize that it might be a contributing factor to the sky-rocketing obesity epidemic in humans. He next looked for evidence of infection with the chicken virus in a group of fifty-two obese people. Ten showed signs of infection. An avian-spread virus was postulated as the cause: it was the 'bird-'flu' model that could be imagined as spreading to human beings. 'Their work on obesity-related viruses has a strong experimental base in animal models and their descriptive epidemiological data appears sound. Whether or not their hypothesis holds up in appropriately designed prospective human studies remains to be answered as far as I know', observed Steven Heymsfield of the Columbia University College of Physicians and Surgeons in New York City.[41]

Commentators immediately responded to the potentiality 'that obesity is a viral disease'. This had serious social consequences (at least before Tommy Thompson), as 'it may give people ammunition to fight for insurance coverage for weight-loss treatment because they could argue: "I've got a reason. I'm not just a fat slob." '[42] The moral claim that obesity was simply a public sign of the lack of will, one of the most powerful notions driving the moral panic about obesity, could be stilled by the very idea that its cause was beyond the individual (even beyond the individual's genetic makeup) and was to be found in the ever more dangerous world of infectious diseases. 'The implications are enormous,' said John Foreyt, a behavioral psychologist at Baylor College of Medicine. He called the research 'startling', and 'potentially a real breakthrough' in explaining the swift rise of the obesity epidemic.[43] 26 percent of American adults were obese in 1980 and 35 percent or more are now. The idea of obesity as an infectious disease also could help explain the odd demographics of the 'obesity epidemic' as it moved from the coasts and then toward the mid-section of the USA. 'People are still struggling with why this enormous increase in obesity', since 'diet, sedentary lifestyles, genetic predispositions and metabolism problems don't explain the whole trend,' Foreyt noted.[44] Infectobesity would answer multiple problems, and a drug that could combat it would be a world-wide blockbuster.[45] While clearly important, Dhurandhar's research was not the first attempt to define obesity as the symptom of an infectious disease. Jules Hirsch, the noted Rockefeller University geneticist, attempted to do so very early in his career. In a 1982 paper, he and his colleagues found an obesity syndrome in adult mice infected with the canine distemper virus (that is, a morbillivirus related to measles). But nothing came of this initial research.

In 2006 Leah Whigham, who had earlier collaborated with Dhurandhar, published a further study of Adenovirus 36 as well as of two other viruses, including the Ad–35 strain.[46] Looking at chickens ('We chose chickens as our in vivo model because these animals respond very rapidly to infection with Ad–36') and at human beings, the study argued that such infection 'increases adiposity and reduces serum triglycerides'.[47] Of the 500 overweight individuals examined, between twenty and thirty were infected with Ad–36, compared with five in the non-overweight group. 'The evidence from the animal studies, the high prevalence of Ad–36 antibodies in obese people compared with non-obese, and the increased BMI and body fat of Ad–36 antibody-positive twins suggest that some cases of human obesity are due to adenovirus infection' (p. 191). When interviewed about this claim, Whigham stated that people who wanted to stay thin should 'eat right, exercise but also wash their hands. The prevalence of obesity has doubled in adults in the US in the last 30 years and has tripled in children. With the exception of infectious diseases, no other chronic disease in history has spread so rapidly, but the factors producing this epidemic have not all been clearly identified. It is difficult to explain by changes in food intake and exercise alone'.[48] The assumption is that such findings bring promise of an eventual vaccine for obesity, as Frank Greenway states in the journal in which Whigham published her findings. Response to the study in the United Kingdom on the part of the 'fat-acceptance' lobby Big People UK was that:'[t]here is too much stigma for being fat. People are perceived as thick, stupid, dirty and lazy'. Being diseased seems not much of a rebuttal compared to being stupid.

In the summer of 2007, a further explanation of the 'obesity epidemic' was identified in the potential of 'the nature and extent of the person-to-person spread of obesity as a possible factor contributing to the obesity epidemic'.[49] Looking at a large social network of 12,067 people who had been closely followed for thirty-two years, from 1971 to 2003, in Framingham, MA, researchers reported that 'obesity is a product of voluntary choices or behaviors' (p. 370). It would seem that an argument based on the internalization of social imagery, in which the model is not 'infection' but 'impression', would argue against any idea that obesity is somehow infectious. 'The fact that people are embedded in social networks and are influenced by the evident appearance and behaviors of those around them suggests that weight gain in one person might influence weight gain in others. Having obese social contacts might change a person's tolerance for being obese or might influence his or her adoption of specific behaviors (e.g., smoking, eating, and exercising)' (ibid.). What is prevalent seems to become accepted, whether it is smoking or being overweight. Yet such social arguments seem to fly in the face of somatic explanations for obesity, and here too the researchers capitulate: 'In addition to such strictly social mechanisms, it is plausible that physiological imitation might occur; areas of the brain that correspond to actions such as eating food may be stimulated if these actions are observed in others' (ibid.). As the *New York Times* reported it: 'Obesity can spread from person to person, much like a virus, researchers are reporting today. When one person gains weight, close friends tend to gain weight, too'.[50] The use of 'viral epidemic' as a metaphor is actually a weakening of the real claim of this research, namely that 'even infectious causes of obesity are conceivable'.[51] Here the notion of social modeling is translated into a medical metaphor parallel to that of AIDS. We are in the midst of an 'obesity epidemic' no matter what its sources or form are.

An antidote may well be a recalibration of obesity from a disease resulting from the lack of will power to one caused by an infection. It is striking how such claims parallel the debates about obesity that dominated the turn of the twentieth century. There the advocates of an endocrinological imbalance as the sole source of obesity confronted those who claimed that the obese simply suffered from aboulia, a weakness of will.

What is remarkable about the notion of infectious diseases in the age of HIV/AIDS is that it couples the idea of the origin of disease in a distant foreign place with the fear of an uncontrolled spread, answered almost simultaneously by the desire for a cure, a quick fix, a magic bullet. Remember E.B.R. Desapriya's warning that 'A 1 percent increase in the prevalence of obesity in such countries as India and China leads to 20 million additional cases'.[52] Imagine each of these cases being a potential source of infection for the West!

3 DISEASES OF THE FOOD CHAIN COME FROM THE 'ORIENT'

It is no accident that the assumption of a global, evidence-based medicine is that such plagues – specifically, those which display transmission of a disease from animals to human beings – begin in the East. 'Bird 'flu' in the twenty-first century has not crossed the 'species barrier' any more than bubonic plague did. But bubonic plague had animals (rats and lice) as its vector. The relatively small number of cases of bird 'flu today seems to be the result of direct exposure to injected animals. Bird 'flu is being treated much like bubonic plague, in relation to 'animals' which are seen to be its cause and (more importantly) seen to pose the risk of the disease crossing the 'species barrier', so that human beings could infect human beings without an animal vector.

In 1896 the plague appeared in China, and then it moved within two years to India. Basing his work on the appearance of the plague in Hong Kong, Patrick Mansion showed that the fact that 'lower animals, especially those . . . that are intimately associated with man, play an important part in the transmission of human disease is now only becoming to be appreciated'.[53] It was rats, and then the fleas on the rats, that provided the mode of transmission for the disease. Yet rats and fleas exist throughout the world. Was it pure accident that Asia – China and India – was the source of such animal-to-human transmission? The assumption was that Asia provided a culture of disease. This was the claim seventy-five years later that 'in parts of China it is also common for animals and people to occupy . . . the same room. The close association between man and animals has been going on in central Asia for seven thousand years'.[54] Not that such an association did not exist in many other parts of the world, including rural Europe; it still does. While it is true that western thought often separated the notion of animal from that of the human being, it is equally true that that separation never was nor could be completed. The idea that animals and humans in Asia (or, in the case of HIV/AIDS, in Africa) provided a unique culture of disease meant that the illnesses themselves could be seen as invading the space of 'civilization', which is intrinsically 'free' of such infection.

The fascination of a viral cause for obesity comes in the context of the SARS (severe acute respiratory syndrome) as well as of other, more recent Asian avian influenzas of the past decade.[55] The view that these diseases invade healthy spaces through an infectious process seems to be a commonplace. That they are also 'probably best . . . seen as a harbinger of future events' is part of a historical pattern (sometimes quite accurate) in imagining the invasion from beyond one's own borders as being the prelude to even greater disasters.[56] Such anxiety (justified or not) reflected the potential for mass death associated with an earlier disruption of the food chain: namely that of BSE (the Bovine Spongiform Encephalopathy), which haunted Europe – and North America – when it entered the public's awareness in 1990 with the publication in European newspapers of its association with neurological diseases such as vCJD (Variant Creutzfeldt-Jakob disease) in human beings.[57] While the origin of BSE was initially not connected with the exotic reaches of the orient or Africa, this disorder quickly became the 'English' disease on the continent or the Canadian disease in the United States.[58] BSE, caused evidently by the use of technology, which introduced ground animal offal into animal feed, became the model for the notion that food kills – not any food, but that which infiltrates from beyond our borders.

Recently, the argument has been made that BSE originated in the consumption of animal feed which had been made from bones and organic scraps imported for animal feed from Bangladesh, India and Pakistan in the 1960s and 1970s. Rather than being an 'indigenous' disease, having its source in the viral disease Scrapie among sheep in Europe, it spread from the ingestion of diseased organic matter from the bodies of infected 'orientals'. Or, as the authors of a recent study stated, 'the route of infection was oral, through animal feed containing imported mammalian raw materials contaminated with human remains;

and . . . the origin was the Indian subcontinent, from which large amounts of mammalian material were imported during the relevant time period. Human remains are known to be incorporated into meal made locally, and may still be entering exported material'.[59] Cannibalism (as the debate about this topic over the past two decades reveals) is always a significant charge in drawing the line between acceptable and unacceptable levels of civilization and health. The authors conclude with the statement that 'both importing and exporting countries are likely to be sensitive to the implications of our hypothesis, and may feel pressurised to issue denials without adequate investigation' (p. 860). In the same issue of the *Lancet*, an editorial by members of the National Institute of Mental Health and Neurosciences at Bangalore decries the cultural bias of the piece, noting that there has been not one single case of BSE or Scrapie in India and that the authors' representation of Hindu burial practice bears no resemblance to the actual practice. The editorial stresses that the remains of those individuals who have died of vCJD are not simply cast into the Ganges.[60] But the argument does present yet another attempt to place food-born illnesses beyond the boundaries of the West.

Our 'borders' are symbolic and should be moral barriers protecting us. 'Meat kills', reads one attack on meat in general, highlighting the dangers of BSE in the food chain.[61] But this was very much in line with the modern awareness of the role of animal consumption in nutrition as the source of disease.[62] This is not to deny that such connections can be made; but the question is, why they are made now at the exclusion of other potential explanations?

4 SARS

Obesity is part of a string of moral panics about food, the food chain, and disease which haunt our present age. Tied to real diseases with real health implications, these moral panics signal a world in which food is the cause of potentially over-whelming epidemics, epidemics that threaten not only the individual but also the very fabric of social life. Where does danger lie? It lies in that one thing we can never do without: our sustenance. Thus SARS, which seemed to begin as a moral panic about infectious disease, turned quickly into the pursuit of the source of the disease.

When it first arose in southern China in 2003, SARS was called 'severe acute nervousness syndrome' (*feidianxing shengjing bing*) because it was accompanied by almost paranoid fear.[63] Here the model of infection as having a psychological component, a public hysteria about vulnerability, is made manifest.[64] The new disease was seen with much the same anx-iety and paranoia in the West as the new cholera or influenza spreading from the East along travel and economic routes. Real infectious disease can also have a powerful psychological impact. SARS quickly became a 'moral panic' which spread world-wide, being accompanied by a true sense of stigma.[65] In the twenty-first century, spreading quickly by plane rather than slowly by ship, SARS was set to invade and destroy 'civilization'.

The initial response in China was panic:

Anti-SARS has now become a political movement in China. All officials are living in nightmares of being sacked. Police force has been enforcing to carry out anti-SARS measures. Curfews have been introduced; people have been arrested for any minor illnesses. SARS is not only headlines; it has become the only topic of conversation. Ordinary people are living in great fear . . . though thousands of people are dying each day in China as result of building accident, no one seems to care and one hardly reads about them in the paper. Three thousand school children were poisoned by soymilk, but they were not allowed to be treated outside of the local hospital, in order that the news would not spread. However the hospital was poorly equipped to cope with the situation.[66]

The general response was chaotic:

> After the national Minister of Health and the Major of Beijing were fired for 'covering' up the extent of the SARS epidemic, a historian in Beijing wrote me that 'Sacking two people is just another way of covering things up and continuing to tell lies. It happens all the time in China, I am so used to it. Though I don't think I should get used to it. Sometimes I really feel I should say something . . . or perhaps not. Beijing is in total panic right now; people have lost their faith in the official report and the government. Everyone knows they are telling the lies, people don't know what to believe anymore. As a result, they turn to everyone and rush into drug stores to buy every imaginable medicine. They won't get killed by SARS but they are going to drug themselves to death! It's really quite awful.'[67]

And, according to public health authorities, it all began in the food chain.

The animal origin of SARS was highly contested. Was it spread by chickens and other domestic animals raised for food or by wild animals, such as civet cats, used for food?[68] It seemed to be transmitted through the food chain. Soon it was clear that 'food handlers working in Guangdong's busy markets [were] heavily represented among those who became ill with the mysterious disease'.[69] In the winter of 1997 millions of chickens had been killed and the corpses burned in Hong Kong because of the fear of a lethal avian influenza that had the potential of infecting human beings.[70] As with the public discourse about obesity, our very food seemed to be striking back to kill us. With 813 deaths out of a total of 8,437 infectious people before SARS was declared in July 2003, SARS was touted as the next great pandemic. Even the jokes that circulated in China made this association: 'What the Party has failed to do, SARS has succeeded in doing'; 'The party failed to control dining extravagantly. SARS did.'[71] Or the benefit a wife received from SARS: 'The husband who self-indulgently gorges on meat in restaurants all of a sudden turns into a rabbit and takes a fancy to the various vegetable dishes cooked at home, contending that eating vegetables may boost his immune system' (p. 164). And the disease itself was seen as originating in the food chain. SARS created a 'moral panic' about the spread of infectious diseases through global travel, as the disease moved from Asia to Europe to North America. While the number of cases was limited, the powerful association of disease with the 'problems' inherent in food chain made pinpointing the origin of the disease in exotic foods a means of controlling the panic associated with the disease.

What if, as with obesity, food itself is seen as the source of this new global epidemic? The very notion of a viral cause for obesity comes to limit this anxiety to those foods which are now seen as inherently 'dangerous'. One can think of this in the light of the identification by the then Surgeon General of the United States C. Everett Koop, in October 1988, of the consumption of dietary 'saturated fat' as the prime cause of obesity and other related illnesses such as cardiovascular disease and cancer. This identification was based on the findings of researchers who needed to pinpoint a single cause of what was seen, even in 1988, as a major public health problem. The debate on whether the excessive ingestion of animal fat or carbohydrates causes obesity had framed the question of the causation of this condition since the mid-nineteenth century (as we shall see in Chapter 3). As a result of Koop's report, 'diet foods' flooded on to the shelves of the American marketplace.

However, sugar replaced fat as the prime ingredient which made such diet foods palatable. By the beginning of the twenty-first century, 'high fructose corn syrup' was labeled as the new 'prime cause' of obesity. It had come to prominence to replace the dangers of dietary fat, which now is no longer seen as the major source of our anxiety about obesity. Indeed, Robert Atkins' high-protein, high-fat, low-carbohydrate diet, first proposed, to public derision, in his 1972 book, *Dr Atkins' Diet Revolution: The High Calorie Way to Stay Thin Forever*, came by the end of the twentieth century to be the diet of choice to control obesity. 'Fast food' was likewise condemned at that point, because it contained sugars and other carbohydrates as the source of the new illness haunting the 'Fast Food Nation'. Such shifts seem to be a permanent part of our new concern with localizing our moral panic about the food chain: we must always know where the danger lies!

5 AVIAN INFLUENZA

Parallel to the growing anxiety about obesity (or globesity, as the World Health Organization would have it), there was an ongoing anxiety about other risks presented by the food we eat. Following the model of SARS in 2005, avian influenza again became a focus of anxiety about epidemic death beginning in the food chain. A version of the coronavirus which was the cause of SARS was found in our domestic fowl, even though this was discounted as a reservoir for the illness.[72] Though there was no avian 'flu epidemic in 2004, 2005, or 2006, the World Health Organization continued to map the spread of such *potential* epidemics. Thus in the spring of 2005 the maps revealed that cases of avian influenza caused by the H5N1 virus were present first in south-east Asia (in Cambodia, Vietnam) and then in China. More recently infected wild animals were claimed to have been found in North America.

Thus in November 2005 Ron Dehaven, the Administrator of the Animal and Plant Health Inspection Service of the United States Department of Agriculture (USDA), gave testimony before the Senate Agriculture Committee about the risk of a massive epidemic with origins in Asia. We need to head this epidemic off at the pass:

> [I]t is critical to effectively address the disease in the poultry population in Southeast Asia. Implementation of effective biosecurity measures and control and eradication programs will go a long way toward reducing the amount of virus in these H5N1-affected countries and minimize the potential for the virus to spread to poultry in other areas of the world. These actions, if effectively implemented, would diminish the potential for a human influenza pandemic. I have traveled extensively in Southeast Asia in an effort to evaluate the animal health infrastructure in Southeast Asia and determine what steps can be taken to improve disease safeguarding and surveillance programs in the region. I can report that there is widespread concern in Asia regarding avian influenza, as well as a strong commitment to working with the international community to address the disease and improve the animal health infrastructure in countries like Vietnam, Cambodia, Laos, Indonesia and Thailand. This is why it is imperative that the United States remains engaged and share resources and expertise with officials in these countries.[73]

With the spread of avian influenza, there was a pattern of human deaths, always small in number, among those who, it was claimed, had been infected by direct contact with fowl. They died 'after developing a fever and pneumonia-like symptoms following contact with sick and dead poultry'.[74] That there were perhaps much greater numbers of individuals who were asymptomatic or had minor symptoms from animal to human transmission meant that there was no real way of estimating the risk of mortality and morbidity in such cases. Hundreds of millions of domestic fowl, from China to Rumania, were slaughtered.

Initially the official Chinese news service was quick to present this as a world-wide epidemic, not as an 'oriental' disease.[75] The Chinese Premier Wen Jiabo, however, much later, stressed the need for transparency in a speech to The International Pledging Conference on Avian and Human Pandemic Influenza (January 18, 2006, in Beijing): 'Acting in a prompt, open and transparent manner, we have informed the international organizations and countries concerned of the epidemic situation among birds and cases of human infection in China. We have hosted and attended international conferences on avian influenza and have provided China's neighbours with financial, material and technical assistance within our capacity to assist their prevention and control efforts'.[76] If it is an 'oriental' disease, China, at least, wishes to work actively to contain it. Migrating wildfowl were seen as the means of transmission across continents which replaced the airplane, the central focus of SARS transmission, as the source of risk. 'Since February, the virus has cut a wide swath across the globe, felling tens of thousands of birds in Nigeria, Israel, India, Sweden and elsewhere. Health officials in the United States say bird flu is likely to arrive in North America this year, carried by wild birds migrating thousands of miles to their summer breeding grounds.'[77] Nature rather than technology was suddenly seen as conspiring to spread the potential epidemic.

The anxiety that tracked this rapid (though 'natural') spread was the prediction of millions of world-wide deaths from a mutated virus.[78] But 'avian 'flu', with its potential to 'cross the species barrier', came to be the major public health menace of 2005. The movement was seen to be from wild birds to domestic birds and eventually to human beings. And indeed, a relatively small number of such cases of animal to human transmission seems to have been documented. It was the curse of the chicken, seen on the one hand as the healthy alternative to 'red meat' and on the other hand as the source of infections, which could cause obesity (in the form of infectobesity) or death from avian 'flu. Obesity was a danger, but it was a slow-moving, chronic danger that impacted on health only after decades of overweight. Suddenly a new and present danger, an epidemic which acted like the traditional epidemics of the past, was on the horizon.

George W. Bush, then the President of the United States, saw it as the equivalent of the 1918 influenza epidemic and posited it as the world's greatest risk – replacing international terrorism, at least for the moment. He called upon Congress in October 2005, asking it to give him power to use the military to enforce quarantines.[79] 'White House officials said Bush's fears were heightened last summer when he read "The Great Influenza", a nightmarish account of the 1918 pandemic by writer John Barry. In that outbreak, an avian flu virus passed to humans and left a trail of death across the globe. Most of the victims developed an extremely virulent form of pneumonia'.[80] In October 2005, 'speaking at his first press conference in four months, Bush said he has been studying the 1918 influenza outbreak in order to gain a better understanding of what his "decision-making process" would be in the case of an avian flu outbreak . . .'.[81] This became the model to be followed. The federal Centers for Disease Control in Atlanta presented a set of quarantine laws in the fall of 2005 which aimed as intercepting infected individuals at the borders.[82] Seemingly ancient maritime rules against epidemics and contagion are reappearing in the same discussions, which are rooted in debates about vaccination and genetic mutation.

Popular fiction began to reclaim the 1918 influenza epidemic, which it had not done since Katherine Anne Porter's 1939 novella, *Pale Horse, Pale Rider*. Porter's text reflected her experience of the 1918 pandemic, in which her fiancé died. Today the past is being reclaimed in the light of the potential for a new epidemic, which would replicate the earlier one. In 2005 Myla Goldberg's *Wickett's Remedy* appeared, which had its origin in reporting about influenza in the context of a renewed anxiety about epidemic and contagion. '[Goldberg was] inspired to write the book five years ago after reading a *New York Times* article on the outbreak. "The fact that I hadn't heard of the epidemic, and it was listed as one of the five worst, and I was thinking, 'If it was that bad, why hadn't I heard of it?'" she recalled. "As I was reading about it and learning what a big deal it was, I became fascinated"'.[83] Public anxiety mirrored in public policy, as well as popular fiction which is already the product of the general discussion of SARS, are the major symptoms of the new avian 'flu. In the week of 8 May 2006, a 'sweeps week', two television programs featured an outbreak of avian 'flu. ABC's 'Fatal contact: Bird flu in America' was followed on 12 May by an episode of the CBS series 'Numb3rs', entitled 'Undercurrents', in which Chinese boat people are found to be infected with the virus. As one commentator noted at the beginning of his review of the ABC film: 'Scientists have discovered a deadly and resilient strain of the avian flu that can be passed between humans. It's already infected thousands and threatens to explode into a pandemic that would dwarf the 1918 Spanish Flu, which killed up to 100 million. It's not reality, though. It's a scare-'em May sweeps movie. But it could happen'.[84] But, in the world, reality is not the movies, nor a novel.

The risk of the historical past returning was made all too real when in the recent historical and epidemiological work on the 1918–19 pandemic of influenza was evoked and sustained by the notion that, if it can happen once, it certainly can happen again.[85] Given that between fifty and one hundred million people most probably died of an influenza which seemed to originate in southern China, this fear was easily evoked. (It was called 'Spanish' because the Spanish newspapers were the first widely to give it space. All of the other combatant nations kept it a relative secret, at least in its first phase.) At the end of February 2004, I debated with John Oxford, Professor of Virology at St Bartholomew's and the Royal London Hospital, who is a great advocate of taking the 'Spanish 'flu' as a model for all future epidemics of infectious diseases: 'You can ask anyone about the bubonic plague, and they'll say, ah yes, the plague killed a third of Europe. But it still didn't have the impact of the 1918 flu, because bubonic plague killed people over periods of 10, 20, 40, 50 years. Influenza in 1918 killed 50 million souls in a period of one year, and that's why, to my mind, it's the biggest outbreak of any infectious disease the world has ever known'.[86] The action he wants taken is to prepare massive amounts of vaccine to secure the future of the world. That microbes mutate constantly; that some create diseases in a limited population or in no one at all; that we live in a world which is full of such events concerning all species, with the potential of diseases crossing 'species' barriers (a notion constructed by the 'negative' case where it seems that such crossing does not take place or takes place only after mutation) – these are facts which raise anxiety in all of us.

It turns out that it was an avian 'flu that caused the 1918 outbreak. It has now been genetically reconstructed as an aid to combating future epidemics. 'By identifying the characteristics that made the 1918 influenza virus so harmful, we have information that will help us develop new vaccines and treatments,' stated Dr Terrence Tumpey, the Centers for Disease Control senior microbiologist who recreated the virus. 'Influenza viruses are constantly evolving, and that means our science needs to evolve if we want to protect as many people as possible from pandemic influenza'.[87] Yet there were substantial differences between the avian version and the mutated human version of the virus, even though the virus was indeed a version of an avian 'flu rather than a human virus that had adapted some avian genes – as had happened in the last two pandemics we had: the Asian 'flu in 1957 and the Hong Kong 'flu in 1968.[88] Again, the spectre of this model of the 'flu returning with catastrophic results is blamed on the food chain.[89] As if it were the chicken's fault!

Looking at the 1976 swine 'flu debacle, Richard E. Neustadt and Ernest R. May spelled out the dangers of 'Unreasoning from analogies'.[90] Swine 'flu too was a disease of the food chain which was seen as an imminent danger to human beings. The science seemed to bear this out, as the virus's antigenic characteristics linked it to the 1918 influenza epidemic, at least in terms of the science of the day. There seemed to be an analogy between its first appearance, at the army base at Fort Dix, New Jersey in February 1976, and the outbreak of Spanish 'flu in army bases in the midwest in 1918. In 1976 the Spanish 'flu seemed to be a matter of 'folk memory' (p. 48). Its evocation made possible the moral panic about swine 'flu. Yet it was clear that it was the immediate memory of the 'flu epidemic of 1968, hardly on the same scale as the 1918 epidemic, that actually motivated the civil servants to act. The public health officials were revealed to have been woefully unprepared for that epidemic, which was seen as a political disaster, given their claims of being in charge of the nation's public health. 'Beat '68' was the mantra in 1976; the 1918 influenza epidemic was the rationale.

The head of the Center (later, Centers) for Disease Control (CDC), David Sencer, needed to be seen in 1976 as being prepared, unlike in the panic that had been the response in 1968.

As he noted: 'The Administration can tolerate unnecessary health expenditures better than unnecessary death and illness, particularly if a flu pandemic should occur' (p. 54). Here the model for avian 'flu was set: money is no object when confronted with the very possibility of a repetition of 1918. But the avian 'flu (and perhaps even the obesity virus) had a major precursor – the moral panic about SARS and the contamination of the food chain. The power of Sencer's argument rested on the inescapable fact that there had been an unrelated outbreak of Legionnaire's Disease. This 'epidemic' reinforced the public's acceptance that there might be potential for an epidemic of the proportions seen in 1918.

The public health claim was that all that was known about influenza pointed to quick action through vaccination as the most certain means of heading off the epidemic. The CDC used the horrors of 1918 as their 'worst case scenario'. They saw a safe, easily manufactured vaccine as the only rescue. The power of the presidency was harnessed to this claim. The reality turned out quite differently. The scientific community was not unanimously in support of this action. The swine 'flu vaccine caused harm to children. The epidemic never materialized. The power of the threat and the attendant panic were real; the epidemic was not.

In 2004, the overarching threat from the 'orient' was neither SARS nor infectobesity, but rather Islamic terrorism. For that, there clearly was never to be a vaccine. Whatever the reality of avian 'flu, the force that propelled much of the anxiety was the notion of this disease being a threat which could be combated, which could be countered, which could be defined clearly in its manifestation as well as in its point of origin. For Neustadt and May, the parallel moment in 1976 was the Cold War memories of Korea and the real experience of the Vietnam War. At least, as the argument might have gone, we can protect the homeland from this invasion.

Avian 'flu's appearance as a public health threat caused the swine 'flu debacle to be re-fought in the CDC's journals in 2006. And re-fought it was. Two of the senior administrators of the time quickly published their memoires. Richard M. Krause, who had been a member of the Infectious Disease Advisory Committee of the National Institute of Allergy and Infectious Diseases (NIAID) from 1970 to 1974, used the language of war as recently presented by Donald Rumsfeld, the former Secretary of Defense, who in 1996 spoke constantly about the 'fog of war'. Krause argued that they had believed that there was a 'real' link between 1918 and 1976: 'the belief [was] that the 1918 virus was eventually transmitted to pigs in the Midwest, where it persisted and caused sporadic human cases'.[91] He sought confirmation by examining the spread of swine 'flu in the southern hemisphere during 1976. He argued that the response to swine 'flu may have been too fast, but the public's response to the subsequent outbreak of HIV/AIDS was too slow. The implication of his argument is: better to be too fast than too slow. David J. Sencer, who had been the head of the CDC, also recapitulated the claims of swine 'flu, ending his potted history with a similar claim that:

When lives are at stake, it is better to err on the side of overreaction than underreaction. Because of the unpredictability of influenza, responsible public health leaders must be willing to take risks on behalf of the public. This requires personal courage and a reasonable level of understanding by the politicians to whom these public health leaders are accountable. All policy decisions entail risks and benefits: risks or benefits to the decision maker; risks or benefits to those affected by the decision. In 1976, the federal government wisely opted to put protection of the public first.[92]

His argument is for supporting the present reading of the swine 'flu response as purely a public health response. That the response could not fulfill its own claims for the protection offered, that the vaccine could neither be assured in mass application nor be seen as secure, echoes at least two of the problems with avian 'flu. But, most importantly, the question of what the political context for such decisions is is never put into play. It is always a case of the brave public health officials working to protect the public – beyond the political world in which they, too, function.

The pattern of the interest in avian 'flu began with SARS in 2003 but continues today. If there is an obesity epidemic that now exists and is the focus of a 'moral panic' about weight and disease, each new influenza outbreak in Asia becomes the cause of a potential pandemic of influenza, with all of the anxiety that accompanies such images. It is precisely the notion that the Ad–36 virus has crossed the species barrier in a far and distant world that makes the notion of 'infectobesity' so powerful – with India, not China, as the land of 'origin'. But, like China, India is part of an 'oriental' world endowed with the notion that it breeds and disseminates plagues, from cholera to SARS. Yet it is also, in the fantasy of the West, the land of famine and starvation, in which obesity can be imagined only with great effort. India may answer our collective desire that obesity, too, can be quickly fixed, once it is recognized as 'merely' an infectious disease or an invasion from without, rather than a reflection on our national or personal character. No quick fix, social or medical, is truly possible; why not hope for a vaccine against modernity, hopelessness, and fat, all at once, asks the dreamer in each of us? Simply because such quick fixes never truly eliminate the moral panic associated with each new epidemic, whether obesity, SARS, or Avian 'flu.

2

CHILDHOOD OBESITY

In contemporary Australia, a culture defined by the beach and by hard, brown bodies, the lot of the fat person is not a happy one. Ironically so, since Australia is the fattest of all the developed nations, with one out of two women being overweight or obese. And they are exposed to all the ridicule reserved today for fat people. They are characterized as 'ugly, stupid, mean, sloppy, lazy, dishonest, worried, sad, self-indulgent, unlik[e]able, and emotionally [more] impaired than normal weight individuals'.[1] In Canada, a nation hardly defined by the beach culture, little is different. The stupidity of the obese is defined by their refusal to acknowledge their own obesity: 'Not only are we fat and lazy, we're apparently stupid as well. . . . 58 per cent of us think our weight has no effect on heart health'.[2] In the Republic of Ireland, when you are seen as fat, you are considered stupid, as one overweight woman noted: 'When you're fat, people think you're stupid and are surprised to hear intelligent sentences come out of your mouth.'[3] But this image of the overweight adult as stupid and self-destructive is hardly one produced by the new 'global epidemic' of obesity that the World Health Organization declared in 1998.[4]

Yet the concern of contemporary culture seems to be even greater when obesity 'attacks' a child. In the United Kingdom there has recently been an obsession with childhood obesity, which, it is claimed, 'has trebled in 20 years'.[5] In Singapore, as elsewhere in the developed world, 'parents and caregivers need to realize the importance of healthy weight, and the long-term consequences of obesity', stated a leading pediatrician.[6] Here it is not 'stupidity' that reigns as the sole model, though 'an overweight child or adolescent may face poor self-esteem and reduced quality of life', but a wide range of physical ailments that will preclude the fat child from taking his or her rightful place as a citizen in the national state. Childhood obesity comes to hold a special role in defining the dangers – to society as a whole – that the perception of increased bodily weight implies, as it seems, across both political and economic divides, from the United States to Iran to South Africa. Fat children signify a basic change in society for the worse.[7]

Stereotypical images of the obese individual are already fixed in the worldview of nineteenth-century Anglophone high culture. The 'fat' stereotype permeates the metaphors (and thus the minds) of even the most radical of thinkers of the time. Thus on October 16, 1851, Frederick Douglass, abolitionist and fighter for women's rights, announced that '*The [New York] Herald*, in noticing the [Liberty Party National Convention] nominations, thus exhibits its innate vulgarity: "Mr D. is white, which shows some progress during the past year even with the old Liberty party." We do not see what complexion has to do with a man's fitness for an office requiring an active and a well informed mind; but we do see, that gross obesity, as tending to induce mental stupidity, as coarseness of feeling, might seriously disqualify a man for such an office'.[8] Obesity was a sign of mental vacuity and of an insensitivity of emotional response. The stupidity and crudity of emotions that Douglas gestures at is that of the senior James Gordon Bennett, the corpulent and conservative editor of the *New York Herald*. It is a sign of the impairment of one's intelligence and emotions. Thus at the beginning of the nineteenth century William Wadd, the Surgeon Extraordinary to the Prince Regent, stated that, 'if the Goddess of Wisdom were to grow fat, even she would become stupid . . . Fat and stupidity, says the accomplished Lord Chesterfield, are looked upon as such inseparable companions that they are used as synonymous terms'.[9] While this is an ancient claim, it is clear that the assumption that fat people are stupid was also contested in unusual ways.

1 DICKENS AND THE PHYSIOGNOMY OF OBESITY

The most evident literary encapsulation of the image of the stupid fat man seems to be found in Charles Dickens' *Pickwick Papers* (1836). This is the last great eighteenth-century novel of travel, making Dickens the heir of Fielding and Smollett.[10] But it is also the first Victorian novel in which, as V. S. Pritchett noted, the desire for food replaces the 'eighteenth-century attitude to sex in the comic unity of Dickens'.[11] In *Tom Jones* food is a path to sex; in Dickens it seems to be a substitute for it. The representation of desire is made socially acceptable by being placed at the table rather than in the bed. Still, desire remains the hallmark of what is truly human.

Dickens uses his readers' expectations as to which characters should or should not be able to experience desire in order to criticize the very notion of the lack of an emotional (and intellectual) life for the obese. The shift in imagining desire plays upon the physiognomy of the characters as a means of undermining these expectations. In Dickens' early *Sketches by*

Boz (1833–6), he presents the idea that, if 'the agitation of a man's brain by different passions' can shape his skull, so too can it shape the form and function of his street-door knocker.[12] Many years ago, I tracked this social–physiognomic phenomenon in Dickens' work on insanity, showing how his representation of the insane provided a critique of the assumptions concerning madness in the world of the reformed asylum.[13] Relying on the physiognomic presuppositions of his time (and on the rise of psychiatric photography, pioneered by his friends), Dickens was able to provide the reader with insight into their own visual expectations of insanity.

What is striking is that, when one turns to the *Pickwick Papers* to examine the question of obesity, not only is the question of physiognomy central to the author's concern, but there is an explicit critique of these assumptions when it comes to our ability to read the physiognomy of the obese as opposed to the merely corpulent. From the standpoint of a contemporary reader (and a viewer of the illustrations by 'Phiz', i.e. Halbot K. Browne), everyone in the *Pickwick Papers* is fat. (One can note that the initial images of Pickwick by Robert Seymour, who committed suicide in 1836, had more in common with the body of Don Quixote than with that of Sancho Panza.[14]) Juliet McMaster argues convincingly that Dickens presents two kinds of 'fat' people: The first is Mr Samuel Pickwick (and his middle-class friends), who, to use her words, are 'fat-cheery' instead of 'fat-bloated'.[15] Pickwick and his friends are plump and 'charged with energy, solar or otherwise. He bursts, he beams, he bulges . . . His fatness . . . is scarcely even heavy' (p. 338). But the 'fat-bloated' form of obesity seems to be incorporated in Mr Wardel's 'boy', his servant, Joe. He is 'better known to the readers of this unvarnished history by the distinguishing appellation of the fat boy' (p. 338), whose body mirrors his soul, or so it seems.

Joe, the comic parallel to Mr Pickwick's clever (and thin) servant Sam Weller, is defined in the novel by his blank expression, huge appetite, and ability to avoid work by falling asleep instantaneously. He is a version of Sancho Panza, only that all of the Quixotes in this novel are 'fat-cheery' except him. He is regularly described as snoring 'in a low and monotonous sound'. Joe is comic because of his girth and what it implies:

> 'Come along, Sir. Pray, come up,' said the stout gentleman. 'Joe! – damn that boy, he's gone to sleep again. – Joe, let down the steps.' The fat boy rolled slowly off the box, let down the steps, and held the carriage door invitingly open. Mr Snodgrass and Mr Winkle came up at the moment. 'Room for you all, gentlemen,' said the stout man. 'Two inside, and one out. Joe, make room for one of these gentlemen on the box. Now, Sir, come along,' and the stout gentleman extended his arm, and pulled first Mr Pickwick, and then Mr Snodgrass, into the barouche by main force. Mr Winkle mounted to the box, the fat boy waddled to the same perch, and fell fast asleep instantly.[16]

In this description, we are presented the stereotype that fat men like Joe move their buttocks comically (like an animal) and they are lazy, falling asleep whenever they cease moving, as a sign of their almost medieval sinful sloth and stupidity. Joe is *seen* as fat, and fat means that he is mentally 'slow' and without the appropriate emotional responses. But what that actually means in Dickens' world of false appearances is not at first quite clear.[17] And that is reflected in the very nature of how Joe is seen. Sam Weller calls him 'young dropsy' (p. 340), ironically seeing his sleepiness as a reflection of illness. Pickwick calls him a 'young opium eater' (p. 344). He is a freak, a body that 'had never [been] seen in or out of a traveling convoy' (p. 675). His is a truly obese body, unlike those of the bourgeois characters. And it is seen as neither healthy nor 'normal'.

The 'fat boy' in Dickens' novel seems to be ill, as one commentator in a Philadelphia African–American newspaper of the 1860s noted about obesity:

> A voracious appetite, so far from being a sign of health, is a certain indication of disease. Some dyspeptics are always hungry; feel best when they are eating, but as soon as they have eaten they enter torments, so distressing in their nature, as to make the unhappy victim wish for death. . . . Multitudes measure their health by the amount they can eat; and of any ten persons, nine are gratified at an increase of weight, as if mere bulk were an index of health; when in reality, any excess of fatness is, in proportion, decisive proof of existing disease; showing that the absorbents of the system are too weak to discharge their duty; and the tendency to fatness, to obesity, increases, until existence is a burden, and sudden death closes the history. . .[18]

Obesity for the Victorian is an illness unto death.

But is Joe truly ill in this sense? Gail Turley Houston notes: 'Dickens expects the reader to differentiate between Pickwickian gentlemanly gusto and the ludicrous gorging of the poverty-stricken hangers-on such as . . . the fat boy'.[19] Thus Mr Pickwick, when awakened by the first rays of the sun, 'was no sluggard . . . he sprang like an ardent warrior from his tent-bedstead' (p. 75). He is plump but quick of body and mind – and therefore healthy and wise. But Joe's 'illness' is clearly not physiological but 'social', not an illness of his own making but a reflection of the society's perception of obesity. What differentiates Joe from Mr Pickwick is the work's definition of true masculinity.

The boundary which defines the masculine seems to run along the fault line of obesity in the Anglophone nineteenth century. In the Victorian epic of Canada, *Idomen; or, the Vale of Yumuri* (1843) by Maria del Occidente (i.e. Maria Gowen Brooks, 1794/5–1845), the protagonist is described thus:

> His age at this time was twenty-three years;
> his stature much exceeded six feet, and his figure,
> though still supple and slender, had attained
> enough of obesity to give that roundness
> of surface so much admired by painters.
>
> The ancient Romans, sometimes fed their
> gladiators with a chosen food, to make them
> look more beautiful; – but here, what tints and
> contour had been refined by a process of nature,
> from the snowy earth of Canada![20]

The body of 'the stranger' is full and yet masculine, formed by his experience on the frontier. Here is the male body in all its glory, just 'obese' enough to be attractive. This clearly is not the body of the fat boy, who never seems to be the object of any one's desire.

There is one odd but effective moment very early in the *Pickwick Papers* where the question of the inferior mental and emotional status of Mr Wardel's 'boy' Joe is called into question. Joe accidentally observes an attempted seduction taking place in the garden. Mr Tracy Tupman is wooing the 'spinster aunt' Rachael Wardle, an odd match even in the world of Pickwick, for 'young men, to spinster aunts, are as lighted gas to gunpowder' (p. 94). Joe observes them and the seducer looks at Joe being 'perfectly motionless, with his large circular eyes staring into the arbour, but without the slightest expression on his face that the most expert physiognomist could have referred to astonishment, curiosity, or any other known passion that agitates the human breast. Mr Tupman gazed on the fat boy, and the fat boy stared at him; and the longer Mr Tupman observed the utter vacancy of the fat boy's countenance, the more convinced he became that he either did not know, or did not understand, anything that had been going forward' (p. 89). This is a clear misapprehension.

But, of course, Joe had understood all too well. As Tupman walks off, 'there was a sound behind them, as of an imperfectly suppressed chuckle. Mr Tupman turned sharply round. No; it could not have been the fat boy; there was not a gleam of mirth, or anything but feeding in his whole visage' (p. 89). His fat physiognomy was unreadable, but he recognized what he had observed and turned it to his own advantage! Later on he goes to his employer's aged mother, to whom he wishes to reveal all. She is initially frightened at his desire to speak, because he had been marked by a silence that reflected his girth. She protests that she had always treated him well and given him enough to eat. He responds with the emotionally ambiguous statement: 'I wants to make your flesh creep' (p. 3). In revealing what he has seen in all of its detail, with all of its 'kissin' and huggin'' (p. 93), he shows that not only does he recognize ill-placed desire, but he can also tell the story for his own betterment. (The reader first meets a similar character in a similar mode in the *Sketches by Boz*, when a 'corpulent round-headed boy' peeps through a keyhole.[21])

In Wilhelm Ebstein's late Victorian study of obesity, the first standard medical presentation of obesity as a physiological problem, the author quotes the eighteenth-century German essayist Georg Lichtenberg, who says that 'there be people with such plump faces that they may laugh under their fat, so that the greatest physiognomist shall fail to notice it, while we poor slender creatures with our souls seated immediately beneath the epidermis, ever speak a language which can tell no lies'.[22] Joe seems to be inscrutable in his obesity, but the tale he tells will make all notice him. He tells stories that will indeed 'make your flesh creep', but at his own pace and in his own time. James Joyce knows the power of this moment when, in the Scylla and Charybdis chapter of *Ulysses*, he has John Eglinton say that Stephen Daedelus 'will have it that Hamlet is a ghost story. . . . Like the fat boy in Pickwick he wants to make our flesh creep'.[23] And our flesh does creep at these ghost stories because of the anomalous nature of the narrator, our seemingly stupid and insensitive 'fat boy'.[24]

This is the reader's introduction to Joe at the very beginning of the novel. His stories may make the characters' flesh creep only because they seem not to be able to read his face. For the physiognomy of 'fat boys' seems not to mirror their character. And yet, at the very conclusion of the novel, Dickens returns to the same scene in a different setting. He stumbles into another seduction, now between partners of an appropriate age, seeing Mr Augustus Snodgrass with his arm about his beloved Emily Wardle's waist:

'Wretched creature, what do you want here?' said the gentleman, who it is needless to say was Mr Snodgrass.

To this the fat boy, considerably terrified, briefly responded, 'Missis'.

'What do you want me for,' inquired Emily, turning her head aside, 'you stupid creature?'

'Master and Mr Pickwick is a-going to dine here at five,' replied the fat boy.

'Leave the room!' said Mr Snodgrass, glaring upon the bewildered youth.

'No, no, no,' added Emily hastily. 'Bella, dear, advise me.'

Upon this, Emily and Mr Snodgrass, and Arabella and Mary, crowded into a corner, and conversed earnestly in whispers for some minutes, during which the fat boy dozed.

'Joe,' said Arabella, at length, looking round with a most bewitching smile, 'how do you do, Joe?'

'Joe,' said Emily, 'you're a very good boy; I won't forget you, Joe.'

'Joe,' said Mr Snodgrass, advancing to the astonished youth, and seizing his hand, 'I didn't know you before. There's five shillings for you, Joe!'

'I'll owe you five, Joe,' said Arabella, 'for old acquaintance sake, you know'; and another most captivating smile was bestowed upon the corpulent intruder.

The fat boy's perception being slow, he looked rather puzzled at first to account for this sudden prepossession in his favour, and stared about him in a very alarming manner. At length his broad face began to show symptoms of a grin of proportionately broad dimensions; and then, thrusting half-a-crown into each of his pockets, and a hand and wrist after it, he burst into a horse laugh: being for the first and only time in his existence.

'He understands us, I see,' said Arabella.

'He had better have something to eat, immediately,' remarked Emily. (pp. 685–6)

Joe certainly understands. He understands the moment of seduction he has observed. He certainly understands the double sense of Arabella's statement that she will not forget him, a two-edged statement that has to do with monetary reward, but is also an acknowledgement of him as a human being. He may be 'slow', but he clearly understands the sexual tension in the room and the power that it grants him. His physiognomy is completely readable by all. He smiles and he laughs, as for once he is in control of the situation – or is he?

And the company sends the servant Mary off with Joe, to make sure that he does not again expose lovers to the forces of social control. It is the laughter (which had also signaled Joe's first sense of awareness in his observation of the earlier seduction) that makes them anxious. They immediately sit down to feed Joe's appetite. Mary's feeding of Joe is intended to draw his attention away from the desire shown by the lovers, and Joe unexpectedly offers Mary some of the food with which she was bribing him:

> The fat boy assisted Mary to a little, and himself to a great deal, and was just going to begin eating when he suddenly laid down his knife and fork, leaned forward in his chair, and letting his hands, with the knife and fork in them, fall on his knees, said, very slowly –
>
> 'I say! How nice you look!'
>
> This was said in an admiring manner, and was, so far, gratifying; but still there was enough of the cannibal in the young gentleman's eyes to render the compliment a double one.
>
> 'Dear me, Joseph,' said Mary, affecting to blush, 'what do you mean?'
>
> The fat boy, gradually recovering his former position, replied with a heavy sigh, and, remaining thoughtful for a few moments, drank a long draught of the porter. Having achieved this feat, he sighed again, and applied himself assiduously to the pie. (p. 686)

The question of Joe's unexpected attraction to Mary startles the reader in Dickens' use of the image of the cannibal. He ironically has us see the fat boy reducing Mary, from an object of erotic desire, to one of gustatory pleasure. Yet the 'heavy sigh' points to a very different desire. He knows what object of desire is available to him. Following this exchange, Joe returns to Pickwick with a note from Emile Wardle. He comments to Sam Weller about the servant girl Mary (in whom Weller is more than interested): 'I say,' said Joe, who was unusually loquacious, 'what a pretty girl Mary is, isn't she? I am SO fond of her, I am!' Mr Weller made no verbal remark in reply; but eyeing the fat boy for a moment, quite transfixed at his presumption, led him by the collar to the corner, and dismissed him with a harmless but ceremonious kick' (pp. 712–13). Even fat boys can show desire! And here V. S. Prichett's claim about the transformation of the erotic into the pleasures of the table is undermined by our recognition that Joe is motivated by much more than food. His desire for status (in reporting the first seduction) and our awareness of his potential for love (in the latter case) change the way Joe is seen, both within the text and by the reader. Masculinity is not canceled by what has been apostrophized in the novel as pathological obesity. Joe can desire and can express this desire.

Yet there is the unstated question of whether the 'fat boy' can have desire, whether he can be a sexual being. In 1859, the British colonial surgeon W. G. Don reporting from India presented the case of a twelve-year-old 'Hindoo boy, known in the streets of Bombay under the soubriquet of the "Fat Boy"'.[25] The echo of Dickens in this colonial report is clear. Don's 'Fat Boy' had become very fat at the age of two, until 'his whole body is now encased in an immense mass of solid adipose tissue, which hangs in pendulous folds over his chest and hips, and the flexures of his limbs.' At twelve he is forty-eight and a half inches tall, weighing 206 pounds. He seems in good health except for 'a difficulty breathing', but his 'appearance is extremely odd' as he 'walks with difficulty, and when tired rests himself by leaning his pendulous abdomen against a wall'. While he seems normally developed for a twelve-year-old, 'the genital organs, however, are not larger than those of an infant, while the testes are very small, and seem either to be undeveloped or to have become atrophied'. He is, however, 'highly intelligent' (p. 363). Here the unstated 'secret' of Fat Boy seems to be revealed. Can Victorian fat boys have sexual desire? Or is their physiognomy the hidden secret of their seeming lack of desire?

The idea that the fat man's physiognomy was misread and that the 'rules' of physiognomic interpretation lead to flagrant abuses was a topic before Dickens. Thomas Love Peacock (1785–1866) in his *Crotchet Castle* (1831) presents the reader with Dr Folliet, who, while quoting Greek poetry to a nightingale, is attacked by two armed robbers and drives them off with his walking stick. He is able to do so in a rage, because he imagines them looking at him and thinking that he is an easy target because he appears to be a fat old man:

> One of them drew a pistol, which went off in the very act of being struck aside by the bamboo, and lodged a bullet in the brain of the other. There was then only one enemy, who vainly struggled to rise, every effort being attended with a new and more signal prostration. The fellow roared for mercy. 'Mercy, rascal!' cried the divine; 'what mercy were you going to show me, villain? What! I warrant me, you thought it would be an easy matter, and no sin, to rob and murder a parson on his way home from dinner. You said to yourselves, doubtless, 'We'll waylay the fat parson (you irreverent knave) as he waddles home (you disparaging ruffian), half-seas-over' (you calumnious vagabond). And with every dyslogistic term, which he supposed had been applied to himself, he inflicted a new bruise on his rolling and roaring antagonist. 'Ah, rogue!' he proceeded; 'you can roar now, marauder; you were silent enough when you devoted my brains to dispersion under your cudgel. But seeing that I cannot bind you, and that I intend you not to escape, and that it would be dangerous to let you rise, I will disable you in all your members . . .'[26]

His fat only appears not to be masculine; in reality he is 'plump', not fat – and dangerous too. His anger, like Joe's desire, may be masked by a misreading of the body but reveals itself in his actions. Fat Boys can mislead!

2 JOE AND THE OBESITY OF CHILDREN

The image of the active, angry plump middle-class man is quite the opposite of that of the servant Joe, whose fat seems to have 'its customary association with inertia'.[27] Joe, however, became a case study of pathology against Dickens' much more complex image of limitation and awareness. It was read as an example of obesity of the youth. As Edward Jukes noted in 1833:

> Fat, when moderately diffused over the body, indicates a sound state of health, and an easy disposition, gives a symmetry to the figure, and (which by many is valued more than all these) it contributes much to the beauty of the countenance; but on the contrary, where it accumulates to excess, it becomes an absolute disease, and is frequently the cause of death, particularly in habits where some chronic disorder has preceded it, or where acute attacks of disease have been aggravated by its presence.[28]

The causes, according to Dickens' contemporary, are either 'occasioned by indulging in the use of highly nutritious foods' or, as in the case of the fat boy, 'a peculiarity of constitution predisposing to this state' pp. 289–90). Fat boys can be a separate class (in both senses of the word), born to be fat. Dickens' fat boy has no childhood; he is the product of his class and of the immediate world in which he lives. He exists well before the category of adolescence, which was created to be the transition between childhood and the adult world.[29] Yet he is not a 'boy', but a fat man in waiting. Dickens wrestles with the question of the meaning of inheritance, as his world comes to be that of Spencer's struggle of the fittest and of Darwin's evolutionary model. In the *Pickwick Papers* Dickens rejects the very notion of a child being able to inherit acquired characteristics, so that Joe could not be the son nor the father of obese men.[30] Joe inhabits his own world and is neither degenerate nor the son of degenerates.

In the Enlightenment, Christoph Wilhelm Hufeland had captured a social explanation for adult obesity in his extraordinarily popular *Art of Prolonging Life* (1796).[31] Fat is simply bad for Hufeland and Enlightenment luminaries because most people eat much more than they need. 'Immoderation' is one of the prime causes of early death (Hufeland (1797 translation), II: 43). Invoking the Aristotelian golden mean, eating too much and eating too richly will kill you. 'Idleness' is also a cause (ii, 64). Human beings have lost their natural ability to determine how much we need through childhood overindulgence. In ploughing the fields, notes Hufeland, natural man has purpose, exercise, and food appropriate to long life. 'His son becomes a studious rake; and the proportion between countrymen and citizens seems daily to be diminished' (ii, 217). The fat child is now the father (and mother) of the fat adult. At the very beginning of his list of things that will certainly cause an early death, Hufeland places a 'very warm, tender, and delicate education' in childhood, one in which children are stuffed 'immoderately with food; and by coffee, chocolate, wine, spices, and such things . . .' (II: 9). Not sin, but middle-class overindulgence begins to be seen as the force that creates fat boys. In the nineteenth century, the 'science' of diet seems to replace the morals of diet. The hidden model remains the same: the normal, reasonable man is always contrasted with the fat boy, and always to the latter's detriment. And the reward for the thin man is life, life extended, while the fat man dies young and unhappy.

Unlike the pampered children of Hufeland's middle class, fat children came to be seen as primal beings through the lens of the various models of evolutionary theory that dominated Dickens' world. These children lacked the specific sense of 'masculinity' inherent to Victorian ideas of manliness.[32] Louis Robinson, in the middle-class journal *The Nineteenth Century*, asked: 'Why should babies be so fat, when the children of their pithecoid ancestors must have been lean? ... The suicidal swallowing capacity of the modern baby is an inheritance from the habits of the crawling cave-dweller'.[33] An anonymous wag in *Punch* replied:

> Baby boy, whose visage chubby
> Doting mother marvels at,
> Full of health, albeit grubby –
> Why are you so fat?
>
> How unlike your rude forefather –
> Prehistoric, pithecoid!
> Who with nuts he chanced to gather
> Filled his aching void . . .
>
> No! but later generations
> Come, in which the infant staves
> Hunger off by dint of rations
> Picked up in the caves.
>
> Holding future meals in question,
> Grasping all with eager fist, –
> To the mill of his digestion
> Everything is grist.
>
> Consequently, you, who follow
> Him in lack of self-control,
> With atavic impulse swallow
> Dirt, and pins and coal.[34]

By the end of the century, post-Darwinian fat was the product of an evolutionary development, which gave purpose to actions in the past but had become atavistic at the present.

Fat had a true function, at least in our distant past, but today such 'fat boys' are primeval throwbacks, unable to function in contemporary society. On such a Darwinian reading, Joe's body is different from that of Pickwick and of all of the other plump, middle-class adventurers in Dickens' novel. His body comes to be read not merely as a symptom of his class (Sam Weller's body is the body of the healthy and wily servant), but as an example of the physiognomy of the primitive that haunts this world of work. Joe is the 'fat boy', the young man who, unlike Sam Weller, will never be able to accomplish anything because of his girth. He is a curiosity, kept by Mr Wardle precisely because of this fat. It is often the worker who is portrayed as lacking will power because of his ancestry and background. At the extreme, it is the worker as alcoholic and criminal. Here, it is the worker as 'fat boy', condemned to live out his desires because of his physical inheritance.[35]

William Thomas Moncrieff dramatized the *Pickwick Papers* under the title *Sam Weller or The Pickwickians* (1837) so quickly that Dickens was just able – just as quickly – to satirize him as 'the literary gentleman' in *Nicholas Nickleby* in 1839. Moncrieff presented Joe as the exemplary British somnambulist in a ditty sang in the British music-halls during the 1840s, well before the Darwin craze:

> Don't disturb yourself, pray – 'tis but Joe, the Fat Boy,
> Who was never known any one's rest to destroy.
> I've come here quite by chance, so, for company's sake,
> I'll just sing you a song – it will keep me awake.
> For we are all noddin', nid, nid noddin',
> We are all noddin', abroad and at home.
> People scold because sometimes I sleep in the day,

Although I might answer, so do they –
For I think I can prove, if you'll list to my rhymes,
Every one of them may be caught nodding at times.
Yes, they're all noddin', nid nid noddin',
They are all noddin', abroad and at home.
The Parson, who tells us to watch and to pray,
And will not on Sundays at home let us stay,
Nods at church o'er his sermon, and makes us, the elf,
Nod long ere it's finished as much as himself.
For they are all noddin', nid nid noddin',
They are all noddin' to church when they come.
Both Houses of Parliament nod, too, you'll find –
When one party speaks, to sleep t'other's inclin'd –
One nods till the other side's said all their say,
And as or the Speaker, he nods night away.
For they are all noddin', nid nid noddin',
They are all noddin' to the House when they come.
Young folks, when the old folks to nod are inclin'd,
And her lover's entreating that she will be kind,
That she neither may grant nor deny him the bliss,
Will appear to nod, too, while he steals a sweet kiss.
For they are all noddin', nid nid noddin',
They are all noddin at our house at home.
But I'm getting quite tir'd – no doubt you're so too –
Ya-aw! I really beg pardon – I'll bid you adieu,
'Tis high time, for I scarce my eyes open can keep,
And I'm sure that I must have walk'd here in my sleep!
For we are all noddin' – yaw-aw! – nid nid noddin' –
We are all noddin' – yaw-aw! – to the end when come!
    [Yawns – sinks into chair – falls asleep – snores, and
    is carried off, first having a nightcap put on him.[36]

For Moncrieff, everyone has a bit of 'Joe' in them, the primitive hidden within. And this is tied to social norms, including

rituals of seduction and desire. But it is the lover who mimes sleep in order to permit the seduction. What is sham here is inherent in the makeup of the fat boy. It is a sign of his being a throwback to the world of the primitive. Joe is Moncrieff's exemplar of fat; his obesity is present in him to a greater extent than in anyone else, and from his very inception.

In the early nineteenth century there was a concern about the association between childhood obesity and moral character. The medical literature expressed some anxiety regarding the overfeeding of infants in the nursery.[37] However, fat babies were seen as healthy babies until the late twentieth century. One of the decisive works on pediatric illness, Johannes Joachim Becher's posthumous *Medicinische Schatz-Kammer* of 1700, lists the entire range of diseases that were seen to befall children (including syphilis), but obesity is never mentioned.[38] After the Enlightenment, where the child was seen as future father to the man, obesity in children becomes a topic of medical interest, illustrating the desire to distinguish between healthy fat and the risk of morbidity. In a standard handbook of 1879, cases of morbid obesity in children from 1815 to 1845 were used to document these rare occurrences.[39] In American popular fiction after Dickens, the 'fat boy' appears as a set character. In 1863 Stephen C. Massett produced one in order to characterize the homespun nature of his frontier characters:

> on one side of the house, upon a piece of canvas, was displayed a painting of a 'Fat Boy'. Immediately upon entering, the showman, pointing with his short stick to a perfect mountain of fat, proceeded as follows: 'Master Villiam Fiddes – or the Hinfant Goliath. He is the seventh son of Joel (that's me) and Helizabeth Fiddes, who is industrious and respectable persons, as resides in Manchester, which was in the month of November he was born. He is only six years of

age, and is considered one of the greatest venders which this world as ever produced by the Supreme Being. Ladies and gentlemen, when this Fenominer of nature were born, he had four regular teeth, and very shortly after that possessed twenty-two teeth. He is a remarkable healthy child when he is well, and is very amusing, and possessed of very pretty features. (Show the gents your leg, Billy.) His food consists of a common and wholesome description, and is generally boiled in hot water, as the doctor says his hinside requires soft things, and is considered the greatest wonder of the world. It would be morally unpossible to describe everything belonging to this great wonder of nature, as he is endowed with every necessary qualification vich adorns the human frame, as such should be produced, and is mild, sensible, and pleasant.'[40]

This 'fat boy' is displayed as a freak, but is actually no more 'freakish' than the other characters inhabiting Massett's world, including his own father.

Even at the beginning of the twentieth century, the public health concern about children's bodies was with malnutrition and the diseases associated with it in children – not with obesity.[41] To be sure, the beautiful (fat) baby contests became part of the eugenics movement, to assure a healthy breeding-stock of human beings delighted in the fat baby.[42] However, through the 1930s and 1940s, fat babies came to be increasingly pathologized, as they were seen as the origin of fat (and sick) adults. This is a decisive shift from regarding moral degeneracy as the cause of obesity.

By the beginning of the twentieth century, the universal argument that such infants suffered from illness – either an endocrine imbalance or a neurosis – provided the means of defining the fat baby as ill. A debate followed between those who argued that obesity was a product of external (exogenous) forces and those who saw it as a symptom of a physiological pathology.[43] The former are well represented by the work of Carl von Noorden, who saw most obesity as exogenous. The latter picked up on the work of Alfred Froehlich, who had described a case of pituitary tumor in a fourteen-year-old male with massive obesity and sexual infantilism.[44] 'Froehlich's syndrome' became the catchword for all physiological theories of obesity.[45] More importantly, it drew an absolute line between sick and healthy children, and was considered to have predictive force.

3 JOE'S AFTERLIFE IN MEDICINE

Joe does have a life beyond nineteenth-century popular culture. Various pirated versions of the tale of Joe, as well as Toby jugs with his visage circulate in the wake of his initial popularity.[46] This is equally true of the medical literature, which adopted Joe as the litmus test for obesity. In 1893 *The Lancet*, citing an American case study, reported on a 'case of narcolepsy'.[47] A soldier who regularly falls asleep is accused of dereliction of duty because he did it at his post. It is revealed that he seemed 'well nourished and all his organs were apparently healthy. Mentally he did not seem to be lacking, although "not very bright" best described his condition' (p. 100). He had fallen asleep on horseback while on parade, as well as frequently falling 'asleep at meals, on one occasion with a spoon in his mouth'. His treatment consisted in putting him on light duty. 'Later he was placed on duty in the kitchen [where] he fell asleep and let the fire out and so delayed the meal.' The author of the note concluded: 'We have sometimes wondered whether Dickens had any knowledge of this as a distinct pathological condition when he described his immortal Fat Boy in "Pickwick".' Dickens' character seems to be the appropriate reference for the readers of *The Lancet* to understand the nature of the soldier's ailment, and narcolepsy seems to be the appropriate diagnosis for the fat boy's problem. Here the mental acuity of the soldier seems also to play a role in his diagnosis. He is not very bright, and that seems to be part of the diagnostic symptomatology of narcolepsy. Being diagnosed with a disease, he is found innocent of a very serious breech of military discipline and transformed into a case that needs treatment.

Dickens' 'fat boy' seems to provide the paradigm for all cases. When in 1904 the parents of 'the fat boy of Peckham', Johnnie Trundley – a boy of five years and a half weighing eight stones and five pounds – are accused of violating the 1894 Act for the Prevention of Cruelty to Children by exhibiting him as a freak, it is Dickens' character to whom the comparison is made.[48] The author of an editorial in *The Lancet* notes that 'every traveling showman would testify that obesity has always been as highly appreciated by the public as abnormal stature, and the youthful Trundley has had the advantage, or disadvantage, of living in an age in which notoriety is easily achieved' (p. 106). But this celebrity, the author notes, pales in comparison to that of the 'heroes of fiction [who] have the advantage in the matter of lasting glory and the names of Daniel Lambert and the Fat Boy of Peckham sink into insignificance beside those of Falstaff and the Fat Boy in "Pickwick".' Conspicuousness as the ultimate case study of childhood obesity is assured through the medium of literature.

In an account written by William Ord at the close of the nineteenth century, the conspicuousness still attendant upon Dickens' character materializes in a case of obesity associated with hypothyroidism.[49] Ord provides an easy reference to how one of his patients is imagined as Dickens' fat boy Joe. He describes a case of Graves' or Basedow's syndrome (or disease), the standard labels for hypothyroidism at the close of the century (the choice between them depending on whether you were a British or a German patient). His patient, a thirty-year-old waiter, is admitted to St Thomas's Hospital in London in 1892 in the ending phase of the disease. Diagnosed some six years earlier, he had developed a set of psychological and physiological symptoms: 'He began at first to feel heavy, dull and depressed, and became clumsy especially with his hands. . . . His abdomen and body generally began to swell and his face became round, puffy, and yellowish-brown with flushed cheeks, earning for him the nickname of "the fat boy in Pickwick", which replaced the nickname of "Skin and Buttons" which had before the illness been bestowed upon him on account of his pale and hollow-eyed countenance' (p. 1246). He developed a 'sort of Mongolian change of physiognomy' (p. 1246). That there are specific physiognomic manifestations associated with this disease was even then well known, having been described for the first time in Sayyid Ismail Al-Jurjani's medieval *Thesaurus of the Shah of Khwarazm*: goiter and exophthalmosis (bulging eyes) were the most evident signs. The altered mental state, too, had become a standard part of the representation of patients suffering from this illness. Treated with thyroid extract, the patient's symptoms diminished and he was able to return to work, even though he seemed clumsier than before at his job of waiter. The case has a negative outcome as the patient stopped coming to the clinic for the thyroid extract and eventually became an alcoholic, dying of symptoms associated with Grave's disease in 1895. Ord's case study notes that the patient's nickname seemed to fit both his mental and his physiological state. On the other hand, Dickens' Joe was developing somatic obesity, but hypothyroidism, with the diminished mental capacity incumbent upon it, seemed an etiology insufficient to explain the power of his character.

With the shift in the explanation of childhood obesity onto a focus on the endocrine system, Dickens' fat boy becomes an illustration of Froehlich's syndrome rather than of Graves' disease. The reason for this lies in the image of the asexuality of the 'fat boy', a quality not present in the traditional definition of hypothyroidism (or indeed of goiter, in its historical construction). By 1953, E. Watson-Williams dismisses 'the well-known but irrelevant case of endocrine obesity recorded by Dickens'.[50] But the endocrine error is not hypothyroidism; it is an error of the pituitary gland. As early as 1922, H. Letheby Tidy had diagnosed Joe as a case of hypopituitarism (Froehlich's syndrome) or 'dystrophia adiposogenitalis'.[51] In addition to having its onset before puberty, in the form of morbid obesity ('adiposity'), other salient features include deficiency of growth and 'genital dystrophy or atrophy.' The 'fat boy' can have no desire because his sexual development is stunted! But, Watson-Williams observes, this does not impact on his awareness of the world, or on his innate intelligence. His face seems to deny this awareness. This type of hypopituitarism 'may produce the appearance which was described . . . as the "pudding-face type"' (p. 600). And yet this type, exemplified by Joe, is neither intellectually nor emotionally retarded. 'Many of the famous Fat Boys have belonged to this group; the Fat Boy in Pickwick may be considered to be an example, and Dickens was by no means inaccurate in picturing him as possessing an acute intelligence in his waking moments' (ibid.). Joe is suffering from a childhood somatic illness, not from a weakness of the will or mind. He has now become a somatic case study with a more specific etiology, unlike the 'Hindoo fat boy' reported some seventy-five years earlier. Yet he, too, is seen as being without desire (or at least without sexual capacity.)

It is in the world of mid-twentieth-century pulmonary medicine that the conflict between the psychological and the metabolic etiologies of obesity, at least in regards to the 'fat boy', is momentarily resolved. This is accomplished through

the creation of the 'Pickwick syndrome',[52] a phrase coined by
C. Sidney Burwell and his colleagues at Harvard in 1956.[53] It
designates a form of obstructive sleep apnea (lack of respiration), the condition where people stop breathing for very
short intervals of time during their normal sleep periods. This
results in the patient having a marked loss of oxygen in the
blood system and being lethargic while awake. Burwell's paper
presented a single case study of the 'association of obesity,
somnolence, polycythemia and excessive appetite' and defined
a new syndrome. Despite its name, the eponymous figure is
not – to anyone's surprise – Charles Dickens' Mr Samuel
Pickwick from *The Pickwick Papers* (1836–7), but rather Mr
Wardle's 'fat boy', Joe.[54]

Instead of considering the societal and stigmatizing ramifications of obesity, as Dickens had done, Burwell sees Joe solely
in terms of his pathophysiology and not in terms of the morality read into his body. Burwell strengthens his argument that
Joe is a case study by citing William Wadd's early nineteenth-
century medical account of 'corpulence.' There have been
claims of a greater antiquity for this syndrome;[55] for instance,
there was the case of 'a country tradesman aged about thirty,
of a short stature and naturally of a fresh, sanguine complexion and very fat . . .', who was suffering from the combination
of symptoms that Burwell finds in Joe. The Burwell article
presents a *single* case study, of a man aged fifty-one, five feet
and five inches tall, who weighed 263 pounds. The salient
incident in this patient's life that brought him to the hospital
was the fact that he fell asleep during a poker game while holding three aces and two kings! His was neither an error of intelligence (he recognized after the fact what he had done) nor an
inappropriate emotional response. He was a somatic 'fat boy'.
In a completely phenomenological description of the case,
Burwell and his colleagues see excessive eating both as a
cause and as a symptom, but they avoid any discussion of the

etiology of the patient's (and Joe's) illness. The case presented by Burwell was that of an adult.[56] Burwell could not use a child, a real 'fat boy' for his example, as these cases were the stuff of the debate about the etiology of obesity, not about its phenomenology.

Contemporary psychoanalysis was at the height of its American prominence in the 1950s. The debate about the nature of Joe's illness was engaged by the psychiatrist and popular writer on body image, Hilde Bruch (1904–84), who countered the rather mechanistic reading of the 'fat boy'. The breadth of Bruch's work and influence is discussed in substantial detail in Chapter 4. In her classic study of *Eating Disorders* (1973), Bruch too cites Dickens, employing the passage where Joe awakens abruptly when he is offered food:

> (Sundry taps on the head with a stick, and the fat boy, with some difficulty, roused from his lethargy.) 'Come, hand in the eatables.'
>
> There was something in the sound of the last word which roused the unctuous boy. He jumped up, and the leaden eyes which twinkled behind his mountainous cheeks leered horribly upon the food as he unpacked it from the basket.
>
> 'Now make haste,' said Mr Wardle; for the fat boy was hanging fondly over a capon, which he seemed wholly unable to part with. The boy sighed deeply, and, bestowing an ardent gaze upon its plumpness, unwillingly consigned it to his master. (p. 48)

She continues: 'During the 1930's and the 1940's [*sic*], Joe's behavior was often cited as evidence of the sleepiness of the pituitary type of obesity. During the 1950s the eponym "Pickwickian Syndrome" was given to the clinical picture of extreme obesity associated with alveolar hypoventilation and hypoxic somnolence. Yet I doubt Joe suffered from it. I have never seen an organically determined somnolence in which one word had such a vitalizing influence'.[57] Bruch sees Joe through a response to the purely biological underpinnings of obesity in the 1940s, when her work began. Her work actually builds on her own dissertation written in 1928, where character and body size are clearly linked. Her image of a lazy, stupid fat child comes to be more differentiated in her later reading of Joe. Her image, as her earlier work in Weimar Germany, endows Joe (and all fat children, real or imagined) with a family that cannot love them as the cause of their obesity.

The psychoanalytic work on obesity that rested upon Bruch's model of neurosis and its aetiological connections with the family also saw the male patients, the 'fat boys', as more tractable. Such patients – as one paper of 1970 noted – 'become obese partly in relation to over-nurturient influences in foetal life or early childhood. Such influences will sometimes have had neurotic determinants based in the mother, in the family, and in the specific maternal attitude to the patient as an infant'.[58] The fact is that the male patients do better: 'some patients, despite remaining massively obese for the meantime, may have the capacity to make a more healthy social adjustment auguring better for the future. The male patient and our last case seem to demonstrate this' (p. 342). Joe can be saved in terms of these psychodynamic models of obesity, while his morbidly obese sisters, now the focus of the psychoanalytic literature on body size, are captured by their past. And yet at this point any reference to the literary figure vanishes, even where the scholarship quotes Bruch's work.

In the twenty-first century, the pendulum has swung very much in the other direction. Obesity has become defined as physiological rather than psychological. Certainly the central thrust of this, recently, has been the examination of 'leptin'. In 1994, Jeffrey Friedman of The Rockefeller University led the team that discovered the obesity hormone, leptin, by studying genetic mechanisms of weight regulation in mice created in the laboratory as 'obese mice'.[59] Leptin is secreted in response to the amount of fat in the body of the animal. The release of leptin decreases appetite and tells the mouse to stop eating. If the gene producing leptin is missing, the mice will not stop eating and will gain significant amounts of bodily fat. When the animals are injected with leptin, they will stop eating and return to normal weight. The genetic mechanism of leptin in humans has come to define obesity, as scientists have equated the genetics of fat production and retention with the totality of the phenomenon of obesity. Thus obesity is the underproduction of leptin.

In 2006, the French researcher Claudio Rabec presented a paper on the 'New adventures of Mr Pickwick' in which he reanimates 'Fat Joe'. There he documents that 'leptin seems to have miscellaneous effects on respiratory function in obesity'.[60] With this he provides a 'pathophysiological explanation to the "phenotype"' of Joe, 'this fat red-faced boy, that snores as he waits at table, becomes easily asleep and then stops to breathe'. Joe is simply a massive sufferer from the underproduction of leptin. To cure him, just provide him with a shot of leptin. (As an aside, this does not seem actually to work in practice with obese individuals except for the tiniest fraction of those who suffer from very specific and very limited genetic error. Clearly, if this were the cause of obesity and its attendant somatic ills, the obesity epidemic could be cured with an injection.) But of course the opposite is also true today: an Italian research team has recently used 'Fat Joe' as the model for the retrospective diagnosis of 'obstructive sleep apnea syndrome' in the widest range of historical figures, including Napoleon Bonaparte, Queen Victoria and Franklin D. Roosevelt, none of whom, of course, was obese.[61] Of course, retrospective diagnosis using fictional characters as one's model provides a very high degree of certainty, since fiction (as we have seen) lends itself to infinite reinterpretations.

Joe is a case trapped between purely physiological and purely psychological explanations of obesity. He is the fat boy who will become the fat man, or, as in the case of the patient described by Burwell, he has already become him! Thus the case of the 'wonderfully fat boy' in Dickens forms the case material that Burwell and Bruch assembled for their argument. Yet each runs quite contrary to Dickens' own comic notion of our personal inability to read obesity and of the mistakes inherent to this misreading.

4 TODAY'S FAT CHILDREN

Today's obsession with fat children provides an odd continuation of many of the earlier concerns about a world of childhood perceived as being out of control. In the twenty-first century, dieting has become the norm for children, and their image of the world is now shaped by the dieting culture. Like Joe, today's children who dieted in order to lose or gain weight expressed diverse motivations, including avoidance of being teased, of pressure from family, of feeling embarrassed about their weight, and a desire to look 'better', to improve sports abilities, and to 'be healthier'.[62] However, popular culture – specifically, diet commercials and diet-related teen magazines – has also been seen as the cause of disordered dieting and eating behavior in adolescents, and this influence may also extend to pre-adolescents, who also read magazines designed for teen readers.[63] 55 percent of children reported learning about dieting from the media, and several children actually cited specific commercials for weight-loss products like Jenny Craig and Slim Fast.[64] A 2003 study also found that 'girls who read magazine articles about dieting and weight loss are more likely to engage in weight control behaviors'.[65] This influence also extends to young men, who reported that they, too, read magazines with dieting articles.[66] In addition, many studies have emphasized the role of parental weight concerns and of eating behavior as contributing to the early onset of dieting in children.[67]

Adult-like body dissatisfaction and dieting behaviors can be measured in children as young as between five and seven, and the methods which children use to diet may also resemble adult dieting practices. A 1999 study of children's dieting practices and understandings found that children as young as seven did participate in 'identifiable restrictive eating behaviors' when they dieted. These restrictive behaviors ranged from eliminating specific foods, which were perceived as 'unhealthy', to limiting food intake overall, exercising, abstaining from food completely, and even purging.[68] Kostanski and his collaborators found that children defined dieting as 'feeling fat' and trying to lose weight by eating better.[69] A small percentage of children believed that dieting meant severely limiting food intake or not eating at all (pp. 493–4). Shur and his collaborators also found that, while children do not generally conceive of dieting in terms of caloric restriction, they did define dieting as 'eating less' and exercising more, and some even mentioned the use of diet pills as a method of weight loss.[70] These findings, researchers agree, demonstrate that children have a sophisticated understanding of what dieting is and how to do it.

The early onset of dieting in school-age children has various consequences, including unanticipated weight gain and the development of eating disorders. A 2003 study published in the classic journal of childhood medicine *Pediatrics* demonstrated that dieting in childhood may be predictive of weight gain during three years of follow up. Reasons for potential weight gain were cited as changes in metabolic rate and dietary attrition.[71] A Harvard study also found that, 'regardless of their intake of calories, fat, or carbohydrate or their physical activity or inactivity, the frequent dieters were significantly more likely to become overweight than those who never dieted'.[72] Nevertheless, correlations between dieting behaviors and overeating/obesity are still debated by medical researchers.

While weight gain in children is certainly a concern in the context of a growing obesity epidemic, perhaps of greater concern is the possible link between the early onset of dieting and the development of eating disorders in children and adolescents. A 1987 study of bulimia and binge eating behavior in school-age populations found twenty years ago that, of 126 school children surveyed, 53 percent reported engaging in some form of binge behavior. While not directly linked to dieting behaviors, the prevalence of binge eating was found to be closely associated with 'unwanted thoughts about food'.[73] The 'predominance of young people at risk for bulimic behavior' was also found to be high in a 1999 study of unhealthy eating behaviors in adolescents.[74] Studies have also shown that rates of anorexia among pre-adolescent girls has been increasing every decade since the 1950s.[75] Such studies and others demonstrate that in a dieting culture even young children are susceptible to eating disorders like anorexia, bulimia, and binge eating disorder.

Since the late 1980s, research has demonstrated that much younger children have internalized gendered expectations about body size and feel unhappy about their bodies. They have a fairly sophisticated knowledge of dieting, have attempted to lose weight through dieting, and are at risk of contracting eating disorders. Behaviors predictive of later disordered eating may appear in children as young as five, and children in elementary school regularly show response to the dieting imperative. Pediatricians and other medical professionals agree that these findings are disturbing and recommend early intervention programs targeted at elementary, as well as middle school and high school, students.

The obesity problem among children is being examined outside of the US. In the United Kingdom, in particular in Hull, which is the country's most obese city, a slimming club has started for children. The club, Slimming World, invites children from 11 and up to attend weekly classes which will help them lose weight. The director, Clare White, stated: 'It's not about dieting, it's about healthy eating and education'.[76] School children in Hull are given one piece of free fruit each day to help them promote a healthy diet and contend obesity.

Schools around the world are making changes in their lunch programs and in their vending machines, in hopes of promoting healthier eating habits among their student body. While this movement within schools is somewhat modern, there has been speculation for years that healthy diet leads to better performance in school. A study of the diet and health of school children in South Carolina over fifty years ago showed those with better diets to be superior in health, in posture, and in scholastic progress.[77] While posture is no longer a main concern in the twenty-first century, health and scholastic progress certainly are.

For this reason, celebrity chef Jamie Oliver began something of a revolution in various London schools in 2004. Oliver has taken on the challenge of going into schools and of swapping the usual unhealthy foods with healthful and tasty foods. His ideas, struggles, and successes have created another successful TV show for Oliver. Oliver's campaign, Feed Me Better, has been launched on the internet, using the website to attract anyone wanting to support the campaign. Oliver far exceeded his expectations for support. He set up an online petition that explained his goal, and hoped to get 10,000 signatures. The petition signatures broke barriers, as his site was hit by over 5 million people while the TV show was on air.

Within weeks of the TV airings and site creation, people all over England were sharing Oliver's disgust with the lack of quality and nutrients in the food served at schools for lunch and dinner. The revolution Oliver started became the talk of the nation. An editorial in *The Lancet* stated: 'it is a sad indictment of public health in the UK that it took a television programme hosted by a celebrity chef to make the government realize that radical changes are needed in the way we feed our children. The obesity epidemic is widespread and well-documented. . . . Oliver . . . genuinely cares about food and nutritional standards and for that he should be applauded'.[78] Unlike earlier European-wide attempts to change the politics of school lunches, Oliver's approach paid off, as the former British Prime Minister, Tony Blair, announced that the government would take immediate action over school meals by upping the cost per pupil from 37p (=.70 cents) to 50p (=.95 cents).

An analogous approach to reform the eating habits of children was undertaken in 2004 by Arthur Agatson, the creator of the 'South Beach Diet' – a version of the low carbohydrate diet. Using the Osceola Country (Florida) school district as his 'laboratory', he created HOPS (Healthier Options for Public School Children). Working on the assumption that a change in diet would impact on the short and long-term health of the child, Agatson created gardens to show children how food was grown and to encourage them to eat 'fresh'. The researchers included nutritional information in other classes, such as math or social sciences, so that food became a general topic of conversation. Most importantly, HOPS provided the cost difference between the school district's food budget and the increased budget for healthier foods. Thus white bread was replaced by whole-grain bread; 'tater tots' by sweet-potato fries. While the program was successful in changing the eating patterns of most children (and in impacting on the eating pattern of their parents), as Jamie Oliver also saw, there seems to be little evidence that such changes actually reduce 'obesity', which was the public health rationale for such undertaking.[79]

Children's nutrition has become a concern all over the world. While it is important not to place weight pressures on children because these can lead to several psychological and emotional problems, it is nevertheless just as important for healthful eating to be part of a child's daily routine. In order to stop the obesity and weight-related health problems, changes need to be made among children. Overweight children today may well lead to overweight adults tomorrow, but it is just as likely that the dieting culture creates obese children through its emphasis on bodily perfectibility. Fat Joe is still alive and well: today, however, he no longer reads Dickens but watches Jamie Oliver on the TV.

3

THE STIGMA OF OBESITY

As early as 1968, the great German–Jewish sociologist Werner Cahnman wrote that while 'obesity is a complex phenomenon . . . the interpersonal factor, which is the truly sociogenic factor and which in its extreme manifestation stamps obesity with the stigma of moral turpitude . . . has consequences for therapy'.[1] The social diagnosis of obesity demands therapy, as obesity comes to be just another term for ill health. The boundary between the 'just right' ('well proportioned') and the 'too much' ('obese') fat is constantly negotiated within the general culture and within medicine. The litmus test is whether the 'fat' is a sign of actual or potential ill health. The moment when 'fat' comes to be a sign of pathology is the moment when it becomes a target for therapy. It is no wonder, then, that when fat is stigmatized individuals rarely 'see' themselves as fat in terms of their self-evaluation. Look in the mirror: the person you see there is 'healthy', even if you sense that you are too fat. There is always the attempt to trans-value fat into a sign of health.

The view that we are in the midst of an 'obesity epidemic' means that there is a demonization of the 'excessive' body and a marketing of everything related to it, from 'fat camps' for children to medications or surgical procedures to 'cure' fat. Fat must be cured, but only if one sees oneself as the object of therapy. (Actually, the industries dedicated to curing fat work on the assumption that they must be ultimately ineffectual in doing so. For without individuals being seen as 'too fat' they are out of business.)

Yet at the very same moment manufacturers discover that the obese are an ever expanding market for the widest range of objects, from 'hospital beds to coffins to car and subway seats'.[2] I may be heavy, says this approach, but I am not to be considered the object of a 'cure'. This compromise is seen by those advocating 'fat acceptance' as positive: 'I think they are behind the times in taking care of those things, but every change is a step in the right direction,' said Peggy Howell, who represents the National Association to Advance Fat Acceptance (NAAFA).[3] At a national convention of that group, Carole Cullum, its co-chair stressed that 'people need to accept who we are. It is important to give us rights, to give us acceptance, because we are part of what this country is made of. We are little bits of the whole, and we have to be included.'[4] 'Little bits of the whole' means that the obese have now become a victim group, seeing the bad jokes and open discrimination about being overweight as a violation of their 'rights'.

When it was stated that the editor of American *Vogue*, Anna Wintour, 'does not like fat people' on talk television, Sandy Schaffer of the National Association to Advance Fat Acceptance immediately shot back that the pudgy editor at large, Andre Leon Talley, who made this statement must be self-hating: 'That you can make that statement and not realize it's hateful, in this day and age, is shocking. Either he thinks the world hates fat people and that's an okay thing, or

he's so self-hating that he didn't see how hurtful this statement is'.[5] And she may not be wrong. A recent study in *Obesity
Research* from Yale University's Rudd Center for Food Policy
and Obesity argued that even overweight people preferred
thin people to fat ones.[6] Perceptions could be changed, but it
was clear that 'fat acceptance' was simply a 'Romantic trans-
valuation' of the pathological aspects of overweight into the
victim status, implicit in their claims for the 'right' to be fat.
What is striking is that contemporary stigma associated with
excess weight within the world of health is an artefact of the
nineteenth century.[7]

1 THE SHAME OF FAT BODIES

In 1863, William Banting sat down and penned his autobiography. In it he accounted for his obesity and for the way he
overcame it. In doing so he showed his mental as well as physical health. His *Letter on Corpulence Addressed to the Public* was
an account of how a successful, middle-class undertaker and
coffin maker (he had actually supplied the coffin for the Duke
of Wellington) overcame his paunch.[8] He was not fat because
of inaction or lassitude: 'Few men have led a more active life –
bodily or mentally – from a constitutional anxiety for regular-
ity, precision, and order, during fifty years' business career . . .
so that my corpulence and subsequent obesity was not through
neglect of necessary bodily activity, nor from excessive eating,
drinking, or self-indulgence of any kind' (pp. 10–1). And yet,
at the age of sixty-six, he stood at about five feet five inches tall
and weighed 202 pounds. He sensed that he had stopped being
corpulent and had become obese. A 'corpulent man eats,
drinks, and sleeps well, has not pain to complain of, and no particular organic disease' (p. 13). But obesity was now a source of
illness. He developed 'obnoxious boils' (p. 15), failing sight
and hearing, and a 'slight umbilical rupture' (p. 16). He could

neither stoop to tie his shoes 'nor attend to the little offices humanity requires without considerable pain and difficulty' (p. 14). Indeed, he was 'compelled to go down stairs slowly backward' (ibid.). All of these ailments were seen by Banting (and his physicians agree) as the direct result of his obesity rather than of his aging. In the appendix to the second edition, still distributed for free, Banting states that 'I am told by all who know me that my personal appearance is greatly improved, and that I seem to bear the stamp of good health; this may be a matter of opinion or a friendly remark, but I can honestly assert that I feel restored in health, "bodily and mentally", appear to have more muscular power and vigour, eat and drink with a good appetite, and sleep well'.[9] Health is beauty.

Most galling for Banting, however, was the social stigma: 'no man labouring under obesity can be quite insensible to the sneers and remarks of the cruel and injudicious in public assemblies, public vehicles, or the ordinary street traffic. . . . He naturally keeps away as much as possible from places where he is likely to be made the object of the taunts and remarks of others.'[10] Underlying Banting's desire to lose weight is the fact that he was seen as a fat man and his body was perceived as useless and parasitic. One of his critics saw this as the core of Banting's personal dilemma. It was not fat but a 'morbid horror of corpulence' and an 'extreme dislike to be twitted on the subject of paunchiness' that is at the core of Banting's anxiety about his body.[11] But he was certainly not alone. The French critic (and self-described sufferer from obesity) Brillat-Savarin tells the story of Edward of New York, who was 'a minimum of eight feet in circumference. . . . Such an amazing figure could not help but be stared at, but as soon as he felt himself watched by the passersby Edward did not wait long to send them packing, by saying to them in a sepulchral voice: 'WHAT HAVE YOU TO STARE LIKE WILD CATS? . . . GO YOU WAY YOU LAZY BODY . . .

BE GONE YOU FOR NOTHING DOGS . . . and other similarly charming phrases'.[12] Stigma, as much as physical disability, accounted for Banting's sense of his own illness. It was stigma that separated him from the universal experiences of his contemporaries.

Having been unable to achieve weight loss through the intervention of physicians, Banting was desperate. One physician urged him to exercise, and he rowed daily which gave him only a great appetite. One physician told him that weight gain was a natural result of aging and that he had gained a pound for every year since he had attained manhood.[13] Indeed, the medical literature of the mid-nineteenth century had come to consider obesity a problem of medical therapy; it condemned self-help: 'Domestic medicine is fraught with innumerable evils – it is false economy to practice physic upon yourselves, when a little judicious guidance would obviate all difficulties' (p. 20). Banting took the waters at Leamington, Cheltenham and Harrogate; he took Turkish baths at a rate of up to three a week for a year, but lost only six pounds in all that time and had less and less energy. Nothing helped.

Failing a treatment for his weakened hearing, he turned to William Harvey, an ear, nose and throat specialist and a Fellow of the Royal College of Surgeons in August 1862. Harvey had heard Claude Bernard lecture in Paris on the role which the liver had in diabetes.[14] Bernard believed that, in addition to secreting bile, the liver also secreted something that aided in the metabolism of sugars. Harvey began to examine the role which various types of foods, specifically starches and sugars, had in diseases such as diabetes. He was involved in a rather acrimonious scientific debate about whether the consumption of animal fat or carbohydrates was the primary cause of overweight. He urged Banting to reduce the amount of carbohydrates in his diet, for he argued 'that certain articles of ordinary diet, however beneficial in youth, are prejudicial in advanced life, like beans to a horse, whose common food is hay and corn' (p. 17). The aging body could not use the common diet and needed much less sugar and starch. Not the reduction of animal fats from meat would cure the body politic. Indeed it could not, in an age in which the 'simple, honest roast beef' defined 'Englishness' more than any other icon. For the French of the time, the English were simply 'les rosbifs' (the roast beefs).

Banting's body finally began to shed its excess weight. He lost thirty-five pounds, could walk downstairs 'naturally', could take ordinary exercise, and could 'perform every necessary office for himself'; his rupture was better, and he could hear and see.[15] But, equally importantly, his 'dietary table was far superior to the former – more luxurious and liberal, independent of its blessed effect' (p. 21). He remained at a 'normal' weight until his death in London in 1878, at the age of eighty-one.

Banting's pamphlet became a best-seller and started the serious, scientific concern as to the meaning of obesity. It was actually one in a number of such pamphlets of the day. Another, by A. W. Moore in 1857, cited earlier cases of people who had been able to drop weight and become healthy.[16] Watson Bradshaw, a physician who had written on dyspepsia before Banting's pamphlet appeared, countered it in 1864 with his own work on obesity, warning against 'rash experiment upon themselves in furtherance of that object'.[17] For Watson Bradshaw, the ideal of the fat body in cultures such as those of China and Turkey, where the 'ultima thule of human beauty is to posses a face with a triple chin, and a huge abdomen', had become impossible in the West. It was impossible because the 'assimilative function has changed its character – the absorbents have varied their duties – fat forsakes the lower extremities and other parts of the body; and persists in concentrating itself in the abdomen, giving rise to what is called "Corpulence"' (p. 6). Corpulence is a condition of the modern, western age, and, concentrated as it is in the gut, it is a quality of men. It is clear that this is a pathological state for Bradshaw, but it is only the extreme cases that he sees as diseased.

But it is Banting who sets the tone. In an anonymous pamphlet of 1865, 'a London physician' wrote about 'How to get fat or the means of preserving the medium between leanness and obesity'.[18] He begins by saying that the one question which everyone asks is: 'Have you read Banting?' and this has 'invaded all classes, and doubtless, will descend to posterity' (p. 7). 'Corpulence is a parasite, . . . the parasite is a disease, and the close ally of a disease, and the said parasite has been exposed and his very existence threatened' by writers such as Banting and William Harvey. This pamphlet then turned to the emaciated body, which is seen as being equally at risk and in need of diet and reform.

But it was Banting's text that became most popular, because it was sold as autobiographical. People spoke of 'banting' when they tried to shed weight. Even today, the Swedish term for dieting, is 'banting'. S. Weir Mitchell noted in 1877 that ' "[b]anting" is with us Americans a rarely needed process, and, as a rule, we have much more frequent occasion to fatten than to thin our patients'.[19] The obese patient was the subject of reform, and, for a rather long time, the patient was seen as a European one. Banting's mentor, William Harvey, turned to this topic in 1872, spurred on, he wrote, by Banting's success.[20] Harvey stressed that the new scientific advances in 'physiology and animal chemistry' have made it possible to treat obesity as a disease. To that point, he cited the case of Daniel Lambert, the fattest man on record to that time, who died in 1809 at the age of forty, weighing 739 pounds.

It was suggested that there seemed to have been no attempt to 'arrest the progress of the disease' in Lambert's case.[21] Banting began his pamphlet with the argument that obesity was a 'parasite affecting humanity'.[22] Suddenly, sufferer and physician saw it alone as the product of forces beyond the will.

But Harvey agreed with Banting that, until this stage of pathology is reached, 'persons rarely become objects of attention; many have even congratulated themselves on their comely appearance, not seeking advice or a remedy for that which they did not consider an evil . . .'.[23] One of Banting's severest contemporary critics, William E. Aytoun, observed that: 'We are acquainted with many estimable persons of both sexes, turning considerably more than fifteen stone in the scales – a heavier weight than Mr Banting ever attained – whose health is unexceptionable, and who would laugh to scorn the idea of applying to a doctor for recipe or regimen which might have the effect of marring their developed comeliness'.[24] Is fat a definitive sign of disease? Even Daniel Lambert was seen as healthy until his death.

Banting and Harvey needed to redefine obesity as a physiological disease rather than as a fashion or a moral failing. Yet Harvey could not make a sufficient leap between his knowledge and the actual mechanism by which 'respiratory foods' (carbohydrates) caused obesity and then other ailments. It was Felix Niemeyer from Stuttgart who later argued that it was the ingestion of more or less pure protein that would reduce the toxic effects of sugars and starches.[25] All believed that the body – in light of the views of materialists such as Johannes Müller – was a collection of chemical processes. Questions of will and of its attendant diseases were eliminated.

2 FALSTAFF AS A MEDICAL PHENOMENON

Soon after the popular movement of obesity into the realm of disease – and treatable disease at that – through the good offices of William Banting, 'Patient Zero' appears in the clinical literature. In 1864, William Shakespeare's Sir John Falstaff graces the pages of the British medical journal *The Lancet* for the first time.[26] He is evoked in a letter to the editor not as a case of obesity but as an example of how Shakespeare dealt with death. Here it is the Falstaff of *Henry V*, and the author describes the fever of the dying Falstaff. But it was soon to be the obese Falstaff who came to the fore in clinical literature. The fat man is – like Banting – in need of a cure, and Falstaff comes to play the role of the exemplary fat man.

It is in the scientific literature on obesity that Falstaff now comes into his own, as a case study. In Wilhelm Ebstein's classic study of corpulence, a study that went through some twenty editions from the 1870s to the 1920s, the author makes the portrait of 'fatty degeneration'.[27] This phrase, still used today, is presented as describing a specific model of illness. According to Ebstein, it develops in three stages. In the first, the individual is a 'person to be envied'. 'We admire his stoutness, his embonpoint, the body grows fatter, the outlines become rounded off, the muscular system still keeps pace with the increase of fat' (p. 10). This is the young Falstaff, whose memories of his earlier life (and body size) haunt the Henry plays.

In the second stage of fatty degeneration in the case study, there is progression to a comic figure, 'the corpulent becomes ridiculous'. Falstaff himself is the example here: 'The ancients jeered at the . . . capacious Falstaff who is the popular embodiment of low comedy. The works of the poets are so full of drastic descriptions of the various aspects of corpulency, that pathologists might learn many a lesson from them. In the first period of this stage the corpulent bear with a certain dignity the inconveniences entailed on them by their increasing bulk, and greater bodily weight' (p. 10). Here is the figure of Falstaff at the very beginning of the Henry plays, but the progressive expansion of his figure ultimately leads to his physical collapse: 'Such people of the Falstaff type with bellies of a hundred pounds are subject to many discomforts. Falstaff bemoans his own fate: "A man of my kidney . . . .. That am as subject to heat as butter; a man of continual dissolution and thaw"' (p. 11). Falstaff has, at this moment, become a classification for morbid obesity. He is the 'Falstaff type'.

It is at this last state of gross size that Falstaff's body and mind fail, according to Ebstein: 'In this third stage the corpulent become seriously ailing and pitiable objects of commiseration' (p. 12). And this is Falstaff in the *Merry Wives of Windsor*. If one examines the sequence of Shakespeare's plays, a very real degenerative pattern emerges, which struck a chord with medical practitioners of the nineteenth century. Ebstein quotes Dr Cantini of Naples: 'Fat quenches the divine flame of the mind even before old age has deprived it of the oil of cerebral nourishment' (p. 13). Falstaff's sexual exploits and dissipation of vital bodily fluids marked him as the sort of individual who would decay into a type of sexuality – asexuality – and he is granted comic, hypersexual gestures. This view was a mainstay in the sexology of the late nineteenth century and persisted well into the twentieth. Max von Gruber, in his standard study of the hygiene of sex, argued that the retention and reabsorption of seminal fluid heightens its functioning capacity; its dissipation leads to decay and to collapse.[28] Ebstein also sees the 'etiology of corpulency' as the result of the 'derangements of the sexual functions. . . . In the male sex, also individual cases of obesity are on record, which at the time of puberty somewhat suddenly set in, associated with a defective development of the penis and the testes' (p. 18). Sexual dysfunction is either the cause of, or the result from, morbid obesity. With Ebstein's taxonomy, Falstaff becomes the exemplary patient in studies of obesity. His figure is culturally available in ways that few fat men are.

And yet there is another side to medicine turning Falstaff into the exemplary obese man who eats his way into death. In one of the first overviews of obesity, Heinrich Immermann evokes the figure of Falstaff as the sign of a healthy and less dangerous past: 'Sir John Falstaff's careful words of wisdom and corpulent moods charm us . . .we always feel ourselves moved, we, sober children of a measured and balanced century. . . Falstaff is an example of what a central place the corpulent paunch [behäbiger Fettwanst] as a comic type has in the heart of the masses. . .'[29] Falstaff is a comic, healthy character; perhaps in Ebstein's 'second stage', who will never move on the disease and pathology because he is fixed as a literary character suspended between the nostalgia for fat in the past and the dangers of fat in the present age. In 1878, *The Lancet*'s correspondent at a spa in Germany writes that at Bad Homburg von der Hohe we meet 'old friends innumerable. Sir John Falstaff, Sir Tunbelly Clumsy, Squire Western, Prince Grogenuff, and the Gräfin von Güzzelmoch are all here in the flesh, and every shade of plethora presents itself as a clinical study to the eye. . . . Here is one whose lot it is to "laugh and grow fat" . . . but there is another, with beading brow and fair round belly, whose dull face and short breathing seem to speak of downright physical annoyance'.[30] The range runs from the happily fat to the pathologically obese, who have come to the spa there to be cured of ' "plethera [*sic*] seriosa", an unhealthy condition which is best described in the English vernacular as "flabbiness" ' (p. 342). This view of the healthy, comic Falstaff does not vanish. As late as 1929, an essay on mid-life psychoses comments: 'At the other end of the scale [from Cassius] is the fat, boisterous, jovial Falstaff, in whom a psychosis – if it occurred – would most probably be of the benign type'.[31] Fat men like Falstaff are inherently healthy, this argument goes, if only they think themselves healthy.

The notion that the paunch of the fat man represents, not a morbid condition but a state of health, or at least of happiness, appears in a programmatic way in Sir W. S. Gilbert's 'A discontented sugar broker', which was included in *The Bab Ballads* in 1869. It is a clear answer to the cult of Banting and to the pathologization of male fat. It portrays a 'gentleman of City fame' who

. . . had one sorrow – only one –
He was extremely bulky.
A man must be, I beg to state,
Exceptionally fortunate
Who owns his chief
And only grief
Is – being very bulky.

'This load,' he'd say, 'I cannot bear;
I'm nineteen stone or twenty!
Henceforward I'll go in for air
And exercise in plenty.'
Most people think that, should it come,
They can reduce a bulging tum
To measures fair
By taking air
And exercise in plenty. (p. 133)

But, as with Banting, it was the 'the sneers and remarks of the cruel and injudicious in . . . public vehicles' that caused real unhappiness:

He braved the gay and guileless laugh
Of children with their nusses,
The loud uneducated chaff
Of clerks on omnibuses.
Against all minor things that rack
A nicely balanced mind, I'll back
The noisy chaff
And ill-bred laugh
Of clerks on omnibuses. (ibid.)

And, like Banting, the gentleman slipped into considering his unhappiness to be the result of a 'disease process' over which he seemed to have no control:

His bulk increased – no matter that –
He tried the more to toss it –
He never spoke of it as 'fat',
But 'adipose deposit'.
Upon my word, it seems to me
Unpardonable vanity
(And worse than that)
To call your fat
An 'adipose deposit'. (p. 134)

The end result was that his unhappiness was not the result of his 'adipose deposit', but the internalization of the public humiliation caused by his appearance. It was the problem of matter over mind.

I hate to preach – I hate to prate –
– I'm no fanatic croaker,
But learn contentment from the fate
Of this East India broker.
He'd everything a man of taste
Could ever want, except a waist;
And discontent
His size anent,
And bootless perseverance blind,
Completely wrecked the peace of mind
Of this East India broker.[32]

Wealth and happiness can never, at least in Gilbert's mind, be vitiated by mere bulk. When you have everything, he opines, then you have the luxury to worry about your gut and its understanding as a sign of social and physical pathology. Here Banting's preoccupation with health and paunch stands as the godfather to Gilbert's 'East India broker'.

3 VERDI, AGE, AND EXHAUSTION

It is in this world, of the debate as to what the paunch of the 'established' fat man signifies – health or illness; happiness or desperation – that Arrigo Boito proposed to the seventy-six-year-old Guiseppe Verdi that they set to music the Falstaff figure (not just the Falstaff of *The Merry Wives of Windsor*). When Verdi began to write the opera *Falstaff* in the summer of 1889, his anxiety about the exhaustion of age was clear. He had had a major success with Boito's version of *Otello* when it was premiered on February 5, 1887 at the Teatro alla Scala in Milan. What could follow this success? Boito, who composed the libretto, suggested a great comic opera, which under Verdi's tutelage became the great opera of the happy fat man. Here Verdi's own understanding of old age must have played a role.

According to Verdi's friend Italo Pizzi, Verdi took seriously the advice of the noted physiologist Angelo Mosso, who argued that older people were at risk from various pathologies if they overindulged in any area.[33] Brain fatigue was the great villain of creativity, especially in the aged. Mosso, who had studied in Leipzig and later with Claude Bernard, was at the time professor of physiology at Turin and a noted exponent of a materialist reading of creativity.[34] He strongly believed that 'psychic functions are . . . intimately united with the phenomena of nutrition and reproduction. . . (p. 60). Since 'mental phenomena are a function of the brain' (p. 62), exhaustion of the brain could be the result of inappropriate intellectual overexertion. Mosso cites Charles Darwin, who claimed that, in himself, 'excessive intellectual work was apt to produce vertigo. . .' (p. 225). Mosso stressed that all creativity should be limited to specific limited periods during the day. Goethe, he notes, worked in the morning; Rousseau at night. However, in general, the best work is done during limited periods of time in the morning. Central to Mosso's presentation of the creative process is that it, too, is a form of work, and as such it can be debilitating, especially to those with pre-existing nervous weakness as well as to the aged. He quotes the noted Dutch physiologist Jacob Moleschott saying that 'in artists and scientists the material change promoted by their intellectual exertions is again moderated by their sedentary life. And it is a well-known fact that artists and scientists, in spite of their sedentary life, rarely suffer of fat' (ibid.). In his 1852 book *The Circuit of Life*, Moleschott likewise noted his belief in the material base of emotion and thought. For him, healthy artists are thin artists, as their body reflects the very work of creativity. Artists may have increased rates of urination, Moleschott claims, but this is simply a sign of the work that can, in some, result in intellectual fatigue. The relationship between stress and blood pressure, a relationship central to his understanding of the perils of aging, is paramount. Thus all old creative men should be advised that they would live longer and more productively if they worked only two hours a day.

After working two hours a day for two years, due to his anxiety that the expenditure of vital energy would lead to his own collapse, Verdi finished *Falstaff*. As a review in the daily newspaper *L'Italia del popolo* stated, *Falstaff* was considered a work that presented the composer as an 'example of a virtuous, severe, and serene life'.[35] The opera was, therefore, the product of the aged but productive composer – a composer who was thin as a rail in his old age. The absence of fat was a sign of the validity of his creativity.

Falstaff, the figure created by Boito and Verdi out of the material of Shakespeare's multifaceted character, renders a true late nineteenth-century reading of obesity. This is reflected in Verdi's music as well as in the libretto. In earlier operatic versions, Falstaff was sung by a comic basso. This was the means by which fat male characters could be differentiated vocally from all of the other set roles in the opera. Falstaff, perhaps more than any of Shakespeare's characters, seemed to lend itself to operatic interpretations from the eighteenth and nineteenth century on, at least as a *buffo* character. In *Falstaff* operas – beginning with Antonio Salieri's opera buffa *Falstaff* (1798), on a libretto by Carlo Prospero Defranceschi – Falstaff is a comic figure and his voice, like those of other comic bassi, marks his divergence from other masculine voices on stage. Certainly, the high point of this 'Falstaff' trend for mid-nineteenth century opera was Otto Nicolai's comic creation *The Merry Wives of Windsor* (*Die Lustige Weiber von Windsor*) (1849). Coming after the great wave of German Shakespeare translations, which started with Christoph Martin Wieland in the eighteenth century and led to the (now standard) Romantic translations by Friedrich Schlegel and Ludwig Tieck, Nicolai's opera was set to a libretto by S. H. Mosenthal. Mosenthal followed, in very rough form, a theatrical translation of Shakespeare's *Merry Wives of Windsor*. In this opera, Falstaff, to no one's surprise, is a comic basso.

Giuseppe Verdi's Falstaff, too, seems to stand in this tradition, yet with a rather important difference. The figure, as drawn in Boito's libretto, presents a new twist on the idea of 'fat' music. Central to this twist is the fact that Verdi set Falstaff as a baritone. How, then, is the audience to understand the character and its musical representation? It is clear that, on one level, Verdi is reaching back to a comic tradition of Italian opera, best represented by the work of Rossini and Donizetti. He also seems to be presenting an answer to the 'fat music' and the 'fat singers' of Richard Wagner (perhaps especially the comic twists of *Die Meistersinger*). And yet it is clear that *Falstaff* is neither a traditional Italian opera buffa nor a post-Wagnerian *Gesamtkunstwerk*.[36]

What is Verdi's version of what becomes the new comic opera? Fundamental to this question is the ambiguous relationship between the voice, the body, the text, and the music representing Falstaff. These altogether present a comic, fat body, but with a powerful change. The power of Verdi's Falstaff is such that Edward Elgar's tone poem 'Falstaff – A Symphonic Study in C minor' (Op. 68, 1913), commissioned for the 1913 Leeds Festival, reflects the psychological complexity of Verdi's representation. For Elgar, too, the 'comic' Falstaff is hidden within the texture of the composition; he uses the bassoon to represent this quality. This is part of the quality of the symphonic poem, as Elgar noted in a written commentary on his text, published in *The Musical Times* on September 1, 1913, before the work's premiere. Interestingly, Elgar also added a section which expands on Boito's short mention of Falstaff's thin youth, when he could fit through a ring; this is a short dream interlude in which Falstaff recalls his time as a boy, when he was page to the Duke of Norfolk, and wonders how different his life might have been had he been given a greater sense of his own self. This echoes the pathos that may be heard in Falstaff's aria of his handsome youth, 'Quand' ero paggio del Duca di Norfolk', which evokes Shallow's comment on Falstaff's youth in *Henry IV/2* (III: 2). Influenced by the whimsical poem, Ralph Vaughan Williams wrote his own *Falstaff, Sir John in Love*, first performed at the Royal College of Music on March 21, 1929. Falstaff as represented here is, of course, a baritone. This version of the character is more lyrical than Verdi's comic version. The baritone voice of Falstaff is not the comic *basso*, but neither is it the *Heldentenor*. Indeed, the vocal range of those who sang (and sing) Verdi's role often bridges between both.

In operatic terms, Verdi's Falstaff was a clear break from the fat, comic tradition of the Osmin figures as well as from the early Falstaffs, especially that of the widely popular Nicolai.

Under the guidance of Verdi, Boito provided a textual break
in the libretto which enabled the opera to present a rather different 'comic' Falstaff to his late nineteenth-century audience.
The result is a comic opera with seemingly profound over-
tones, in which the fat of the central character is also to be read
as the prime indicator of his character. The fat of the character, however, is not simply equated with the false pseudo-
masculinity of the comic basso. Falstaff is a baritone. This
baritone voice (and what Verdi chooses to do with it) seems to
represent the decay of 'real' manhood into the pathology of
aging. The text and the voice mark the distinction between
the older opera buffa settings of Falstaff and those of Verdi, as
well as the difference between the body of Falstaff and all of
the other 'fat' male bodies on the stage. Verdi's Falstaff is different from the inherently pathological character represented
by the comic basso as well as from the merely 'fat' males on
the stage. The pathology represented by Falstaff is found in
the voice of the character as it sings within the structure of the
libretto.

Something else changes in the space between Boito's
libretto and Verdi's musical interpretation of Falstaff. Both
Boito and Verdi employ the double image of Falstaff, using
translations of *The Merry Wives of Windsor* as well as passages
from the *Henry IV* plays, translated by Giulio Carcano into
Italian and Victor Hugo into French. Boito self-consciously
interpolates some selected passages from the *Henry* plays into
a text based on the *Merry Wives of Windsor*. These passages
build a contrast between the early image of Falstaff as a knight
in decay and the later comic image, found in the *Merry Wives
of Windsor*, of the decayed knight. And yet in doing so, the
libretto (and the music) undermines both images by merging
them. Verdi and Boito present an amalgam of Falstaff in his
first stage, that of the bragging soldier, and in his second stage,
that of the comic fop. To achieve this, the first aria given to

Falstaff is an interpolation of Falstaff's monologue on the nature of honor, and especially on the nature of the relationship between honor and the body. Boito's version of this monologue, which comes early in the first act of the opera, delineates Falstaff's 'fat' character. He does not represent *all* old men but rather the pathological case, the old man in decay:

Honor!

Scoundrels! You dare talk of honor! You!

You swear of debasement; tell me of honor.

Who can always live by honor? Not even I. I can't even.

Ever so often I must go in the fear of Heaven

When I am forced by want to veer from honor with hellish lies

And half-lies and stratagems: to juggle, to embellish.

And you, with rags and tatters, the look of half-dead owls,

And lice for comrades, who go through life surrounded by scornful howls,

Talk honor now! What honor? You swine! You filth!

How funny! What rubbish! Can this honor fill your paunch?

When you are hungry? No. Can this honor heal a leg that's broken?

No, so. A shoulder? No. A finger? No. Not a thumbnail? No. For honor's not a surgeon. What is it then? A word.

What's in this word? There is a vapor that scatters.

What a structure! This honor, think you a dead man feels it?

No. Lives it with the living? Not either. Our lust conceals it.

Our vanities corrupt it, our enjoyment infects it.

And calumnies debase it; as for me I reject it! Yes!
Will I miss it? No! But to come back to you, you
  scoundrels!
Now I am full up and dismiss you![37]

Falstaff's monologue of the cowardly soldier on the risks run
in battle, risks to life and limb, becomes an aria that begins
with the pathetic, gestural cry of 'honor' and ends in anxiety
about infections and collapse. As in Shakespeare, this signals
the anxiety about disease, now in the decaying, ineffectual
body of the old man. The audience, however, sees this (with
the singer) as an indicator of the ambivalence of the warrior
figure, now aging and facing the inevitable decay of old age.
Verdi marks this 'serious' decline with the increased speed of
Falstaff's aria. It begins with the opening *L'onore*, marked as
allegro sostenuto ('lively, sustained'), with a marking of 112 for
the quarter note. It slows down to *poco meno mosso* ('a little less
agitated'), at 100, and *poco più mosso* ('a little more agitated') at
the line that 'honor is not a surgeon'. In the line before the
music becomes 'more agitated', at the point where Falstaff
announces that honor can not heal even a broken fingernail,
the orchestral line includes two solo double basses, whose
mocking tone 'profoundly' underlines the irony of Falstaff's
notion of the inviolate body. Verdi directs one of the basses to
do a 'drop-D tuning' (lowering the 'e' string to a 'd'), to enable
it to hit the lowest note in the aria. Here, and only here, do we
have Verdi's signaling of the hidden and missing comic *basso*
aspect of Falstaff's character. The baritone voice of the warrior (in his comic version) is also the voice of the 'fat man'
hidden within the character of Falstaff. Falstaff is not the
comic bass in the opera; the soldier Pistole, his comic side-
kick, is the true comic bass in the opera – he is a shadow of
Falstaff. Yet Verdi places in the music a key to understanding
the complexity of Falstaff's character and body. Comic and yet

not comic; diseased and yet only aging; threatening and yet ineffectual, Falstaff dominates the stage.

The 'drop-D tuning' of the bass is the figurative shadow of Verdi's use of 'fat' music, which only the attentive listener can note. As the aria steadily increases in tempo, Falstaff picks up a broom and flails it about to clear the stage! What begins as a mock gesture to honor ends as a comic, feminized sign of the anxiety about the body. It is a suspension of Shakespeare's opposition between 'fat and effeminate Egypt to the lean and virile Rome'.[38] For Falstaff is not a woman, nor is he overtly feminized in the opera. He is a de-sexed male whose virility is in question (he desires the 'merry wives'' money more than their love). He uses the broom as a weapon, since drawing a sword would have been impossible in his middle-class world. This defines an aspect of Falstaff's character, but one which is not dominant. This is not the old man on the stage, not the standard comic character of the opera or theatrical stage, but the immoral figure whose decaying body is captured in the words of the monologue. The sexual desire of Falstaff is pathological because the old man, unlike the healthy follower of Mosso, who is promised a long and healthy sexual life, is now neutralized. The desire is a mirror not of his character, but of his old age. Vanity and lust are the causes which explain why some bodies decay into fat and licentiousness as they do. And Falstaff, in Verdi's aria, marks the new notion of a 'fat' voice, a voice in decay because of the wasteful immorality of the character's life. Thus there is never any chance that Falstaff could fool the female figures in the opera. They hear the *basso* under his baritone voice. His vocal body seems to reveal his character, and his dissipation seems to reflect the danger he represents for the institution of marriage through his role as a braggart who claims much more than he can actually deliver.

By the end of the nineteenth century, Verdi and Boito were able to stage the ultimate comic opera: the opera of old age, in which the central comic character was not the representative figure of aging but its anomaly. Verdi's Falstaff is comic because his decay is evident to all as a pathological sign, present in the aging of those old men who have dissipated their vital fluids. Thus the 'happy' conclusion of the opera, when all conflicts are resolved, is fated to take place at the dinner table. Falstaff's dangerous private acts of seduction have been unsuccessful. No matter how the women of Windsor view him, it is not as a potential lover. In the audience, we have seen the private (read: sexual) made public through Falstaff's humiliation, when he is dumped in the river after the women of Windsor discover his hypocrisy (he sends them all the same letter of seduction, promising love and adoration). Falstaff's need is not sex but money, and this, the audience quickly realizes, makes him a comic figure. But the opera does not conclude with Falstaff being dumped into the Thames in a basket. It concludes with the ultimate reconciliation of all the figures, including Falstaff, over food. Ford invites everyone for a meal – to be paid for by Falstaff. This is so very different from the conclusion of Shakespeare's play, in which all are commended to return to their own hearth. The desire for food, as V. S. Pritchett noted in a classic study, replaces the 'eighteenth-century attitude to sex in the comic unity of Dickens' – and, one can add, in the comic unity of other nineteenth-century texts such as Verdi's *Falstaff*.[39] In Henry Fielding's *Tom Jones*, food is a path to sex; in Verdi, it comes to be a substitute for it. No seduction does or can take place. Food (or drink) always trumps it. Indeed, in the world of Banting and of dieting, as W. S. Gilbert noted twenty years before Verdi's *Falstaff* appeared on the stage, you have to have worldly riches to worry about your paunch. When you don't, your paunch becomes something that needs preserving. The death of sexual desire is at last presented as a positive force in the reconstitution of social order. Sexual desire is replaced by the communal breaking of bread, a communion which now truly links God with the act of eating. We, members of the audience (and here we all are the old Verdi's substitute as we all will age), find this comic because we know in our heart of hearts that we are different from Falstaff – we hope against hope that we will never become a laughing stock. We are not as fat as he is; our sexuality will remain vital even into our old age; our sins are not written upon our bodies. We are not to be bought off by a good meal for which we must pay. Or are we?

4

OBESITY AS AN ETHNIC PROBLEM

Let me evoke two moments two hundred and fifty years apart:

In 1745 a man appeared in the dark room of a London inn to the hungry and tired Emanuel Swedenborg, then a member of the royal Swedish mining commission, and said to him: 'Eat not so much', and then disappeared. After dinner he soon reappeared and revealed himself as God. Swedenborg, who has a 'thin and hungry look' in portraits of the time, took his advice and lived to be an 84-year-old theosophist.

In June 2004, Renate Künast, the Consumer Affairs Minister of the Federal Republic of Germany, declared there to be an obesity epidemic. In her position paper 'Plattform Ernährung und Bewegung', she warned that one out of three boys and one out of four girls at the time of entering the school system were overweight and that Germany stood on the edge of an obesity epidemic. 'Every third child, and every fifth teenager, is massively overweight', Künast told a German television program.[1] The intent of the program was to compel German children to learn to eat better and get more exercise.

According to Künast, the increase in obesity is due to two factors: the soaring growth of the fast food industry over the past twenty years, and a lack of exercise resulting from the increase in computers and television sets in the home. Obesity is not a disease but a failure of will due to the pressures of modern life. As an essay by Richard Friebe and Gerd Knoll in the *Frankfurt Allgemeine Zeitung* noted on June 27, 2004 that this so-called epidemic is an artefact, both of reporting and of desire. How could the Germans be any less modern than the Americans?

Swedenborg's God is heard today in different voices but with much the same message: 'Eat not so much.'

1 THE MORAL PANIC ABOUT OBESITY AND THE JEWS

Obesity presents itself as a world-wide 'moral panic'. The moral panic about obesity is not only a reaction to waist size; it is part of a discourse on race that surfaced in the nineteenth century, shaping the very manner by which obesity is understood in today. Race and obesity have a long and fraught history. As with other explanations for 'fat', this association is reductive and provides a clearly defined explanation for the impression that obesity is pathology. Yet even here the implications of such an association reveal the moral panic associated with body size. Let us focus on one moment in that history of that panic – the tale of 'fat Jews' and the meanings associated with them in the world of nineteenth-century scientific anti-Semitism.

Historically, the Jews placed relatively little focus on the representation of the obese body. Such a body is evoked by the biblical figure of Eglon, King of Moab, who oppressed the children of Israel for eighteen years.[2] His fat, male (*ish bari me'od*) body was destroyed by the left-handed hero Ehud (Judges 3: 17, 22). (As the Jewish body was defined by circumcision, it was usually represented by the male body.) It is even described how Eglon's fat closed around the blade when he was pierced. Ehud smuggles his sword in the presence of the king by wearing it on the 'wrong side', at least the wrong side for right-handers. He is 'treacherous and sneaky; perhaps the culture of ancient Israel thought those descriptions to be synonymous, at least stereotypical'.[3] As for the fat king, his guards do not even notice that he has been disemboweled until they smell his feces. Is this the case of one deviant body destroying another? The Talmudic obese body was a deviant one, but not a particularly dangerous one. Rather, it held a certain fascination.

The Talmud even asks whether very fat men, such as Rabbis Ishamel ben Yose and Eleazar ben Simeon (end of the second century BC), could ever reproduce because of their huge bellies. There the metaphor is of a body which also represents a hidden truth. The idea that the fat body thinks intuitively, or has intuitive knowledge, is an inherent aspect of Talmudic discourse. In *Baba Metzia* 83b–85a, so ably explicated by Daniel Boyarin, the tale of Rabbi Eleazar, the son of Simeon, reveals that Eleazar intuitively knows the truth because of his fat body. As a Roman turncoat, he makes judgments that seem destructive, arbitrary, or foolish, but because he knows the truth intuitively he is always right. His solutions turn out always to be accurate, even though at first glance they appear to be false. One day he has a 'certain laundry man', who had insulted him, arrested. Before he can come to his senses, the man is hung. As Rabbi Eleazar stands below the body and weeps over his error, he is told that the man had violated a number of *mitzvoth* (laws) that would have condemned him to death anyway. When his judgment is accredited this way, 'he placed his hands on his guts and said: "Be joyful, O my guts, be joyful! If it is thus when you are doubtful, when you are certain even more so. I am confident that rot and worms cannot prevail over you."' But in spite of this, he remains unconvinced of his inherent ability. When he is drugged, 'baskets of fat' are ripped from his gut and placed in the July sun. 'And it did not stink. But no fat stinks. It does if it has red blood vessels in it, and this even though it had red blood vessels in it, did not stink.'[4] It is the belly, now separate from the body, which has a life of its own. It represents the intuitive ability of this otherwise suspect figure to judge truth from falsity; it is a gut feeling, quite literally.

But Jewish attitudes toward obesity were clearly defined by the model of the lack of self-control. Unlike the much later Christian theological enumeration of the 'seven deadly sins', gluttony is not included in either version of the Ten Commandments presented in the Hebrew Bible. Gluttony is, of course, not praised among the Jews. It can be seen as a sign of human failing, as in Proverbs 23: 20–1 ('Be not among winebibbers; among riotous eaters of flesh; For the drunkard and the glutton shall come to poverty: and drowsiness shall clothe a man with rags'), or of violation of human order, as in Deuteronomy 21: 20 ('This our son is stubborn and rebellious, he will not obey our voice; he is a glutton, and a drunkard; And all the men of his city shall stone him with stones, that he die'). It is only with the Pauline condemnation of the flesh that the desecration of the 'temple of the Holy Ghost' through obesity stains the soul that inhabits the obese body. The fat man is unable to become truly righteous (I Corinthians 6: 19: 'What? know ye not that your body is the temple of the Holy Ghost which is in you, which ye have of God, and ye are not your own?').

It is only in modernity, with the secular transformation of obesity from a mark of sin to a sign of illness, that the Jew's body comes to represent all of the potential for disease and decay associated with the obese body. This is very much in light of the general understanding of the stereotypical 'Jew', both in Christianity and in Islam, as the antithesis of the healthy, true believer. The diseases ascribed to the inherent difference of the 'Jewish' body (now the ill body per se) become the litmus test for 'Jewish' difference. In such a system it is always helpful to have visible signs and symptoms onto which to hang the overt difference of the 'Jews'.

2 DIABETES AS THE JEWISH DISEASE

In modern western medicine, there was a preoccupation with a claimed Jewish predisposition to diabetes. The nineteenth-century practice of labeling Jews as a 'diabetic' race was a means of labeling them as inferior within the terms of nineteenth-century scientific racism. In the fall of 1888, the Parisian neurologist Jean Martin Charcot described to Sigmund Freud the predisposition of Jews for specific forms of illness, such as diabetes, and how 'the exploration is easy' because the illness was caused by the intramarriage of the Jews.[5] Jewish 'incest' left its mark on the Jewish body in the form of diabetes – as well as on the Jewish soul.

However, there are further views on why the Jews are pre-disposed to this illness. The British eugenicist George Pitt-Rivers attributed the increased rate of diabetes among the Jews to 'the passionate nature of their temperaments'. He noted that by the 1920s diabetes was commonly called a 'Jewish disease'.[6] Jews were inherently diseased, a quality that distinguished them from the 'healthy' peoples of Europe and defined them as part of an inferior racial group.

Over and over again, it was the obesity inherent in the Jew's body (and soul) that was seen as the cause of the illness. The 'Oriental races, enervated by climate, customs, and a superalimentation abounding in fats, sugar and pastry will inevitably progress towards the realization of fat generations, creating an extremely favourable soil for obesity'.[7] Even in the diaspora, the assumption is that the Jew is diabetic because of his pre-disposition for fat:

> All observers are agreed that Jews are specially liable to become diabetic. . . . A person belonging to the richer classes in towns usually eats too much, spends a great part of his life indoors; takes too little bodily exercise, and overtakes his nervous system in the pursuit of knowledge, business, or pleasure . . . Such a description is a perfectly accurate account of the well-to-do Jew, who raises himself easily by his superior mental ability to a comfortable social position, and notoriously avoids all kinds of bodily exercise.[8]

Jews inherited their tendency toward fat from their life style: 'Can a surfeit of food continued through many generations create a large appetite in the offspring; alternatively, can it cause a functional weakness of their weight-regulating mechanism?' asks W. F. Christie. And he answers:

> Take, for instance, the Hebrews, scattered over the ends of the earth. Probably no race in the world has so apparent a tendency to become stout after puberty, or is more frequently cited as an example of racial adiposity. It is also probable that no nation is so linked in common serfdom to their racial habits and customs. [Elliot] Joslin says of the present generation of Jews: 'Overeating begins in childhood, and lasts till old age.' The inheritance of large appetites and depressed weight-regulating mechanism may exist in them, although they show no other signs of the latter; whereas the inheritance of fat-forming habits is certain.[9]

Here 'nature' trumps 'culture' even among emancipated Jews.

Thus Jews inherit the compulsive eating patterns of their ancestors and are therefore fat already as children. Their obesity and their diabetes are a reflection of their poor hygienic traditions, precisely the opposite of the claims of nineteenth-century Jewish reformers, who saw Judaism as the rational religion of hygiene. It is the 'oriental' Jew who presents the worst-case scenario for this line of argument. Max Oertel, perhaps the most quoted authority on obesity at the beginning of the twentieth century, states that '[t]he Jewesses of Tunis, when barely ten years old, are systematically fattened by being confined in dark rooms and fed with farinaceous articles and the flesh of dogs, until in the course of a few months they resemble shapeless lumps of fat'.[10] Here the fantasy in the West about the 'oriental' body is heightened by the Jews feeding their daughters non-kosher food. Jews, according to much of the late nineteenth-century literature critical of Jewish ritual slaughter, are inherently hypocrites. They will in fact eat anything and everything, claiming that their religious practice precludes them from anything that is not kosher. Obesity becomes here a sign of that hypocrisy.

Hidden within the modern, acculturated body of the Jew is a racially defined Jew whose body betrays itself. Thus William-Frédéric Edwards, a physician, argued in 1829 that races remained constant all over the world. Edwards' proof for this was the stability of the Jews all over the world.[11] Edwards' friend, the Scottish physician Robert Knox, brought as proof the 'fact' that the portraits of Jews in Egyptian tombs resembled the Jews of contemporary London! Oscar Wilde was, of course, right decades later, when he argued that nature copies art rather than art copying nature. The reality of the world mirrored the fantasies of its observers. The fantasies about the Jewish body demanded such arguments of continuity. In 1841 Hubert Lauvergne, a follower of the phrenologist Franz Joseph Gall, argued that contemporary Greeks bore the proud face and skull of ancient Greece, while the 'immutability of the

Jewish type' proved their degeneracy. One sign of this was the obese body and its predisposition to diabetes.

From the nineteenth century on, diabetes had been seen as a disease of the obese and, in an odd set of associations, the Jew was implicated as obese due to an apparently increased presence of diabetes among Jews. According to one turn-of-the-century specialist, mainly rich Jewish men are fat.[12] But, rather than arguing for any inherited metabolism, he stated that the fault was with the poor diet of the rich: too much rich food and alcohol – this being yet another stereotype of the Jew. And yet the contrary argument is often made.

Jewish scholars reacted in a less than sanguine manner. In the essay on diabetes in the turn-of-the-century *Jewish Encyclopedia*, an essay written by the leading British and American scholars of the diseases of the Jews, Joseph Jacobs and Maurice Fishberg, there is a clear rejection of the premise that Jews are prone to diabetes for 'racial' reasons.[13] The authors state categorically: 'It has also been shown that diabetes is not a racial disease of the Jews' (p. 554). For them, diabetes is a disease of 'civilization', not of the Jews. As Jews become both emancipated and secularized, they come to have all of the diseases of those cultures into which they seem to amalgamate. Hence the dichotomy of Jewish proclivity for and immunity against diabetes. 'Both of these views,' they argue,

(1) that the Jews suffer more frequently from diabetes than other races, and (2) that they are not more often affected – are probably well founded. It is only a question of the nativity of the Jews: the Jews in Germany, for example, are decidedly more diabetic than those in Russia, England, and France; and the difference of opinion among physicians of experience is simply due to the fact that they usually neglect to consider the question of the nativity of the Jews under consideration. In

the United States, where Jews arrive from various countries, diabetes is found to be extremely frequent among the German and Hungarian Jews; while among the Russian Jews it is certainly no more – perhaps it is even less – frequent than among other races (p. 555)

Diabetes is a disease that becomes evident among Jews as they move from one culture to another, from one world in which they feel to be part of the national identity (Germany) or into one where they are alienated (Russia).

Jacobs and Fishberg are forced to confront another theory for the emergence of diabetes among the Jews. Anti-Semitism, in the late nineteenth century, saw the Jews as an essentially 'ill' people and considered the origins of that illness to be incest/inbreeding, labeled in the case of the Jews a 'consciousness of kind'. While the illness that dominated anti-Semitic discourse in science was madness (and Jacobs and Fishberg both confront this claim in their own work and elsewhere in the *Jewish Encyclopedia*), diabetes was also attributed to Jewish inbreeding. Its origin, too, was in the 'dangerous' marriages of the Jews, that is, their refusal to marry beyond the inner group. These marriages were stigmatized as a criminal activity even when such 'inbreeding' was not consanguineous. In historical terms, writers such as Houston Stewart Chamberlain could comment on the origin of the Jews and its 'refreshingly artless expression in the genealogies of the Bible, according to which some of these races owe their origin to incest, while others are descended from harlots'.[14] Chamberlain's polemic also appears at the time under the guise of ethnological description. The Jews are described as not only permitting sibling incest (*Geschwisterehe*) historically, but actually practicing it even after they claimed to have forbidden it. The pathological result of such open and/or hidden practices is premature sexual maturity.[15] The various links between deviant forms of sexuality such as inbreeding (understood as sibling incest) and prostitution (the ultimate etiology of mental illness in an age of syphilophobia) placed the Jews and their marriage practices at the center of 'biological' concern. And yet there was also a hidden economic rationale to this discussion. For, by refusing to marry into the general society, the Jews seemed to be signaling that they were an economic entity – which lived from the general society, but did not contribute to it. 'Inbreeding' was seen as the origin of the economic hegemony of the Jews and was as poisonous as their sexual mores.

In the literature on diabetes, consanguineous marriages are considered to be more frequent among the Jews than among most other races. It is Jewish practice more than anything that is at the heart of diabetes, according to one group of scholars. 'The Jews are the children and grandchildren of town-dwellers,' says Charles Bouchard:

> In the long run the unfavorable hereditary influences are not rectified for them by the frequent intermarriage of the urban with the country people, as is the case with the rest of the population. The Jews marry exclusively among themselves; first cousins from the paternal or maternal side find no barrier to marriage, and immediately on being born the young Israelite receives the accumulated unfavorable (hereditary) influences, which he further develops during his lifetime, and which tend to the diseases that are generated by disturbed nutrition, particularly diabetes.[16]

This they strongly deny. And yet it is clear, in Jacobs and Fishberg's joint essay on *diathesis* (constitution or predisposition to certain forms of disease) in the *Jewish Encyclopedia* that they also rejected obesity as a causal factor in diabetes. Jews may suffer from 'arthritism' – under which the authors

'understand a certain group of diseases, usually due to disturbances of the normal metabolism, which manifest themselves
primarily as chronic rheumatism and gout, but which also
include other morbid processes, such as diabetes, gall-stones,
stone in the kidneys, obesity, and some diseases of the skin'.[17]
But these 'are not racial in the full sense of the word. In the
majority of cases they are due to their mode of life, to the fact
that Jews are almost exclusively town dwellers, and to the anxieties of their occupations' (p. 574). Obesity remains for these
authors a product of civilization, and diabetes is one of its
manifestations.

At the beginning of the twentieth century, scientists began
to explore the relationship between the Jews' predisposition
for diabetes and the assumed relationship between diabetes
and obesity. One physician in 1926 noted that, 'since one in
twelve obese Gentiles develops diabetes, no less than one in
eight obese Jews develop it. This, it is suggested, is to be
explained by the fact that a fat Hebrew is always fatter than a
fat Gentile, and that it is the higher grade of obesity which
determines the Semitic preponderance in diabetes'.[18] The
assumption about fat and the 'oriental' race is one that comes
to haunt discussions of the meaning of fat.[19] When W. H.
Sheldon developed his 'somatotypes' in the 1940s, he
observed that Jews show an exaggeration in each of his body
types. Thus fat Jews are somehow fatter than fat non-Jews.[20]
More recent studies of obese Jews look at the complex behavior patterns that occur when religious demands for fasting and
the psychological predisposition of the obese come in conflict.

Today, Type II diabetes is not generally considered a Jewish
illness. Research now follows the so-called thrifty genotype
hypothesis, which had been suggested in 1964. Simply stated,
it has been observed that, when mice are transferred from a
harsh to a benign environment, they gain weight and become
hyperglycemic. Thus, when one measures first-generation

groups of immigrants to the United States in the late nineteenth century or in Israel today, one finds a substantially higher rate of diabetes. The initial groups, as in the example of the Yemenites, who immigrated to Israel from a harsh environment, showed an extremely low index of diabetes when they arrived in Israel. This index, however, skyrocketed after just a short time of living in their new environment. Thus diabetes and obesity seem to be the index of a failure to adapt rapidly to changed surroundings.[21]

3 PSYCHOANALYSIS, OBESITY AND 'RACE'

The debates about obesity and the Jews shaped one of the central discourses of medicine concerning bodily form and weight. Contemporary psychoanalysis was at the height of its American prominence in the 1950s. The debate about the nature of obesity during that time was shaped to its greatest extent by Hilde Bruch (1904–84). Bruch was a German–Jewish physician who escaped the Nazis to England and then to America, and ended her career as Professor of Psychiatry at Baylor Medical School. Her claim to fame is that she popularized the diagnosis of anorexia nervosa. She was an often cited specialist on obesity who revolutionized the debate between those who saw exogenous or endogenous causes for obesity.[22] She provided the first complex psychological theory of obesity – linking developmental forces with the external world of the pathological family. Her interest seems to have begun with her arrival to the United States in 1934, where, according to her own account, she was amazed at the huge number of fat, truly corpulent children, not only in the clinics but also on the street, in the subway and in the schools.[23] Her work on the 'psychosomatic aspects of obesity' was funded by the Josiah Macy, Jr. Foundation, and its results began to appear in the 1940s; they were summarized in her in her book *Eating Disorders* in 1973, where she presents a form of developmental obesity which develops through specific family interactions from birth. At the core lies her view of the child's struggle to develop its autonomy from the family setting, a view championed by Theodore Lidz, with whom Bruch had worked in Baltimore between 1941 and 1943 (Lidz created the 'schizophrenegenic mother'). As she was undergoing a training analysis with Frieda Fromm-Reichmann in Washington at the time, Bruch began to see more complex implications of the work on obesity which had brought her to Fromm-Reichmann's initial attention.

Typical of Bruch's readings of obesity is the case study of a four-and-a-half-year-old girl weighing ninety pounds. The child had been conceived by accident, during the war, and was initially rejected by her mother (ibid., 138). For the mother, 'feeding showed love and expiation of guilt' (p. 140) for rejecting the very idea of bearing the child. The mother was a compulsive confabulator, always embellishing the tales she told about her daughter's treatments in order to manipulate them. Bruch thus provides obese children with a childhood of rejection which explains their obesity. Now, Bruch's child is a female – as, after World War I, the exemplary patient in questions of obesity shifts from being male (as it had been ever since the ancient Greeks) to being female (which came with the construction of the image of the 'new woman'). But this has a special role in Bruch's system. Here, again, it is the mother who is the cause of the obesity. The child's obesity is a neurotic response to her mother's 'unnatural' rejection of her.

Yet little is known of Bruch's initial work on obesity. In her 1928 dissertation, written under the renowned pediatrician Carl Noeggerath at Freiburg i. Br., she tested the stamina and lung capacity of children with the new instrumentation of the spirometer. She traced how their respiration increased with increased work (turning a weighted wheel). One of the children, Maria O., was, according to Bruch, chronically obese, weighing 58,4 kg (127 lbs., 4 oz.) at the age of twelve. She 'speaks tiredly and in a monotone, complains about constant tiredness and weakness of memory. There is neither determination nor a joy for work'.[24] This case study provides all the negative images about desire and work and intelligence that is found in classic images of obese children. But it is also the classic racist image of the non-productive 'fat' Jew that haunts the medical texts of her time.

Bruch also provides a rationale for the psychological state of the obese child: the absence of love from the mother, the negation of the natural desire of the parent for the offspring. The image of the lazy, stupid fat child comes now with a family which can neither love nor desire. Bruch offers an alternative model for exogenous obesity – one beyond the control of the individual and, more importantly, beyond racial categories. Any child raised badly can (indeed will) become obese.

Bruch had been raised in a religious German–Jewish household and attended a one-room Jewish elementary school in the tiny, mainly Catholic, hamlet of Dülkens in 1910. She was of the very first generation of young women who forced their way into the academic Gymnasium (for her in Gladbach) – rather than following the traditional Höhere Mädchenschule. She had wanted to become a mathematician but settled for the more pragmatic study of medicine. In 1923 she entered the world of somatic medicine in Würzburg, and then in 1924 in Freiburg where she wrote her thesis. This world was the world that demanded an understanding of the inherent relationship between race and obesity. All of the discussions about Jews and diabetes, obesity, and food were part of the medical discourse about eating disorders that shaped her professional training. It was this world that Bruch rebelled against, especially after fleeing Nazi Germany, where the notion of race and hygiene was so explicitly stated within the medical world. Bruch's construction of an alternative, psychological model ran against the dominant racial model in Germany, but also against the implications of the metabolic model that held sway in the United States when she arrived. Psychoanalysis provided a non-racial, non-biological answer to what had been a racial and/or biological explanation.

Sigmund Freud had shown that 'race', a staple of the cutting-edge medical science of Vienna in his day, was not a factor in either somatic or psychological illnesses of his day.[25] As early as the 1890s, Freud had argued for a universal model to explain that 'the relation between body and mind (in animals no less than in human beings)' is as much determined by 'mind' as it is by body', that it 'is a reciprocal one'. Patients whose illnesses are psychogenic have constantly shifting symptoms, which included responses to food: 'A patient who has hitherto been incapacitated by headaches but has had a fairly good digestion may next day enjoy a clear head but may thenceforward be unable to manage most kinds of food. Again, his sufferings may suddenly cease if there is a marked change in the circumstances of his existence. If he is travelling he may feel perfectly well and be able to enjoy the most varied diet without any ill effects, but when he gets home he may once more have to restrict himself to sour milk.'[26] Freud is not interested in questions of body size here, but the notion that all symptoms, including eating disorders, are constantly in transformation is central to his theory of psychopathology.

Bruch's work trumped earlier psychoanalytic approaches to obesity such as that of the Viennese psychosomaticist Felix Deutsch (1884–1964), which were anchored in Freud's views concerning the relative stability of symptoms. Deutsch had stressed the interchangeability of overweight with other somatic symptoms. Very much in the model of traditional psychoanalysis, obesity was but one symptom of an underlying neurosis that could easily transform into other pathological mental states:

> Suppose that a female patient comes to consult us believing herself to be suffering from obesity and demands treatment to reduce her weight. It would be incumbent upon us, not only to prescribe a suitable diet, but to recognize that while by dietetic methods we can certainly influence the body, the prohibition of certain foods cannot fail to reactivate all the unconscious fantasies connected with the oral zone. We know, for instance, that certain states of depression (ranging in degree up to the severest forms) manifest themselves in the form of disturbances in the taking of food, and that these disturbances are connected with the introjection of the lost love object and with severe feelings of culpability, which derive from the attitude to the introjected object. If we were to treat such a patient by the inconsiderate prohibition of certain articles of diet, we might very well find that she would be led to react with an onset of severe depressive states. Not only are there certain patients who tell us that they always become extremely 'nervous' when they try to diet strictly. We actually encounter some in whom an attack of depression has ensued immediately after the enforcement of a reducing diet. Thus now a days medical treatment is being influenced by considerations of an entirely new order.[27]

Indeed the Viennese psychoanalyst Franz Wittels (1880–1950), one of Freud's original followers, was convinced that even 'beauty' could be one of those symptoms that paralleled obesity: 'I became acquainted with a family in which a number of children had to undergo treatment because of neurotic disturbances. A brother suffered from obsessional ideas, another was a schizophrenic, a third showed pathological obesity, and one of the sisters at the age of puberty 'burst out' into glorious beauty, flamboyant with sex appeal, large sensual eyes, vivid colouring, tall slender body.'[28] Obesity was not a primary sign of any specific psychopathological problem and could not be treated as such. It was clearly not to be treated by somatic interventions, such as dieting, because it was not only a psychogenetic response but could easily be transformed into other symptoms. Wittels' family of neurotics presented obesity and narcissistic beauty as equal psychopathogical states.

All of this changed with Hilde Bruch's championing of a family-based definition of obesity, which dominated the discussion in the United States after the 1940s. Obesity came to stand for a specific error in 'mothering' which reflected the developmental problems of the specific individual. In eating disorders (for, later, Bruch's interests expanded into the field of anorexia), the primary symptoms of the disorders resulted from the specific nature of the psychological state of the parent, not of the child. All of her patients suffered from some developmental disruption in infancy, at the stage when the child focused on oral gratification and the bonding with the mother. Inappropriate feeding or rejection by the mother at this early stage led to a pathological relationship with food. Such symptoms could not easily be transformed into other, analogous somatic problems. As A. H. Vander, in 1944, summarizing Bruch's views, stated for the broader psychoanalytic community:

The dominant emotional patterns in the children consisted of aggressive demands on the mother for feeding, dressing, and toilet care; avoidance of physical activity, sports and social contacts; greed in areas other than food (e.g.

addiction to movies); and lack of open aggression to persons other than the mother. None of the children ate a well-balanced diet and generally they preferred starches. The family patterns were quite uniform. In general, the fathers were weak and unaggressive. The mothers frequently gave histories of early emotional deprivation, poverty and hunger. Their attitudes toward the children were ambivalent, combining overprotection and anxiety with overt hostility at the child's demands. The mothers consciously hoped to possess the exclusive love of their children by keeping them in a state of perpetual babyhood. They actively encouraged the children to overeat. Food seemed to symbolize love to both mother and child and also acted as a reassurance to the child against many anxieties arising from his social ostracism and his sexual conflicts. The author believes that such children enjoy their obesity and utilize it to fantasy [*sic*] that they are big, powerful and therefore safe. She concludes that 'obesity in childhood represents a disturbance in personality in which excessive bodily size becomes the expressive organ of the conflict'. Dr Bruch is to be highly commended for placing the study of obesity on a rational basis.[29]

The psychoanalytic work on obesity thereafter rested upon Bruch's 'rational' model of neurosis and its connection with the family. It reflects the obese children's choice of foods as much as their psychological attitude towards their bodies. Fat people were created in their childhood. Fat was a sign of early psychological distress, not of physiological pathologies, systemic or inherited. Such patients, as one paper of 1970 noted, 'become obese partly in relation to over-nurturent influences in foetal life or early childhood. Such influences will sometimes have had neurotic determinants based in the mother, in the family, and in the specific maternal attitude to the patient as an infant.'[30] The fact is that they can undo this influence: 'some patients, despite remaining massively obese for the meantime, may have the capacity to make a more healthy social adjustment auguring better for the future. The male patient and our last case seem to demonstrate this.' The obese patient can be saved in terms of these psychodynamic models of obesity. The baneful influence of the mother can be undone. No such possibility exists within the racial model of obesity. For the racial predisposition to obesity will cause obesity no matter what level of self-control is exerted.

Such psychoanalytic explanations continue to fascinate. Bruch's view dominated the accounts of obesity in the 1940s.[31] Moreover, this approach never quite vanished from within psychoanalytic discourse, even though some work in the 1970s postulated a post-oral origin for obesity – for instance in the Oedipal conflict, in sibling rivalry, or even in early childhood sexuality. In 1971, a study reported on a case in which pregnancy and lactation were accompanied by a revival of the patient's infantile fascination with reproduction while she was growing fat:

> As the regression deepened, her Oedipal fantasies faded into the background and she engaged in much projection and introjection. She was continually preoccupied with her lactating breasts, which were a source of pride and pleasure to her. Daily she expressed the milk, noting its color, consistency, and taste. . . . She also thought that in order to grow big and have a baby inside her, she must eat a great deal and not allow feces or urine to escape (a conjecture that had contributed to her moderate obesity); any act of elimination was accompanied by intense anxiety and withholding.[32]

The focus on the infantile is reflected in further case studies in the age of AIDS, where perhaps a more subtle understanding of ethnicity and its reading in American culture could have been undertaken.

> An obese, handsome five-year-old, José was brought to the clinic by his foster mother because of his aggressive, self-destructive outbursts. The most severe of these culminated in José's puncturing his arm with pins. José's mother had been imprisoned for selling drugs, and the boy's care had been entrusted to his father and paternal grandmother. He was routinely beaten for infractions of the house rules, and his daily needs, such as food and clothing, were not always fulfilled. His father, who reportedly was himself obese and unkempt, contracted AIDS through intravenous (IV) drug use. When word got out that his father was ill with AIDS, José was teased by his peers and quietly ostracized by the staff. . . . José's profound feelings of abandonment and victimization seemed to result in his defensive identification with the powerful, deserting (through illness and death) parent – the aggressor. José's obesity also appeared to be in part a way of maintaining a tie to his dead father, perhaps due to a primitive identification, a result of fusion of self and object images.[33]

It is clear that the interfamilial structures, and not any ethnic or 'racial' quality, still determine obesity in this model.

Bruch's views shaped the medical discourse on obesity as much as her work on anorexia nervosa did. Indeed as late as 1992, her work on obesity as a product of psychodynamic forces is used to provide an explanation for the presence of precisely the opposite, eating disorders, such as anorexia nervosa.[34] But of equal importance was the fact that she wrote widely for popular 'women's magazines' and served as advisor on weight questions to the most popular newspapers as did 'agony aunt' Ann Landers. Bruch's views, shaped against

a world dominated by moral panic about the Jewish difference, came to create a model for obesity rooted in the individual experience of the patient in the context of the family
– not of race. Bruch's world-view permitted a new, if also
troubling, definition of obesity in its relationship to mental
states. But it also allowed for the possibility of 'cure', or at
least treatment – through psychological rather than physiological intervention.

We have not come very far from this view in our public
outcry about the epidemic of obesity today. We seek a new
type of magic bullet to ward off the collapse of the nation.
Obesity remains a 'moral panic' because the obese represent a
true threat to the national state – as Bruch's concern with the
family was echoed in the 1960s and the 1970s by a general
concern in the United States and with the 'death of the
nuclear family' as the potential cause of massive social unrest
within African–American society as the often quoted work of
the sociologist Daniel Patrick Moynihan stressed in 1965.[35]
Such a threat had a real impact later in the century on the shift,
within the African–American community, in understanding
excessive bodily size, not as beautiful or healthy, but as a diseased process which originated within the family and lead to
multiple somatic illnesses. The public discussion on the collapse of the 'Black family' was the major precursor to the shift
within that community towards seeing bodily size as a marker
of illness.[36] In 2008, the blame game has moved from bad parenting to bad genes. A British study published in 2008 in
the *American Journal of Clinical Nutrition* found that differences in bodily mass, index and waist size were 77 percent gov-
erned by genes.[37] Not even good parenting can answer that
claim that inheritance trumps all. In all these views, 'fat' still
points towards social as well as personal catastrophe and it still
has one single cause, which could be identified and treated.
Swedenborg's God, in the form of the public health

authorities advocating dietary change, is still heard today with much the same message: 'Eat not so much.' Neither parenting nor genetics seem truly to play much of a role in our debate on personal responsibility versus external causation. All such approaches to obesity see it as the symptom of a single, underlying pathological problem.

5

REGIONS OF FAT

What strikes me first when I sit in the Café du Monde in New Orleans now is the girth of people in the cars passing by. You can only see them bisected; holding 'phones to their ears, yet everything visible drips of fat. The flesh hanging from their arms, multiple chins, their eyes framed in fat. The 'phone vanishes in their hands, their knuckles being huge and covering completely the ever smaller 'phones. The rest of them is invisible to me, I can only imagine their torso and legs. As we discussed in Chapter 4, when Hilde Bruch – the psychoanalyst who forcefully advocated the notion that it was families that cause obesity – came to the USA from Nazi Germany in 1938, she too was struck by the huge size of the Americans she saw in New York. Had she only landed in New Orleans, that city of food and fat!

Today there is more than a little empirical evidence that the South beats all when it comes to weight. In August 2006 the Trust for America's Health found that 29.5 percent of Mississippi residents were obese and that nine of the ten states with the highest rates of obesity were in the 'old' South. But even in this fattest part of the nation there are further qualifiers as to who is really fat. There seems to be a religious hierarchy of fat – and that not only in the South. In a recent paper, the Purdue medical sociologist Kenneth Ferraro looked at the correlation between belonging to a religious denomination and being obese.[1] Baptists were the fattest of them all, followed by other Protestant groups. The rule seems to be: the more fundamentalist you are, the fatter you will be. Roman Catholics and then Mormons, Seventh-day Adventists (with their vegetarian diet) and other 'non-traditionalist' Christian groups were at the middle on his scale, and Jews (and other non-Christians) made up the thin end of Ferraro's sample. In Baptist churches, one out of four members of the congregation is obese; but only 1 percent of the Temple-attending Jews are obese. Compared with the Jews, Catholics too had a high rate of obesity, about 17 percent of the congregants being obese. Ferraro stresses that, while this is a national problem, the domination of Baptists points to its being very much a Southern problem too.

In 1998, Ferraro concluded an earlier article by observing that food and religion provide 'a couple of the few pleasures accessible to populations which are economically and politically deprived.'[2] According to his work in 2006, it seems to be the 'dietary patterns in the South' that, coupled with the explosion in church membership, point to the ever-expanding waistline of the southerner. Perhaps Marx was right – religion (and here we can add food) is (together are) the opiate of the people.

Evidently, when Jews are considered as a religious rather than an ethnic group, they are thin enough. But this is where the analysis breaks down. For the Jews are simultaneously a religious group of people – let's say 'peoplehood' – and a (self-described) ethnic one, and the flaw of Ferraro's model is that

his notion of religion, especially in the South, maps historically on to older models of ethnicity, in which the world of the
nineteenth and early twentieth century were also models of
race. One of the great historical 'secrets' of the obese South is
that the 'black/white' dichotomy of race provided a means by
which 'black' races in Europe, such as the Jews and the Irish,
were made 'white'.[3] But, for the KKK, the litmus test was, and
is, religion as well as race; they knew on what side of the racial
divide Jews and Catholics were to be found. Yet in the nineteenth century this distinction between religion and race
was rarely made. The Jews and the Irish, like the 'Blacks',
were understood as racially a different people from real
'Americans'. Their beliefs (as well as their bodies) betrayed
them no matter how 'white' they looked. The late nineteenth-
century fetish of light-skinned Blacks 'passing' as white in
order to cross the color bar applied to the Jews and the Irish
as well. The fictional literature on 'passing', from Mark
Twain's *Pudd'nhead Wilson* (1894) to Edna Ferber's *Showboat*
(1926), revealed this obsession with the permeability of racial
categories in a world seemingly convinced of their absolute
nature.[4] Liberals argued that the color bar was arbitrary and
capricious. For those who argued for an inherent racial difference, the 'racial' body, no matter how well disguised, would
eventually betray its 'essence'. And, for the twentieth century,
that body, at least in literature, comes to be obese.

The irony here is that in the United States African–
Americans form a rather special case. As they have extremely
high rates of type 2 diabetes, high blood pressure and other
diseases associated with the 'metabolic syndrome', they have
been recently targeted by the dieting culture. With the charge
that the African–American diet was the cause of illness in view
of the the traditional African–American ethos that 'being
bigger and fat is ok', African–Americans have come to represent a section of American society that is 'ill'.[5] The ideological

position concerning the reasons for this are varied. Was it the continuation of some conspiracy, by slave-holders, to control black bodies? Was it the result of an inappropriate diet from a period of more intensive physical effort? Was it the amalgamation of African dietary traditions with North American foods? Whatever the answer may be, blackness has come to signify illness, as has, in an odd way, white ethnicity.

1 GONE WITH THE WIND

The nostalgic world of the old South, now re-imagined in literature, is the place where we should look for these bodies which betray. No place is better to begin from than my favorite literary place in Atlanta: the Margaret Mitchell house. Mitchell, as James Cobb observes, was hardly a naïve writer evoking a lost antebellum (antebellum is the term always used to refer to the period before the American Civil War) tradition.[6] She reflects constantly on the explosion of vanished ethnicity that made up the old, seemingly homogenous 'white South' – where no one except (in great irony) the slaves was fat. Scarlett's slave 'Mammy' describes herself as 'too old an' fat',[7] but Mitchell makes this quality her icon, as 'Scarlett longed for the fat old arms of Mammy'. The African–American woman, depicted as large and devoted to preparing the food, comes to be a classic icon of early twentieth-century processed foods. 'Aunt Jemima' reigns, from 1905 to the post-World War II period on, as a sign of a 'maternal' and acceptable body – but only within the confines of racial difference.[8]

It is indeed the ethnic vigor of the 'black' Irish Catholics revitalizing and rebuilding the effeminate South in Mitchell's *Gone with the Wind* (1936) that stands behind Scarlett's cry about never being hungry again, 'if I have to steal or kill – as God is my witness, I'm never going to be hungry again'.[9] Her father, Gerald O'Hara, had invigorated the world of the plantation with his rough Irish ways, following to America his too tall brothers, who had flaunted the English occupation of his homeland. (Mitchell was writing at a time when the partition of Ireland was a *fait accompli*.) Gerald O'Hara was a

> small man, little more than five feet tall but so heavy of barrel and thick of neck: that his appearance when seated, led strangers it think him a larger man. His thickset torso was supported by short sturdy legs, always incased in the finest leather boots . . . Most small people who take themselves seriously are a little ridiculous; but the bantam cock is respected in the barnyard, and so it was with Gerald. No one would ever have the temerity to think of Gerald O'Hara as a ridiculous little figure.

His formidable – if short – body and feisty spirit point to a man who had succeed in overcoming hunger and oppression and would add this quality to the South. He was 'fat', but in the most positive sense of nineteenth-century masculinity. He was not 'beautiful', and according to the opening line of Mitchell's novel neither was Scarlett.

Yet when the producer David O. Sleznick (1902–65), together with the scriptwriter Sidney Howard (with Ben Hecht, Jo Swerling, and John Van Druten) made the novel into a film in 1939, all this representation of ethnicity and transformation was eliminated. Without laboring the point, the anxiety about race in the 1930s, in the light of the growing power of fascism and Nazism abroad and the United States, meant that the Hollywood studios, so much labeled as Jewish that they were exceedingly anxious to avoid any such designation, could not even image 'ethnic vigor' as an advantage. Neal Gabler has written about this fear in great detail, noting that Selznick had actually denied his Jewish identity: 'I am an American and not a Jew . . . it would be silly of me to present suddenly that I'm a Jew, with some sort of full-blown Jewish psychology.' [10] When his friends were queried, of course he was seen as a Jew: 'I'd say David Selznick was a Jew,' answered Martin Quigley, publisher of the *Motion Picture Exhibitors' Herald* (ibid., p. 291). This anxiety about ethnic, racial, and cultural difference is clearly present in the stripped down version of the tale presented in the film. Gerald O'Hara (played by the character actor Thomas Mitchell) and his daughter (played by the ethereally beautiful British actress Vivien Leigh) are clearly representative of the antebellum plantation culture as imagined in Hollywood. It is a world without fat – except for 'Mammy', played by Hattie McDaniel, who suffered professionally because of her acceptance of this 'Aunt Jemima' role.[11]

In 1941 the historian W. J. Cash tells the story of his own great-grandfather in *The Mind of the South* as an example of 'ethnic vigor' and of the creation of the 'white' planter culture of the Carolinas.[12] He was a 'stout young Irishman' who came with his bride to the Carolinas and entered into trade in whiskey. He began, almost as an afterthought, to plant cotton and brought the first cotton gin. From that sprang his fortune and his status in the community. He builds a 'big house', paints it in white, buys slaves, enters the legislature. By this time he was 'tall and well-made'. His daughter, educated by the local Presbyterian minister, marries a 'Charleston gentleman' (12–17). Thus the 'ruling class in the great South' is revitalized on the frontier.

This is not the place to rehearse the general claims concerning how the Irish and the Jews became 'white' in America and how contested that shift in racial identity was, especially in the South. The reading of an editorial in the *Charleston Mercury* in 1856 reveals that there had been a reduction of emigration which eliminated the 'Know Nothing' Party's demand for imposed limits as 'quite unnecessary [even] by the most bigoted hater of our Irish and German populations.'[13] After the Civil War the Irish, at least, become white and stout. Both Mitchell and Cash use the Irish as their model, speaking about the body as an unstated place of identity formation. Being 'stout' is a mark of power; being fat is a disease. Men of power (like Gerald O'Hara) are never fat: 'The Pope [Pius IX] is pretty tall and stout, without being obese.'[14] But the diet culture was alive and well in the South before the age of southern nostalgia.

In the antebellum and immediate post-war South, however, there was a great concern with obesity – if only with obesity far from the United States (as this concern had started). As early as 1833, the *New Orleans Commercial Bulletin* recounts how the 'omnibus drivers on the Edgeware Road' in London refuse to take passengers they judge to be too obese and their refusal was accompanied with catcalls and 'great laughter'.[15] Obesity is a 'British disease' which is not the 'combined result of laziness and high living', but 'a constitutional disease'.[16] This was very much in line with the views that American neurologist S. Weir Mitchell (1829–1914) expressed in 1877. He was startled by 'those enormous occasional growths, which so amaze an American when first he sets foot in London'.[17] But such obese spectacles are not limited to England. We can read an essay by Mordecai Noah (1785–1851), the first American-born Jew to achieve prominence as a writer, politician, and utopian advocate of creating a Jewish refuge ('Ararat') in New York State.[18] He reported, in the *South Carolina Temperance Advocate* in 1847, recounting his time as American consul in Tunis, when he saw local women struggling with their fat: 'The more fatness, the greater beauty as a wife – and, therefore, tender mothers begin at an early age to fatten their daughters. They allow them very little exercise, compel them to eat very rich substances, little paste balls dipped in oil, and every kind of food calculated to produce obesity. The result is

. . . a lady weighing some three hundred pounds. . .'[19] Fat may even be 'Northern'. The *Atlanta Constitution* reports in1873 the 'fat man's clam bake' in Norwalk, Connecticut, where 'the monsters . . . numbered 143 persons, or more accurately speaking, 32,942 pounds . . . which is 230 1/3 pounds a head'. This comic report, however, ends with an admonition that 'we have said enough to arouse the emulative spirit of Georgia's fat men. Let them organize. And if Atlanta's does not pull down the scales for the Presidency of the Georgia club – may we never be fat.'[20] Fat is exotic, yet there is also a theme in the southern response to fat which echo the growing understanding of obesity as a disease.

In 1856 the *Charleston Mercury* advocated 'health for the People', seeing some 'deteriorating influences on national health'.[21] Childhood ill health haunts Charleston, and the remedy is 'calisthenic and gymnastic exercises', which assure the removal of 'obesity, or an excess of fat'. The dieting culture is alive and well in the South. The English layman William Banting's (1796–1878) low carbohydrate diet, which was first introduced in London in 1864, had become the rage in the South, 'conferring the benefit of wholesome muscular development' upon its practitioner and upon 'others'.[22] In Georgia, Banting's approach to 'the treatment and cure of excessive fatness in the human race' 'caused a decrease in weight from twenty-five to sixty pounds in the course of a few weeks'.[23] But other remedies were quick on the market. 'Allan's Anti-Fat, the only known remedy for obesity' was sold to men 'whose several weights range from two hundred to three hundred pounds'.[24] Obesity is an 'abnormal condition', though 'many people have erroneously considered it as an evidence of health, and any agent that reduces fat is therefore at once suspected of being injurious'.[25] Not being stout but fat was dangerous or alienating. In the North Georgian realist novel *White Marie: A Story of Georgian Plantation Life* (1889), by Will N. Harben (1858–1919), it is the uppity overseer's wife who is obese and acts out of her class

> The overseer walks about with a prouder strut than has characterized his gait previously. This is owing in part to his having persuaded the mistress of Oaklawn to permit his wife to superintend the household during her absence. Mrs Johnson, round and obese, moves about with an arrogant and weighty tread in what the negroes regard as sacred precincts – the loved mistress's parlor, sitting-room, and dining-room – much to their disgust, for they decry Mrs Johnson's ability to manage the household affairs, and sneer at her uncouthness.[26]

Here fat and poor character are qualities that are even imagined to be linked as signs of social inferiority. This notion vanishes in the 1930s and 1940s and is transformed into Gerald O'Hara's ethnic vigor.

2 A CONFEDERACY OF DUNCES

If the notion of ethnic vigor and bodily form as a model for imaging a new southern identity is linked to the Irish, who become 'white' – at least in part – by becoming southerners, then the great mid-twentieth answer to *Gone with the Wind* is John Kennedy Toole's *A Confederacy of Dunces* (1980).[27] Written during the beginnings of the Civil Rights movement, it provided a parodistic rethinking of 'stout' men and ethnic identity. It was Walker Percy who truly discovered the novel after its author's suicide. He praised the way Toole presented New Orleans' 'ethnic whites – and one black in whom Toole has achieved the near impossible, a superb comic character of immense wit and resourcefulness without the least trace of Rastus minstrelsy' (p. viii). The ethnic whites in Toole's world are without a doubt trying to become 'white', but they sink

ever more in a world of fat. And the soft underbelly to southern identity formation, how ethnics become authentic southerners, is exposed by Toole through these subjects' bodies.

Toole's protagonist Ignatius J. Reilly opens the novel as he is
waiting for his mother in front of a D. H. Holmes department
store and 'shifting from one hip to the other in his lumbering,
elephantine fashion . . . sent waves of flesh rippling beneath the
tweed and flannel, waves that broke upon buttons and seams'
(13–14). He is an ethnic and a Catholic; his obsessions focus on
food and theology. His faith was shattered as a teenager, when
his parish priest refused to bury his pet dog. His huge body is
sustained by jelly doughnuts rather than communion wafers:
'Ignatius says to me this morning. "Momma, I sure feel like a
jelly doughnut." You know? So I went over by the German and
bought him two dozen' (p. 39). It is the 'German' baker who
supplies the food of the 'slob extraordinaire'.

Mrs Reilly is addressing the hapless Officer Mancuso, who
had tried to arrest her son in front of D. H. Holmes as a 'character'. (He had been ordered to bring in 'characters', meaning
'deviants', by his sergeant.) Mancuso's Italian identity within
the world of ethnic New Orleans is established when he takes
Mrs Reilly bowling with his aunt, Mrs Santa Battaglia. Her
mother 'had her a little seafood stand right outside the
Lautenschlager Market. Poor Mamma. Right off the boat.
Couldn't speak a word of English hardly. . . . Poor girl.
Standing there in the rain and cold with her old sunbonnet on
not knowing what nobody was saying half the time' (pp. 91–
2). From her mother's photograph there stared 'little black
coals of Sicilian eyes' (p. 192). But neither Mrs Reilly nor Mrs
Santa Battaglia is corpulent; on the contrary, they are tiny,
hard bodied, and very aggressive.

The other 'white' ethnics are equally slim. Mr Gonzalez,
who employs Ignatius, has his desk ornamented by 'another
sign that said SR. GONZALEZ and was decorated with the

crest of King Alfonso' (p. 108). Gonzalez is a chain smoker, but no attention is paid to his bodily shape. (Ignatius's fantasy of his Spanish roots only reflects the romantic notion of ethnicity imagining lost kingdoms, a feature so well embodied in Gerald O'Hara.)

Beyond the Irish Catholic Ignatius, fat encompasses Toole's Jews. But perhaps we should look at the core Jewish figure that sets the model for Jewish ethnic identity in Toole's New Orleans, a figure who never actually appears in the novel. Mrs Reilly mollifies their high-strung neighbor, Miss Annie, whose life is made a living hell by Ignatius's raucous presence, by giving her a rosary: 'I stopped off at Lenny's and bought her a nice little pair of beads filled with Lourdes water . . . She loved them beads, boy. Right away she started saying a rosary.' Ignatius is dismissive of Lenny's: 'Never in my life have I seen a shop filled with so much religious hexerei. I suspect that that jewelry shop is going to be the scene of a miracle before long. Lenny himself may ascend' (p. 77). Actually Lenny had already 'ascended'. We learn that he had gone to an 'analyst in the Medical Arts building [who] helped Lenny pull his jewelry shop out of the red. He cured Lenny of that complex he had about selling rosaries. Lenny swears by that doctor. Now he's got some kind of exclusive agreement with a bunch of nuns who peddle the rosaries in about forty Catholic schools all over the city. The money's rolling in. Lenny's happy. The sisters are happy. The kids are happy' (pp. 150–1). Mrs Santa Battaglia, too, is happy for having bought her plastic 'Our Lady of the Television' from Lenny: 'It's got a suction cup base so I don't knock it over when I'm banging around in the kitchen' (p. 262). Here one can stop and ask, like Richard Klein, who put the 'Jew' in 'jewelry'.[28] Lenny has been saved; indeed his shrink is described as 'Lenny's savior' (p. 282). The unseen Lenny has become part of the world of New Orleans; he has abandoned at least the superficial sense of ethnic/religious difference which made him uncomfortable with selling rosaries and plastic Mothers-of-God. As the other 'ethnics', he retains a 'Jewish' quality, at least at it is perceived from the perspective of the mid-century – that is, his happiness with worldly success. This is a key, by the way, even to American–Jewish writing through Philip Roth's *Goodbye, Columbus* (1959), where worldly success and loss of identity go hand in hand.

Since Lenny is without a body, it is the figure of Mrs Levy, the wife of the owner of Levy Pants, whose body reveals it all. It is she who had evoked Lenny as the model for her husband's dealing with his business difficulties. She enters the novel 'prone on the motorized exercising board, its several sections prodding her ample body gently, nudging and kneading her soft white flesh like a loving baker' (145–6). Perhaps the 'German' baker? The bodies of Mrs Levy, her daughters, Susan and Sandra, and her mother represent the fantasy of the 'Jewish–American Princess' obsessed by worldly things, including her own appearance. What is clear is that, like Lenny, Mrs Levy no longer has any sense of her own 'Jewish' identity and spends her time looking for meaning, a meaning which her very position in the hierarchy of Toole's world must deny her. Unlike her husband, who overcomes his hatred of his dead immigrant father (who moved from selling pants from a pushcart to the ownership of 'Levy's Pants'), she never acknowledges the burden of the past, or indeed even the burden of the present, present in 'her ample body'.

Yet the Jewish character who 'embodies' Jewish fat in all of its ramifications for Ignatius is his New York Jewish college girlfriend, Myrna Minkoff. She has failed in her many attempts to seduce him because 'my stringent attitude toward sex intrigued her; in a sense I became another project of sorts' (p. 137). Her lust is that of the Jewish woman as succubus; but, even more importantly, of the northern Jew come to New Orleans. She is Ignatius's Rhett Butler.

Minkoff appears in the very opening of the novel, when Officer Mancuso attempts to arrest Ignatius, and Ignatius complains that he will report the officer to the 'Civil Liberty Union . . .We must contact Myrna Minkoff, my lost love. She knows about those things' (p. 6). In the 1960s New York 'agitators', all seen as Jews, 'know about such things'. Myrna 'was only happy when a police dog was sinking its fangs into her black leotards or when she was being dragged feet first down stone steps from a Senate hearing' (p. 125). Myrna, like Levy's daughters, has a father who 'has money' (p. 79). He sends her to New Orleans (to the unnamed Tulane) to 'see what it was like "out there" ' (p. 125), where she meets Ignatius and they so disrupt the slow flow of the History department that they are removed. (Gus Levy sends his children North to college.) Her experience in the 'ghettos of Gotham' (p. 124) had not prepared her for Ignatius and the South, as she believed 'that all humans living south and west of the Hudson river were illiterate cowboys or – even worse – White Protestants, a class of humans who as a group specialized in ignorance, cruelty, and torture'. Here Ignatius interpolates '(I don't wish to especially defend White Protestants; I am not too fond of them myself.)' (p. 124).

Listening to Ignatius' take on the world, she declared him 'obviously anti-Semitic' when he disagreed with her (ibid.). This becomes a leit-motif for her. When Ignatius sends her a letter on 'Levy Pants' stationary, she responds that 'it is probably your idea of an anti-Semitic prank', as her father is in the clothing trade (p. 214).

Myrna haunts Ignatius dreams. In one dream he stands on 'a subway platform, reincarnated as St James the Less, who was martyred by the Jews'. Myrna appears carrying a sign for the 'NON-VIOLENT CONGRESS FOR THE SEXU-ALLY NEEDY' and Ignatius 'prophesied' to her that 'Jesus will come to the fore, skins or not' (p. 242). The dreams morph into life when Myrna appears stuffed in her Renault to rescue Ignatius, when his mother, egged on by Mrs Santa Battaglia, tries to have him committed to the psychiatric ward at Charity Hospital. Myrna whisks him off towards New York City, where, given the picaresque nature of the tale, his adventures in the skin trade would certainly continue.

Like attracts like. Myrna's shapeless, hippy body is the political counterpoint to Ignatius' huge one. There is a parallel in Salman Rushdie's first novel, *Grimus* (1975), a fantasy work centering around a quartet of American misfits living in a fantasy world.[29] One of them, Virgil Jones, 'gross of body' (p. 12), is in love with the hunch-backed Dolores O'Toole: 'they loved each other and found it impossible to declare their love. It was no beautiful love, for they were extremely ugly.' When they finally do make love, their 'disfiguration [is] transformed into sexuality' (p. 50). 'Her hands grasping great folds of his flesh . . . It's like making bread, she giggled, pretending to work his belly into a loaf' (ibid.). We seem to be back again to the 'German' baker. Ethnicity and obesity come to be linked in an odd way, both in their representation in culture and in their living experience of it.

6

CHINESE OBESITY

Over the past decade the nineteenth-century preoccupation with food-related or food-borne illness has reappeared. The older assumption of such diseases infiltrating from the 'orient' has been part and parcel of the newer obsession. From BSE – which, as we discussed in the first chapter, was recently attributed to the consumption of animals fed on human bodily parts and coming from the Indian subcontinent[1] – to the widespread anxiety about 'bird 'flu', the 'orient' has been seen as the source of illness.

1 THE 'ORIENT' RESPONDS IN THE EARLY TWENTIETH CENTURY

The idea that dangerous infectious diseases originate in the 'orient' is not new. The model of the Victorian understanding of the spread of bubonic plague can serve as a model for the anxiety about the spread of influenza today. However, recent studies of obesity in China have come to reverse the claim that such food-borne diseases invade from the primitive 'orient'. These Chinese-based studies are often rooted in the view that obesity and its attendant symptoms are the result of the recent pathological 'Occidentalization' of China and the Chinese. This obsession with the 'contamination from the West' has come to be part of the imagined etiology of obesity in contemporary medicine in China (PRC) as well as in western (US/UK) medicine dealing with the Chinese from the diaspora.

In early twentieth-century China there was a popular fascination with obesity, perhaps as a result of the images of 'famine' that marked western views of the pathological body in nineteenth-century China.[2] When you systematically read the standard 'western' medical journal published in China, the *China Medical Journal*, from the beginning of the twentieth century down to the Japanese invasion of China, the central medical discourse concerning 'diet' and the body is that of famine and starvation. The physicians of the Chinese Medical Missionary Association are concerned that the food made available in their hospitals has sufficient protein and fat, to the extent that they advocate 'crossing foreign and native cows', or the introduction of canned milk to improve the local diet.[3] That diet seems to be regionally differentiated. One physician notes that the 'rich have rice, vegetables, and meats. The poor have rice, vegetables and substitutes for meat.' It is only 'when floods overtake the people year in and year out that so many are driven to our doors for charity.'[4] China is, from this perspective, not a 'famine' culture at all. Rather, it is the distribution of foods that seems to be at the heart of famine from the standpoint of the physicians. In this rather contemporary view, the distribution network is what causes famine.[5] (Amartya Sen's 1981 *Poverty and Famines: An Essay on Entitlement and Deprivation* argues that famine occurs not from a lack of food, but from inequalities built into the

mechanisms for distributing food.) But there is also some sus-
picion that the indigenous foods may not be 'suitable' enough
to maintain a healthy diet.[6] The soybean is seen over and over
again as an adequate substitute for other forms of protein.[7]

Yet when the concern is about true starvation, the sense is
that 'western' cures, for instance a rich, milk-based diet, are
most appropriate.[8] It is the child who is seen as mostly at risk
from the effects of famine. The selling of children is seen as a
major result of the famine culture of China.[9] 'Cannot the
famine relief associations . . . take this matter into consideration and put an end to it', writes one irate physician.[10] In all of
the myriad concerns about the pathological effects of diet, not
a single word is spent on the dangers or effects of obesity.[11]

The concern with obesity first appears in Chinese popular
magazines, where it is already seen as a response to the
view of China as a famine culture in past and contemporary
allopathic medicine.[12] Yet in Shigehisa Kuriyama's brilliant
*Expressiveness of the Body and the Divergence of Greek and Chinese
Medicine*, the standard study of the differences between
ancient Greek and traditional Chinese medicine, the 'model'
bodily type in classical Chinese medical literature and culture
is described as rotund, as opposed to the muscular and svelte
bodies of Greek art and medicine.[13] Obesity seems not to be a
major problem in the various theories of the ill body in
Chinese medicine. This is not to say that there has not been a
constant and intense concern with the 'immoderate body' in
the medical and dietetic literature of traditional Chinese medicine. In the sixteenth century, Li Shizhen (1518–93) wrote in
his *Bencai gangmu* (*Systematic Materia Medica*) that the consumption of fresh crabs was healthy 'in small quantities', but
'gluttons will consume a dozen or more at a sitting together
with various kinds of meat and other foods. They eat and
drink twice as much as they need . . . then blame [their upset
stomachs on] the crabs. But why blame the crabs?'[14] The

culture of excess in the world of traditional Chinese medicine became a hallmark of the degenerate Chinese body in need of regeneration by the early twentieth century. This was quite in contrast to the anxiety about emaciation, which drove thin people to undertake 'special bulking diets' in order to find marriage partners. Such emaciation was often seen as the curse of ancestors, who were 'eating' the health and vitality of a descendant in retaliation for neglect or mistreatment. Plumpness, by contrast, was perceived as a clear indication that the person so blessed was in harmony with the supernatural world.[15] Yet this dominant image of China as a starvation culture had its answer in the counter-example of the degenerate obese body, also present in the world of early twentieth-century China.

Immediately before the revolution that overthrew the Qing dynasty on 10 October 1911, 'reform' was everywhere. A new fantasy of the 'reformed' body had begun to emerge in China. Obesity came to be viewed as one of the signs of the degenerate Chinese body, a body clearly in need of reform. Following the model of 'regeneration' that captured most of the ideologies of the day (from Zionism to Marxism to social Darwinism to colonialism), obesity defines the ability of the society to reform the individual.[16] In one of the most widely read columns 'Ziyoutan' ('Unfettered talk') in the renowned newspaper *Shenbao*, the author Wang Dungen explored the reform of the body. He was a well-known writer and a key figure in the 'Mandarin Ducks and Butterflies School', one of the 'oppositional' cultural movements. Most of the young revolutionary writers were adherents of the 'May Fourth' literary movement begun on that date in 1919. The movement followed the Xinhai political revolution of 1911, during which the Qing Dynasty was overthrown. Wang Dungen had been attacked by the May Fourth progressive writers of the late 1910s and early 1920s, for in 1914 he had created the comic journal *Saturday*. In the comic essay 'Reforming the human body', Wang Dungen envisions a grotesque ideal of the 'new' body. He imagines a body with newly configured mouth, tongue, ear, eyes, nose, skin, eyebrow, hair, teeth, neck, shoulders, arm, hands, fingers and feet. He sees it as having hundreds of mouths, so that a person can eat more and still be able to talk.[17] This is an ironic response to the theme of the starved body, which desires a reform that should permit it to consume ever more. 'Western' models of regeneration, such as structured physical exercise, become the means of reforming the too fat body. Chen Duxiu, the leader of the New Cultural Movement, advocated exercise to make the Chinese physically as well as morally fit, and Mao Zedong in 1917 published a full-scale manual of physical activity to reform the body.[18]

By 1913, the classical Chinese medical literature on obesity is beginning to be summarized for an intellectual readership in China. The essay 'On obesity' by Shuhui and Weiseng was written in classical Chinese for a leading women's magazine. Such magazines came to shape, and be shaped by, the images of the so-called 'new woman' (*xin nuxing*) and 'westernized modern girl' (*modeng nulang*) which came into prominence in the first decade of the twentieth century in China as well as in the West. They were defined in many ways, to no little extent by their 'thin' bodily form. Thinness, even after the establishment of the People's Republic, continued to be a mark of 'bad luck, illness, and early death', as James L. Watson noted.[19] It was the 'stigma of emaciation' which scarred the psyche of the Chinese at the beginning and at the close of the twentieth century. But it was associated not with 'modern' thought, but with village superstition and backwardness among the intellectuals of the early twentieth-century.

The 1913 essay 'On obesity' presents the argument that obesity is an illness which women must not take lightly.[20] The authors refer to male figures and texts from ancient China, such as a man named 'Zilong', who lived in the Warring States period. Zilong felt he was too fat, so he took *Phragmites communis Trirn* (a traditional medicine) to lose weight. The authors use this example to prove that obesity is an illness treatable by medical intervention even in the pre-modern period. One source they mention is *Hanshu yiwenzhi* (*The History of the Former Han Dynasty*), written by the historian Ban Gu (32–92 AD). They argue that, according to the *Hanshu*, too much bodily fat is the cause of obesity. But there are two kinds of obesity. One is obesity with too many blood cells; the other, with not enough blood cells. The causes the former are: (1) not eating appropriately; (2) not having a balanced life style; and (3) not having enough sex. Not eating appropriately means that one eats too many unhealthy foods such as flour, sugar, and alcohol. Obesity of the second type is caused by external injury, overworking, stress, or sometimes after giving birth.

As in the western literature of the late nineteenth century, there are stages of obesity.[21] For the authors, obesity has three phases. Initially, the person looks acceptably plump, which indicates prosperity, so that others admire him; then the person looks overtly obese and funny; and, finally, the person is in danger and others take pity on her. This final stage of obesity presents symptoms which include sweating, fatigue, backache, heart disease, sexual incompetence, and so on. The 'cure' for obesity is a balanced eating and life style: avoid eating things that contain too much fat, don't sleep more than eight hours, take a warm bath two or three times a week, walk two or three hours every day, and be persistent. In terms of medication, one should take either traditional medication such as *wodu* or, better yet, thyroid tablets. The later are the classical pharmaceutical intervention which certainly can reduce weight by making the individual hyperthyroidic, which increases basal metabolism. This will lead to weight loss but can also be conducive to a wide range of pathologies, such as Thyrotoxicosis.

The modern creeps into this world of classical Chinese views on the obese with the suggestion of treating it as an endocrinological deficiency, one of the most up-to-date views in early twentieth-century medicine. For the obese body is the antithesis of the beautiful and healthy body. And this is a special problem for contemporary women. In an essay entitled 'Keep the body slim' and published in a women's magazine in 1922, the author, Daizuo, stresses that people with obesity are not beautiful, especially women: 'A person who is too fat looks very ugly. Women especially can't be fat. If a woman gained too much weight and became fatty, where can one find her beauty?'[22] In addition, obesity is an important medical problem. Obesity is seen as the result of faulty metabolism, the result of hormone imbalance. Yet obesity is not a random occurrence, as some people are more at risk. Specifically, people who eat rich and abundant food, people who are not physically active, people with a family inheritance of obesity, and alcoholics.

Obesity is dangerous in so far as it leads to heart disease. People with obesity have shortness of breath and rapid heartbeats even after walking a few steps. They are more likely to have a stroke. People with obesity have urinary and kidney problems. Dieting is, again, the solution. One should not overeat; one should avoid foods that contain too much fat and eat less meat. Other suggestions the essay gives for weight loss are physical exercises, the use of laxatives, and electric steam therapy to reduce body fat, which according to the essay is very popular abroad. While it was widely used for various ills, electrotherapy was a standard late nineteenth-century western treatment for the 'failure or perversion of nutrition', including diabetes.[23]

It is clearly women who are the target of the growing anti-obesity anxiety of republican China. In one essay the author,

Zhou Zhenyu, states that he is a doctor who often has female patients who need help in order to lose weight.[24] Zhou Zhenyu comments: 'when I was a doctor in Beiping, I often had women patients come asking for the method of losing weight. I would tell them the method, some of them went home and practiced following my suggestions, others would come visit again and want medication. The effects differ because the causes of their obesity vary.' 'The cause and danger of female obesity' is seen either in over-indulgence and the absence of exercise or in the imbalance of hormones. This is the classic argument about obesity that dominated the late nineteenth-century discussion of the causes of obesity. In the United States, which was the home of most of the medical missionaries to China by 1924, the editors of the *Journal of the American Medical Association* had published an editorial entitled 'What causes obesity?' Following a powerful anti-psychological strand in obesity research that began in the late nineteenth century, they argue in it for an etiology in mal-functions of normal metabolic processes. See obesity as a 'scientific problem', they write, and that will free the 'fat woman' from the stigma that she 'has the remedy in her own hands – or rather between her own teeth'. That new object of scientific interest is the fat woman, who had been charged with carrying 'that extra weight about with her unless she so wills'.[25] Women, not 'men' or 'people', are at risk from obesity – a far cry from the evocation of Falstaff as the exem-plary sufferer from obesity in the mid-nineteenth century.[26] According to the anonymous Chinese physician in 1922, although fat people usually eat less than thin people, they do not burn enough calories. There are still large amounts of fat accumulated and stored in their body. While the obese do not eat much at every meal, they snack often. Women specifically can suffer from hypothyroidism, hypopituitarism, or a loss of estrogen. Pregnant women are especially at risk. One woman, after giving birth, had to get up and eat every night. She quickly gained weight and became obese.

The danger of female obesity is the collapse of one's health and thus of one's ability to bear children. This remains the classic definition of women's health. Obese women have compromised immune systems; they are likely to catch colds and coughs, which leads to tuberculosis. They have heart disease. There is danger to one's nervous system. The obese are usually slow and lazy, but oftentimes they laugh and seem happy. Obese women have problems conceiving, have problems when having sex, and are likely to have miscarriages.

By 1941, as the war raged and famine haunted China, a public discourse on obesity remained part of the popular register of the new 'reformed' Chinese attitude towards the body. These attitudes came to be labeled a 'tragedy at the dinner table'.[27] An essay by this title seems to be a free adaptation of a number of foreign medical and popular articles, especially American ones. It presents the pathological consequences of overeating. The author identifies middle-aged people as the ones mostly at risk, because they seem to be more easily taken by the desire for fine eating. The essay defines pathology by quoting a saying attributed to an American congressman: 'fifty, fifty, fifty', which means if a fifty-year-old person is fifty pounds overweight, his life span will be reduced 50 percent. The author also quotes statistics by an American doctor to the effect that, out of 2,000 cases of sudden death, 90 percent were people who died of heart disease. 'Most of them eat too much, are overweight, which causes heart disease.' While other, foreign or historical, cases of overeating are mentioned, for instance the ancient Romans, the American Thanksgiving is picked out as a moment of public gluttony:

Around Thanksgiving time, there are often cases of death caused by overeating to be found in the mortuary. People in

Figure 6.1 An advertisement from the Shanghai newspapers in the early 1930s

The advertisment reads: 'Lipolysin. The heavenly medicine to cure obesity (feipangbing). If one is obese, one can't move easily, one sweats all the time, and one may suffer from stroke and other sudden diseases. Given the harm obesity causes, it certainly should be cured as early as possible. Lipolysin is produced by the German Haier pharmaceutical company; it combines elements that conquer obesity, and will transform a fat and stupid body into a slim and agile one, and therefore cure the disease and achieve longevity.'

charge of the postmortem examinations are often too busy rushing to luxurious banquets to do their work. It's also quite dangerous to eat too much after fasting. One should definitely divide all the nice dishes into several meals, and never eat everything at once. It is nice to be able to enjoy a full table of luxurious food, but one should remember not to gamble with one's own life. Otherwise tragedy would take place in the holiday season, and one would sadly fall onto the bosom of the death.

The result of such gluttony is sudden death, chronic heart disease, or diabetes. A litany of diseases is the result of obesity: high blood pressure, lung disease, cancer, even suicide and accidental death. For, according to the author, people with obesity often have psychological problems and are very slow in reacting to what is going on – thus being prone to accidents. The overweight should consult qualified doctors to decide over his or her individual diet. Yet the 'cure' proposed in the essay of 1941 is to pay minute attention to what and how much one eats. The formula does not have much to do with any specific type of food; rather, the idea is that, as one gets older, one should eat less. When one gets very old, one should only eat light and simple foods, returning to the diet prescribed for infants.

2 A SECOND CULTURE OF OBESITY TODAY

The fear of obesity has reappeared in the past decade in an age that remembers another moment of famine. James L. Watson noted that the dominant sense of fear concerning the body in modern China is the result of the great famine under Mao Zedong.[28] This famine from 1958 to 1961, which resulted from the collectivization of the peasants, killed millions in China and evoked the horrors of the famines of the 1940s during the war against the Japanese, the civil war, and the policies of the nationalist government.[29] For adults in today's China, 'famine' evokes their own experiences under Mao and the tales of starvation during the war, told by their parents and grandparents.

Yet the concern with obesity appears at the close of the twentieth century. In a retrospective analysis of a detailed, nationwide survey of illnesses ascribed to dietary causes in the 1980s and 1990s, obesity was hardly mentioned, except to note that 'obesity was a much less central concern in China'.[30] And yet, in the twenty-first century, the 'obesity epidemic' seems to be the next great fear of Chinese public health officers after smoking:

> chronic diseases now account for an estimated 80% of deaths and 70% of disability-adjusted life-years lost in China. Cardiovascular diseases and cancer are the leading causes of both death and the burden of disease, and exposure to risk factors is high: more than 300 million men smoke cigarettes and 160 million adults are hypertensive, most of whom are not being treated. An obesity epidemic is imminent, with more than 20% of children aged 7–17 years in big cities now overweight or obese.[31]

Being a child in the twenty-first century means being at risk. The transition from smoking to obesity as the most important threat to public health clearly parallels the fear in western sources such as the World Health Organization, which had identified obesity as the next great danger – having 'eliminated' smoking as a public health hazard.[32]

For China, a country with an increasing number of people now smoking and where tobacco remains a major source of state revenue, obesity is the new danger. The fat child, not the Marlboro Man, is the source of anxiety.[33] Smoking is popularly seen as a 'positive' reflection of the process of modernization, while obesity has come to represent the corruption imported from the West. The official journal of 'preventive medicine', *Zhonghua Yu Fang Yi Xue Za Zhi*, acknowledged in 2005 that

> the prevalence of overweight and obesity among people living in rural areas was lower than that of their urban counterparts, while the increment of overweight and obesity prevalence among rural people was greater than that of their urban counterparts. It was estimated that another 70 million overweight and 30 million obese Chinese people emerged in China from 1992 to 2002. The prevalence of overweight and obesity of Chinese people was increased rapidly in the past decade, which had affected 260 million Chinese people. It would continue to increase in the near future if effective intervention measures have not been taken.[34]

The shift seems to be marked. A Body-Mass Index (BMI) of greater than 25 kg/m² is to be found in 18.7 percent of the population in urban areas, as opposed to 13.7 percent in rural areas. (We should note that a BMI of 30 is conventionally held to be obese.) But the increase over the past decades is also striking. These figures are for 1997. They mark a four-fold increase over 1982, when only 3.7 percent of Chinese adults had a BMI of over 25.[35] Chinese medical and epidemiological studies argue that 'obesity has become a global epidemic', although there seems to be little knowledge of the state of affairs in China (meaning the People's Republic of China). Looking at 'a group of 2,776 randomly selected adults (20–94 years of age) living in the Huayang Community in Shanghai, China', this 2002 study argued that, while 'the prevalence of obesity [using western standards] was lower in China than in the West, the overall fat mass-related metabolic disorders were also common'.[36] The Chinese, unlike the Japanese over the past fifty years, seem to be growing 'fat' without

developing greater height or frame size. Rather than the positive aspects of a change in diet being measured, only the
pathological results of overweight preoccupy the medical scientists. Thus the diseases of 'modernity' such as diabetes are
often the proof of a decaying, decadent population, just as it
was in the nineteenth century in studies of diabetes, then
labeled the 'Jewish' disease:

> All observers are agreed that Jews are specially liable to
> become diabetic. . . . A person belonging to the richer classes
> in towns usually eats too much, spends a great part of his life
> indoors; takes too little bodily exercise, and overtakes his
> nervous system in the pursuit of knowledge, business, or
> pleasure . . . Such a description is a perfectly accurate
> account of the well-to-do Jew, who raises himself easily by his
> superior mental ability to a comfortable social position, and
> notoriously avoids all kinds of bodily exercise.[37]

Today the argument is that diabetes is more than twice as frequent in the Chinese (urban) overweight population, even
though this population was of lower weight than the equivalent western population. The visible pathology of obesity was
immediately translated into the invisible disease of diabetes.
But what is the cause?

Westernization and 'economic success' in the new China,
or among the Chinese in the diaspora, are seen as the ultimate
cause of the disease. The urbanization of China is read as the
source both of shifts in patterns of food consumption and of
changes in work habits. Both lead to what is now called 'metabolic syndromes', the diseases associated with obesity.[38] All of
these shifts are read as aspects of 'Americanization', the new
cause of obesity. America is now the source of illness rather
than, as in the early twentieth century, the place 'cure' may
come from.[39] James L. Watson noted that McDonald's is the

test case for the positive or negative implications of 'Yankee imperialism'.[40] Or, as he points out in the 2006 update to his book on 'fast food' in China, McDonald's has become paradigmatic of the new evil: globalization (pp. 186–7). Yet in the eyes of the Chinese authorities and of the public, McDonald's represented 'modernization, hygiene, and responsible management'.[41] In a complex way, it represented a healthy food as opposed to the traditional 'street food', which was seen as dangerous. McDonald's represented the 'invention of cleanliness' in Hong Kong and beyond.[42] In Taipei, McDonald's was actually credited 'with promoting hygiene and etiquette'. A school principal there observed: 'Every set lunch is wrapped in a clean bag. Students become accustomed to using a napkin during meals. They learn hygienic behavior and proper etiquette by eating hamburgers.'[43] Today McDonald's represents the intrusion of a 'homogenous, global culture'. But this is also a hygienic culture, because of its emphasis on its homogeneity as the root of hygiene into what is seen as a purely 'Chinese' food culture, which posed health risks.

3 THE CHINESE–AMERICAN PROBLEM

The medical reading of such changes was, however, solely negative, and had little to do with improved food safety. Tsung O. Cheng of George Washington University's medical school has made the claim, concerning even the recent work on obesity in China, that 'the proportion of obesity among children under the age of 15 increased from 15% in 1982 to 27% today' because of 'fast food and physical inactivity'. 'All of the children in China recognize the image of Ronald McDonald, even though they may not be able to read English.'[44] Zumin Shi of the Jiangsu Provincial Center for Disease Control and Prevention looks at the expansion of obesity-related illnesses such as anemia among adolescents in the new China and correlates it to parental attention and 'overnutrition'.[45] J. X. Jiang at the National Center for Women's and Children's Health examines in terms of family structure, for etiology and intervention, a similar problem.[46] Bin Xie, a social worker based in California, looks at data from Wuhan in order to correlate mental state (depression) and obesity among the newly successful who now lack an adequate social network. The claim is that 'the findings of this study may contribute to our understanding of the influences of psychological correlates in pediatric overweight in the Eastern cultural environment'.[47] All imagine that obesity is a reflex of the alteration in the status of individual, family, and society with the most recent changes in the economic system. Yet there is also a compelling counterview: that the weight of immigrants tends not to shift greatly when they come to the United States.[48] The view seems to be that America provides all the wrong incentives; only traditional values (and diet) preserve health.

What happens when we leave (for a moment) China and move, with the Chinese diaspora, to that land of McDonald's, America? Jyu-Lin Chen and Christine Kennedy examine correlative material in an analysis of over-weight Chinese–American children, to conclude

> that a more democratic parenting style contributes to a higher BMI in Chinese–American children. First, several studies have shown that an authoritarian parenting style in Chinese families may not necessarily reflect the strict parenting that was measured in Western society. Conversely, parents' involvement, care, supervision, and encouragement of academic achievement, all of which typically have been identified as components of an 'authoritarian' parenting style in Western society, are, in fact, a reflection of caring and loving parenting in the Chinese culture.[49]

American-type success breaks down the 'parental control and warmth' that constitutes Chinese child raising and leads to fat Chinese children, who are a pathological sign of that success: 'a democratic parenting style, and poor family communication contribute to higher BMI in Chinese–American children' (p. 115). All obesity comes from the West. Chinese families, understood as a traditional society (certainly not in terms of the cultural revolution), simply don't produce fat kids. Only children raised in the traditional 'Chinese' manner (not children raised in the American manner) are not at risk – unless, of course, they live in Shanghai.

There are, of course, large numbers of 'Asian–Americans' who fall below the poverty line. They are seen to be at risk from the obesity associated in contemporary medical argument with poverty. In this way, too, they mimic 'typical' American dietary patterns. In one study, Asian–American ethnic groups, defined as the Chinese, Vietnamese, and Hmong in California, were the focus. In this study, 'the concept of good health [in these communities] included having a harmonious family, balance, and mental and emotional stability. All groups also expressed the general belief that specific foods have hot or cold properties and are part of the Yin/Yang belief system common to Asian cultures. The lure of fast food, children's adoption of American eating habits, and long work hours were identified as barriers to a healthy, more traditional lifestyle.'[50] Yet the results here are virtually identical with those whose belief systems were very different. All classify the 'poor' as those being at risk from the pathologies of obesity. In fact one recent study has argued that children in China stunted by malnutrition are at substantially greater risk from obesity as they mature.[51]

'America' serves as more than the place where obesity has its origin. In many Chinese studies, the model of a multi-ethnic America, with different rates of risk, becomes the model for understanding different group responses to obesity. What was once a monolithic risk to the 'Chinese' becomes a more differentiated risk, where ethnic sub-groups are seen as being at greater risk because of their implied genetic or cultural difference. Looking at 'ethnic' populations in Xinjiang, a recent study documented that more 'obese' Kazak people developed hypertension, whereas more 'obese' Uygur people developed diabetes. Implicitly, by using the American studies of African–American and Mexican–American obesity and the resultant increase in cases of type II diabetes in these communities, the study suggested the difference in 'genetic' background as the cause. (The People's Republic of China includes fifty-six national minorities, but the 'majority' Han is itself a composite category.) But it is also clear that the Uygur subjects were from rural south Xinjiang and the Kazak subjects from suburban north Xinjiang.[52] Thus the 'Han' become the unspoken parallel to the labels in American majority culture, where they are labeled 'white' or 'Caucasian' and are epidemiologically rarely differentiated into sub-groups. This is just as constructed a 'majority' category in opposition to the other minority groups (now understood as 'racial'), as is the Han.[53] This is a sub-set of the construct of the 'yellow race' which, according to Jing Tsu, is one of the formative myths of modern Chinese identity.[54] Each such construct seeks out some category which risks to stress the 'healthy' nature of the racial category seen as dominant. In the nineteenth century it was the 'healthy' German Jew as opposed to the sickly eastern Jew. The 'rural versus urban' question of healthy versus unhealthy 'ethnicities' replicates this dichotomy. They are here as muddy as those studies of obesity in the developed world which seem to reveal that, for ethnic minorities, as in the West, ethnicity trumps geography (or rather biology trumps class). Indeed there is even the argument that urban sprawl does not impact on weight – it is rather that fat people 'choose to live in more sprawling neighbourhoods' as opposed to 'mixed use' ones, as they would rather get about by car rather than walk.[55]

4 ASIA AND THE WEST

The cause of obesity, even in such communities, is laid at the feet of processed, 'fast' foods, which, if not imported from abroad, are Chinese versions of it. The specter of the 2008 Olympic games should create in China some type of awareness of healthy bodies and healthy lifestyles (at least in theory). A recent essay on the 'obesity epidemic' in China prophesied that the Olympics would add to rather than help cure this malaise.[56] That many of the sponsors are 'directly involved in high-caloric foods' such as 'calorie-dense beverages (e.g., Coca-Cola)' seems to imply that the games will make the Chinese even fatter. That McDonalds is one of the sponsors the authors find 'full of irony', citing Morgan Spurlock's 2004 film *Supersize Me* as their authority for the 'high saturated fat' that will put athletes and spectators alike at risk (pp. 173–4). This, coupled with 'television viewing and motorized transport', will condemn them to 'an increase in the mortality, morbidity and disability' associated with obesity. Among the other sponsors of the games are Volkswagen and Panasonic. It seems apparent, even at first reading, that the 'curse' of high fructose corn syrup as one of the prime re-shapers of the 'fast food nation' has been drawn into question, and that a national stereotype (much like that of the Americans) underlies the work of these researchers from the antipodes.

There are numerous questions which seem to go unanswered in these studies. Is 'obesity' in 'Asia' the same phenomenological category as in the 'West'? Not only are there different histories of the 'large' body and its meaning in 'Asia', but there are different physiological measures that would be used for the definition of the obese body. I use the label 'Asia' in this context rather than 'Chinese' because in 2002 The World Health Association called a meeting in Hong Kong to examine whether the obese body was to be defined differently among 'Asians'. This 'lead to the proposal that adult over-weight could be specified in Asia when the body mass index exceeded 23.00 and that obesity should be specified when the BMI exceed 25.00'.[57] These criteria are substantially lower (almost by 10 points) than the American criteria, which should include that new category, 'Asian–Americans'. Yet it is clear that the Asian–American population is being measured by western public health definitions of overweight and obesity. What are the boundaries of 'Asia'? Do they now contain Taiwan, which sees itself in the context of the Pacific islands? Does it reach north into Mongolia and Siberia? To the Ainu? To the west to India? Or is it a composite that rests in an American fantasy of the 'Asian'? Yet bodily changes have been demonstrated among Japanese–Americans over three genera-tions after immigration. However, there seems to be no increase in obesity except over the past decade, with the impo-sition of 'western' definitions of 'obesity'.[58] Indeed, *Japanese Women Don't Get Old or Fat*, runs the title of a recent book, which claims that Japan has the lowest obesity rate in the developed world, the longest life expenditure and the lowest per capita health care cost.[59] It postulates a 'Japanese paradox' (analogous to the 'French paradox' and the claim of universal thinness in France): 'How can the world's most food-obsessed nation have the lowest obesity rates in the industrialized world – and the best longevity on earth?' The answer given is diet: 'the Asian diet is probably the best on earth' (p. 8). Yet the take-out foods available are western: 'Italian, Chinese, French, and Indian, since food in Japan has been a global affair for many centuries' (p. 25). 'Sushi' (as well as McDonald's and pizza) has gone global since it was first mentioned in the

Ladies'Home Journal in 1929 as not being quite as delicious as it sounds to the untutored reader.[60] The 'sushi' craze does not seem to have altered the American sense of what are healthful foods, even at the glatt kosher Shalom Sushi, a New York restaurant playing to two contemporary senses of what is healthy food. Health promotion, as Richard Parish has noted, is a concept not much older than the 1980s.[61] In that light, 'Japanese' food comes, along with 'kosher' food, to be read as inherently 'healthful' even though such claims are rarely made for it at its point of origin.

No such claims are made about the low impact of western foods, such as pizza and curry, on China. A recent popular American study claims that the Chinese diet is the answer to western obesity![62] Its authors stress that the 'difference between rural Chinese diets and Western diets, and the ensuing disease patterns, is enormous' (p. 75). Their claim is that 'cancer' is primarily the result of the ingestion of animal fats. For them, the paucity of such fats in the traditional Chinese diet may explain the different epidemiology of cancer in contemporary China. There is nostalgia for the food of the 'natural man' living in harmony with nature, which protects people from disease – a nostalgia which haunts such approaches. Indeed, even a recent, more serious epidemiological study of the shifts in Chinese eating and working patterns and of their suggested impact on weight gain begins with the statement: 'The classic Chinese diet based on rice and vegetables is being replaced by increasing amounts of animal products and a Western-type diet profile.'[63] The inhabitants of northern China with their heavily meat- (read pork-) oriented diets would clearly take exception to the creation of a 'classic Chinese diet', which seems to reflect a western homogenization of the wide range of cuisines that exist and existed throughout the broadest reaches of what is now called China. That there is a change in eating patterns may well be the case:

but the creation of an ideal Chinese diet belies both the diversity of Chinese eating patterns and the existence of rural famine, even in areas which do reflect such a reliance on 'rice and vegetables'.

Westernization, both in China and in the Chinese diaspora, may well play a role, but it is a secondary cause – the primary cause is the long-established one-child policy in China and the change in the status of urban children. This change is analogous to the attitudes of many first-generation immigrants (not only the Chinese) to the American urban diaspora. Yet a preoccupation with the diseases of obesity, specifically diabetes (type II), is found within this literature on China. In a paper from 2001 – a study of adults in a population of north-eastern China, specifically in Da Qing City – the author argued:

> increasing waist measurements predicted 10-fold increases in hypertension and a three-to-five times increased risk of diabetes. Suitable waist cut-off points were 85 cm for men and 80 cm for women, with statistical analysis showing waist as the more dominant predictor of risk than age, waist-to-hip ratios or BMIs. Hence, small increases in BMI, and particularly in waist circumference, predict a substantial increase in the risk of diabetes . . . in Chinese adults.[64]

What is being seen is the shift in body size caused by the accessibility of different foods. Perhaps one sees at work here the so-called 'thrifty genotype' hypothesis, which had been suggested in 1964. Simply stated, it has been observed that, when mice are transferred from a harsh to a benign environment, they gain weight and are hyperglycemic. Thus, when one measured first-generation groups of immigrants to the United States in the late nineteenth century, one found that there was a substantial higher rate of Type II diabetes, whereas the initial groups had shown an extremely low index of obesity and of the resultant diabetes. This index, however, skyrocketed after just a short time of living in their new environment. Thus diabetes and obesity seem to reflect a failure to adapt rapidly to changed surroundings.[65] It is the rapidity of change that lies at the heart of the matter.

In China today, rural children are suffering from malnutrition. The Beijing-based Institute of Nutrition and Food Safety found that more than 29 percent of children under five years old in China's poorest regions were growing at a slower than normal rate. This is quite different from the situation in the cities, where too rich a diet has increased the level of obesity. In China's larger, wealthier cities, milk, formula milk powder, yoghurt and many other types of food are available which would prevent childhood malnutrition. Yet, of course, the availability of such foods seems also to be viewed as a causal factor in the new Chinese 'obesity epidemic'. According to Chinese public health sources, severe obesity now affects some 16 percent to 20 percent of the urban youngsters.[66] But, of course, 'urban' itself is a highly problematic category; for it includes the rural diaspora – people who lead marginal lives in the large cities as well as in cities which have had little share in the new boom economy.

5 THE FAT AND HAPPY CHILD

Now, in a China, with a growing urban middle class, obesity seems to have been uncoupled from the official demand under Mao Zedong, in 1979, that only one child per couple should be allowed – which radically reduced the average of three to four children per family in rural areas and two to three in urban areas. China, unlike most societies in transformation which have a reduction in birth rate as a reflex of the increasing economic status, saw the reduction in the number of children per family coming before the development of the new economic

modernization begun under Deng Xiaoping. More food and
more TV are today indeed a means of pampering these children, often called 'the little emperors' (*xiao huangdi*) – but the
number and the status of the children are independent of economic change. These 'little emperors' are 'used to getting
plenty of candy, lavish praise from grownups, and pretty much
anything else [they] want.'[67] And what they want is food, at least
as imagined from the perspective of a western observer writing
for a western audience accustomed to critiques of the 'Fast
Food Nation'. They are imagined being 'weaned on cheese-
burgers from McDonald's, pizza from Pizza Hut, and fried
chicken from KFC'. Their growing obesity has become not
only a public health problem but a source for a new 'weight-
loss business'. 'At the Aimin Fat Reduction Hospital in Tianjin,
a former military institution that launched China's first weight
clinic in 1992, doctors treat 200 patients, most of them under
twenty-five, with a daily regimen of acupuncture, exercise, and
healthy food. Fifteen-year-old Liang Chen reports proudly
that he has lost thirty-three pounds in less than a month at
Aimin. But he can't stop reminiscing wistfully about his regular visits to KFC. (His favorite T-shirt is a souvenir from
China's largest KFC store.) 'I used to be able to eat an entire
family-size bucket all by myself,'he recalls. 'Just one?' snorts his
roommate, fourteen-year-old Li Xiang. 'That's nothing. I used
to be able to eat four buckets – sometimes five, if I didn't eat the
corncobs and bread.'[68]

Childhood obesity is not the only curse of the 'little emperors', as anorexia nervosa seems also to be present. In 1993, an
eating disorders clinic in the Fujien area reported 200 cases of
radical underweight among children, from 1988 to 1990. The
gender balance was remarkable for anorexia nervosa from the
western point-of-view: 112 cases were boys and only 88 were
girls. These cases were not the product of a starvation culture,
but rather of 'non-fat phobic anorexia' caused, according to

the researchers, by the single-child policy, as the children were spoiled by their parents and developed unhealthy eating habits which contributed to their underweight.[69]

As the anthropologist Jun Jing notes on the basis of his fieldwork, things have changed radically since the 1980s. 'Children now have more money and . . . their money goes to candy, cookies, chips, instant noodles, chocolate, nuts, soft drinks, and ice cream.'[70] But even in his serious attempt to plumb the depths of the new obesity, the villain remains 'Colonel Sanders, impeccable in his white suit and goatee, holding a jumbo bucket of Kentucky Fried Chicken' (ibid.). Or at least Chicky (Qiqi), the Chinese cartoon emblem of KFC, the first western food franchise in China (1987). This Chinese capitulation to westernized (modern) food is paralleled by a sense of the nostalgia for a past of ideal foods, not specifically consumed by children. Thus the essayist H. Y. Lowe (Wu Hsing-yuan) is quoted from the period 1939–40 (which ranges towards the end of the first epoch concerned with obesity) as expressing a nostalgia for the 'eighteen kinds of foods and beverages that he had enjoyed as a child'. As Jun Jing notes in his introduction, only two ('dried cake powder' and 'old rice powder') were specifically for children and 'were intended to supplement mother's milk' (p. 9). These were the 'modern', manufactured foods advocated by the missionary physicians to augment the diet of hunger perceived in China.

Here the problem is not 'western' food but the absence of moderation, an absence fostered by the 'little emperor' syndrome. The number of children is a result of the old communist system, and may be exacerbated by the availability of western fast foods. Yet there are studies that minimize the shifts in diet towards a westernization of the Chinese diet. One such study argues that, while in the United States snacks contribute 'more than one-third of their daily calories and a higher proportion of snack calories from foods prepared away from home', in 'China . . . snacks provide only approximately 1% of energy. Fast food plays a much more dominant role in the American diet (approximately 20% of energy vs 2% to 7% in the other countries), but as yet does not contribute substantially to children's diets in the other countries. Urban–rural differences were found to be important, but narrowing over time, for China . . . whereas they are widening for Russia.'[71] What has changed in contemporary China?

Moderation on the part of children is what has been sacrificed – not traditional foods. The status of the child may be linked to the new status of what the child eats, but childhood obesity is not the result of the availability of alternative western foods; it results rather from the perceived special status of the child. No equivalent of this status existed in Japan at the time when the reduction in the birthrate was concomitant to the increase of economic status. In Japan, American fast food has been omnipresent since the 1960s. If there is an increase of childhood obesity (and the argument is that this is reflected in adult obesity), then the phenomenon has occurred only over the past decade. In the National Survey of Primary and Middle Schools in Japan, between 1970 and 1997, obesity in nine-year-old children increased three times, but the focus has been on the past decade, a decade of economic retrenchment.[72]

Yet today in China no one would imagine tying childhood obesity to anything but perceived economic improvement in the 'new economy', as part of 'Jiang Zemin's legacy'. This, of course, mimics the western 'Super size me' rationale, which sees all obesity as a result of the global 'epidemic' of 'junk food'.[73] The Chinese term kuaican (actually 'fast eating') does not have quite that pejorative sense, even though it contradicts the traditional notion that meals, at least, should be eaten slowly.[74] Yet a glance at the food diary of an eleven-year-old boy written from 7 to 14 June 1997 reveals no western 'fast food' but a mix of 'fast' but traditional noodle dishes and some candies and soft drinks.[75] This is much more in line with the traditional idea of *xiaochi* (small eats) which typified the Chinese snack culture. Certainly not an 'unhealthy' diet compared with the claims of the McDonaldization of teenage China.

The treatment for obesity also parallels the introduction of westernized forms of 'traditional' Chinese medicine. Thus 'electroacupuncture' for the treatment of overweight has melded traditional views of obesity and the newest research on human metabolism, including serum total cholesterol, triglyceride, high-density lipoprotein cholesterol and low-density lipoprotein cholesterol.[76] What comes from the West can be cured now by that which (seems) indigenous to the East (but of course is not – just like obesity).

China, like America, is suffering from a new epidemic, but one that documents its modernity; no model of oriental, primitive infectious diseases here. Rather, a claim of 'invasion from the West'. However, the negative aspects of the new economy can be confronted through the importation of models of obesity from western public health. Obesity and its treatment may both be understood as parts of a system of modernization, with all the pitfalls recognized and the 'cure' in sight.

CONCLUSION

'GLOBESITY' AND ITS ODD HISTORY

In 2001, the World Health Organization stated that there was a brand new pandemic of 'globesity' sweeping the world.[1] The present book has looked at the history of bodily fat as it has been played out in different places in the modern world. What is labeled 'globesity' is in fact the most recent iteration of an obsession with control of the body and the promise of universal health. This iteration, however, comes with an unstated and complex history. If, said the ancients, you would only – eat well, sacrifice to the gods, avoid beans – then your health would improve or, simply, never decline. There have always been changes in eating patterns. Perhaps in the twenty-first century these changes speed around the world more quickly than in the past. But the notion of a world in decay on account of the growth of girth carries with it odd and complex subtexts. What are the central implications of 'globesity'?

'Globesity', according a publication of the Pan American Health Organization in 2002, 'places the blame not on individuals but on globalization and development, with poverty as an exacerbating factor.'[2] The focus on what has been called, earlier in the twentieth century, 'diseases of extravagance' postulates a model not so much of change as of invasion: a Gresham's Law of Food in which the bad drives out the good.[3] It is the modern version of a 'degeneracy theory', with the new assumption that the ills of the world are to be traced back directly to the developed world. In this way, the model is a dietary version of the basic global warming thesis: developed nations have destroyed their environment and now they are invading the rest of the world, corrupting it. 'Nature' was benign, even kind; now it has become threatening. 'Globesity' argues that inherently healthy eating practices have been corrupted through the expansion of development and the resultant poverty. 'Fat' is a product of globalization and modernity. The utopian 'undeveloped world' – in Enlightenment jargon, the world of the 'noble savage' – is a world in which 'diseases of extravagance' could not exist, as they are a reflex of a 'civilized' model of exploitation and capitalism. The 'cure' for 'Globesity' in the twenty-first century is 'natural' or 'slow' food as a prophylactic against obesity as well as illness, as we have seen argued in the previous chapter. It is a return to the inherently 'healthy' eating practices of the edenic past.

Such views have a relatively long history. The French food writer Jean Anthelme Brillat-Savarin could write as early as 1825 that 'obesity is never found either among savages or in those classes of society, which must work in order to eat or which do not eat except to exist'. But he provided a caveat, 'savages will eat gluttonously and drink themselves insensible whenever they have a chance to'.[4] This is very much in line with Immanuel Kant's view of 'savages' and alcohol use in his lectures on anthropology, first held in 1772–3 and published in 1798.[5] Obesity, therefore, could be an illness of natural man as well as of civilization. Christoph Wilhelm Hufeland (1762–1836), one of the first modern medical commentators on dieting, recognized this when he commented that 'a certain degree of cultivation is physically necessary for man, and promotes duration of life. The wild savage does not live so long as man in a state of civilization.'[6]

The notion that the exotic can never be obese is one lodged in European tradition. Certainly humoral theory, as it was adapted in the seventeenth century, labeled exotics as being thin by their very nature:

> Besides their scituation, hot and dry,
> Doth alwaies much obesity deny.
> Who ever saw a Spaniard over fat?
> Their Countrey-man (the SUN) prohibits that,
> Who by extensive heats exhals their moist,
> Unlesse perchance some Spaniard the Seas crost,
> And Leiger lay in England then he might
> Return a Shew, and the Madrids delight.[7]

'Fat' here is clearly the preferred state of being. The age of exploration extended the notion of a healthy and an unhealthy fat to the very bounds of the world, to be documented by Enlightenment science.

This notion is also reflected in the memoirs of Georg Forster (1754–94), who accompanied Captain James Cook (1728–79) around the world in the 1770s. In 1773, Cook and Forster found themselves in Tahiti, an island they saw as the perfect natural society. Food abounded, and one did not have to work for it. Therefore gluttony was impossible, as only in a society of inadequacy did the passion for food arise. Fat men were impossible in Tahiti. Except, Forster reports, as he was walking along the shore, he saw a 'very fat man, who seemed to be the chief of the district', being fed by a 'woman who sat near him, crammed down his throat by handfuls the remains of a large baked fish, and several breadfruits, which he swallowed

with a voracious appetite'. His face was the 'picture of phleg-
matic insensibility, and seemed to witness that all his thoughts
centred in the care of his paunch'. Forster is shocked because
he had assumed that obesity of this nature was impossible in a
world of 'a certain frugal equality in their way of living, and
whose hours of enjoyment were justly proportioned to those of
labour and rest'. However, here was the proof that obesity and
society were not linked; for Forster found a 'luxurious individual spending his life in the most sluggish inactivity, and without one benefit to society, like the privileged parasites of more
civilized climates, fattening on the superfluous produce of
the soil, of which he robbed the labouring multitude'.[8] This
contradiction caused much consternation. Later on, Cook
recorded that in the language of the Society Isles the word for
'obesity or corpulence' is Oo'peea.[9]

The belief in the inherent absence of obesity among 'natural man' still echoes in Edwin James' 1819 statement that
'the Missouri Indian is symmetrical and active, and in stature,
equal, if not somewhat superior, to the ordinary European
standard; tall men are numerous. The active occupations of
war and hunting, together perhaps with the occasional priva-
tions, to which they are subjected, prevent that unsightly obesity, so often a concomitant of civilization, indolence, and
serenity of mental temperament.'[10] But this is true only of
men. John Wyeth observed in 1832 that, among the tribes of
the north-west, 'the persons of the men generally are rather
symmetrical; their stature is low, with light sinewy limbs, and
remarkably small delicate hands. The women are usually
more rotund, and, in some instances, even approach obesity.'[11]
Among 'natural peoples', it was shocking to imagine a fat man
then as it is now.

The counterpart to 'natural man' in the thought of the time
was the scholar. Thus there are regimens of dieting for intellectuals. In 1825, the American Chandler Robbins suggested

that the 'evils usually incident to sedentary and studious habits' were the result of poor diet.[12] Yet the author also noted that what was an appropriate diet for one did not always work for others (p. 58). The key was variety, temperature (cool was better than hot, such as with food eaten in nature), frequency (three meals a day, one 'liberal' and two 'slight'), the avoidance of exercise (after a meal one should rest) and 'chewing long and leisurely': 'masticate, denticate, chump, grind, and swallow'. This later becomes gospel by the end of the nineteenth century as it was espoused by Horace Fletcher, but it is, in the end, one thing that 'maintains vigour of the mind and the body, temperance becomes the parent of all other virtues', unlike what reportedly happens in the idyllic world of 'natural man' (ibid., p. 57). In 1836, William Newnham observed in London that 'overstimulation of the brain' caused 'the general health to suffer'.[13] What results is torpor, and the cure is dieting. Mastication is vital but the diet must be 'simple: animal food under dressed, roast in preference to boil'd; let vegetables be very much dressed, and bread very much baked; sauces, made dishes, an pastry to be avoided, or taken very sparingly'.[14] Water should be taken rather than wine. Indeed, the cure for the scholar is the diet of the 'natural man'.

There had been a debate about whether those natives described as 'degenerate' also suffered from obesity. As I have argued elsewhere, the classic example of the degenerate native was found in the Khoi-Khoin (Hottentots) of Southern Africa, who, through the eighteenth century and beyond, were considered to be huge and deformed.[15] Francis Galton made his reputation as one of the first 'scientist/explorers' in South Africa in 1852. His account of that trip catapulted him to fame as a geographer. He was impressed by the girth of the inhabitants, for instance when he met Nagoro, the king of the Ovampo, who was, according to one of his informants, 'the fattest man in the world and, larger than either of my wagons.'[16] He is struck initially by 'an amazingly fat old fellow . . . he was very short of breath, and . . . waddled up looking very severe. . .' (p. 129). Nagoro was indeed 'obese' (p. 202). But he was not the only one:

> Mr Hahn's household was large. There was an interpreter, and a sub-interpreter, and again others; but all most excellently well-behaved, and showing to great advantage the influence of their master. These servants were chiefly Hottentots, who had migrated with Mr Hahn from Hottentot-land, and, like him, had picked up the language of the Damaras. The sub-interpreter was married to a charming person, not only a Hottentot in figure, but in that respect a Venus among Hottentots. I was perfectly aghast at her development, and made inquiries upon that delicate point as far as I dared among my missionary friends. The result is, that I believe Mrs Petrus to be the lady who ranks second among all the Hottentots for the beautiful outline that her back affords, Jonker's wife ranking as the first; the latter, however, was slightly *passée*, while Mrs Petrus was in full *embonpoint*. I profess to be a scientific man, and was exceedingly anxious to obtain accurate measurements of her shape; but there was great difficulty in doing this. I did not know a word of Hottentot, and could never therefore have explained to the lady what the object of my foot-rule could be; and I really dared not ask my worthy missionary host to interpret for me. I therefore felt in a dilemma as I gazed at her form that gift of bounteous nature to this favoured race, which no mantua-maker, with all her crinoline and stuffing, can do otherwise but humbly imitate. The object of my admiration stood under a tree, and was turning herself about to all points of the compass, as ladies who wish to be admired usually do. Of a sudden my eye fell upon my sextant; the bright thought struck me, and I took a series of observations upon her figure

in every direction, up and down, crossways, diagonally, and so forth, and I registered them carefully upon an outline drawing for fear of any mistake; this being done, I boldly pulled out my measuring tape, and having thus obtained both base and angles, I worked out the results by trigonometry and logarithms.[17]

Yet there were counter voices who earlier saw in the Hottentots the 'noble savage', and this quality was measured by their lack of girth: 'The Hottentots are neither so small of stature nor so deformed as some have described them. . . . Both sexes . . . are well made; keeping a due medium between leanness and obesity.'[18] Were the Africans unduly large, or were they healthily 'normal'? This was answered with the development of 'tropical medicine'.

Allopathic medicine 'discovers' the evolving spread of the diseases of civilization to the world of natural human beings as an offshoot of colonial medicine. The standard handbooks of what comes to be called 'tropical medicine' are little concerned with diseases of the West present in the rest of the world.[19] Michael Gelfand, in his *Sick African* (1944), is still concerned only with the differential diagnosis of diseases of westerners in Africa and of the 'natives'. His book is much more focused on the diseases that westerners can get in Africa than on those diseases of encroaching 'civilization' suffered by Africans. Thus the only discussions of nutritional diseases are those of vitamin deficiency (such as pellagra), and the only discussion of obesity is as a specific problem of the failure of the pituitary gland.[20]

Yet there were other voices to be heard. Cyril Percy Donnison argued in 1937 that 'civilization' was the cause of disease, indeed was itself a harbinger of diseases.[21] Cultures, for Donnison, follow a series of developmental changes in terms of their psychological and social constitution. He had worked as a medical officer in Kenya, with 'a primitive native

race in a fairly isolated part of Africa' (p. vii), and was surprised at the lack of 'western' diseases such as 'high blood
pressure, diabetes, exophthalmicgoiter, peptic ulcer', which
he attributed to the absence of western civilization. For him,
western civilization, marked as it is by rapid change, was
inherently different from the ' "primitive" races' where the
'same conditions persist for a large number of generations'.
But by the 1930s he saw 'the spread of the diseases of the white
races to other parts of the world to which White civilization
has spread' (p. 6) – to 'primitive' societies as well as to 'ancient'
civilizations such as China (p. 2). Among these were 'diseases
of nutrition' (p. 29). He contrasted the inherent diseases of
starvation with those 'conditions due to overnutrition':
'Adiposity is rare in the primitive native but is seen occasion-
ally in mild degree in towns and is common in the American
Negro . . . Overnutrition seems to be associated with the civilized state' (p. 30).

The reason given for overnutrition is the 'lessened expenditure of physical energy and increased accessibility to food
supply' (p. 30). Julian Huxley made a similar remark in 1930,
on a trip to Africa, when he observed that 'almost the only fat
woman I saw in Africa worked in a Nairobi brewery' and
mused that beer might be fattening.[22] The evolution of 'western diseases' and the concomitant praise of 'natural man'
becomes the mantra that underlies 'globesity'. As late as 1981,
Hugh Trowell, looking back to the 1920s and to his years of
service in colonial Africa, commented that 'in 1926 when I
started medical work in Kenya obesity was rare. At the present
the towns of east Africa contain many fat upper class Africans,
who are grossly obese.' The cause would be the 'change of
energy foods' and the introduction of 'fibre free fat and
sugar'.[23]

Donnison condemns what seems to underlie many of the
discourses about 'globesity'. He puts both the dieting culture

and the food faddist in the camp of those who misconstrue the nature of causation about 'western diseases':

> The food faddist never finds difficulty in adapting the facts to determine the root of all evil to lie in his particular aversion, whatever that might be, whilst the newer methods of pre-serving, distributing, and preparing food stuffs present, superficially, a tempting target for attack. Others see deficient or ill-balanced diet as responsible for nearly all our ills – the criteria of balance always being obscure. (p. 65)

He notes that civilization provides access to food that 'primi-tive' societies cannot have: 'Few native races have such abun-dant access to food that consistent overnutrition is practicable' (p. 70). In western civilization more food is available because of improved transportation and agricultural methods; food is more elaborately prepared; and is also more attractively pre-sented (ibid.). But Donnison does not fault overnutrition 'in large measure' for the pathologies he associates with civiliza-tion, as he believed that one should not condemn modern dietetic practices for their negative impact. The '"primitive" races' are more often ill because of the 'unhygienic feeding' now eliminated in civilization.

In 1939, a Cleveland dentist named Weston Price (1870–1948) self-published *Nutrition and Physical Degeneration*, which argued that isolated cultures showed no tooth decay and less arthritis, diabetes, cancer and heart disease than people living in urbanized, industrialized nations.[24] This seemed to make some sense at the time, given the politics of food faddism – except that Price, like all the earliest advocates of 'natural man', also saw such societies as better, purer, and more moral than more developed societies, which would show 'character changes' and would be in a state of 'moral deterioration' (p. 353). The communities – including the

dairy farmers in Switzerland's Loetschental Valley, the abo-
rigines of Australia, the 'Gaelics' in the Outer and Inner
Hebrides, the Maoris in New Zealand and the native peoples
of ancient and modern Peru, as well as the Melanesians and
Polynesians (remember Foster) – were so varied and had such
radically different food cultures that Price focused on the
absence of processed foods, such as refined sugar and flour and
hydrogenated oils. His goal was a 'nutritional program for
race regeneration' in which deficient foods for the urban
dweller represented the equivalent of inadequate nutrition
among the 'natives'.

The result of the latter is the encroachment of civilization
on the healthy, natural world (p. 498). For Price – and his
views, on nutrition at least, have lasted – the natural human is
healthy because a natural human eats 'natural' foods – a claim
belied by the complex reality of such cultures, as observers in
the eighteenth century could well have shown him. Indeed,
Price's example comes from 'the high Alps of Switzerland',
where he found 'an excellent state of physical development and
health in adults and children living in the high valleys'. This
state of health persists in spite of the inroads of 'refined cere-
als, a high intake of sweets, canned goods, sweetened fruits,
chocolate; and a greatly reduced use of dairy products' among
the urban Swiss (p. 43). Price's explanation for the innate
'healthiness' of those Swiss, 'isolated' from the spread of
modern, manufactured and therefore corrupting foods, is their
consumption of 'rye . . . the only cereal that developed well for
human food' (p. 509). He took a piece of the rye bread and had
it analyzed, finding that 'it was rich in minerals and vitamins'.

A hundred years before, he would have found the valleys
full of 'cretins' with the stigma of degeneration, the goiter
(Basedow's disease), clearly present, as B. A. Morel (1809–73)
saw them in 1857, when he coined the term 'degeneration' on
the basis of these cases.[25] All would be suffering from severe

mental retardation – caused by the absence of iodine. Or they would have been simply 'mad' from eating rye grain covered with ergot, a poisonous fungus. Swiss public health officials intervened over the subsequent fifty years; they turned the verdant valleys of the Alps into Price's edenic landscape, where only healthy food is consumed. Even the 'natural human' needs civilization.

Today, we are attempting to reverse the argument. Eat organically, eat naturally, eat healthily, eat fat-free, eat high-fiber, eat low-carb, eat slowly (or, at least, eat slow food), and you are by definition a better person than those who don't. Companies such as 'Whole Foods' juxtapose 'conventional' and 'organic' foods much to the advantage of the 'organic', which seems closer to nature. 'Slow' food is more natural that 'fast' food. Ironically, the boom in the sale of kosher food (which only means ritually supervised) in the United States today has much the same health rationale. As one American hot dog maker's advertisement has it – kosher food answers to a higher authority – but it also carries with it the promise of more natural eating. Eat like our Paleolithic ancestors, say the advocates of the *Paleolithic Diet*, and you will be healthier and morally better attuned to the world.[26] It is the claim of the return to a state of nature that is seen as the answer to 'globesity'. Almost everything offers that promise now. But only as long as the strict guidelines of civilization as to health, cleanliness, adequate labeling, workers' rights, and fair-trade foods are not compromised (something I am sure Palaeolithic peoples could not have imagined during their extremely short, brutal, and disease-plagued lives). Maybe at the end of the day our desire to control and reform our bodies is what is truly 'modern', and the obesity epidemic is only proof of our desire to undertake this quixotic task of absolute bodily control.

NOTES

Introduction: Some Weighty Thoughts on Dieting and Epidemics

1 'George W. Bush delivers remarks on the national strategy for pandemic influenza Preparedness and response', *Congressional Quarterly* (1 November 2005).

2 Pete Moore, *The New Killer Germs: What you Need to Know about Deadly Diseases of the Twenty-First Century* (London: Carlton, 2006), p. 240.

3 'Laugh lines', *The New York Times* (6 November 2006), section 4, p. 2.

4 Quoted by George R. Armelagos, 'Emerging disease in the third epidemiological transition', in Nick Mascie-Taylor, Jean Peters, and Stephen T. McGarvey, eds, *The Changing Face of Disease: Implications for Society* (Boca Raton: CRC Press, 2004), pp. 7–22, here p. 7.

5 Cited by Pete Moore, *The New Killer Germs: What you Need to Know about Deadly Diseases of the Twenty-First Century* (London: Carlton, 2006), p. 7.

6 Jean Anthelme Brillat-Savarin, *The Physiology of Taste or, Meditations on Transcendental Gastronomy*, trans. M. F. K. Fisher (Washington: Counterpoint, 1999), pp. 243–4.

7 Hans-Georg Gadamer, *The Enigma of Health*, trans. Jason Gaiger and Nicolas Walker (London: Polity, 1996), p. 113.

8 Giorgio Colli and Mazzino Montinari, eds, *Nietzsche: Sämtliche Werke: Kritische Studienausgabe*, 15 vols (Berlin: De Gruyter, 1980), vol 3, p. 57.

9 *Obesity and Disability: The Shape of Things to Come* (Santa Monica CA: Rand Health, 2004), p. 1.

10 Walt Whitman, 'Poem of many in one', in *Leaves of Grass* (Brooklyn, New York: [s.n.], 1856), p. 181. See Robert Leigh Davis, *Whitman and the Romance of Medicine* (Berkeley: University of California Press, 1997).

11 Stanley Cohen, *Folk Devils and Moral Panics* (London: Macgibbon and Kee, 1972), p. 9. Cohen did not coin this phrase. It first appeared in Jock Young, 'The role of the police as amplifiers of deviance, negotiators of drug control as seen in Notting Hill', in Stanley Cohen, ed., *Images of Deviance* (Harmondsworth, England: Penguin, 1971), pp. 27–61, and has since been used to analyse social 'epidemics' such as 'child abuse' and the 'war on drugs'. See also Gina Kolata, 'Study aside, fat-fighting industry vows to stick to its mission', *The New York Times* (29 April 2005 (Friday)).

12 Sara Bleich, David Cutler, Christopher Murray, and Alyce Adams, *Why is the Developed World Obese?* (Cambridge MA: NBER, [March] 2007), p. 18.

13 Kelly D. Brownell and Katherine Battle Horgen, *Food Fight: The Inside Story of the Food Industry, America's Obesity Crisis and What We Can Do About It* (New York: McGraw-Hill, 2004).

14 Thomas Hobbes, *Leviathan*, edited by J. C. A. Gaskin (Oxford: Oxford University Press, 1998), p. 166.

15 Quoted from 'An indelicate delicacy', *Deseret Morning News* (Salt Lake City) (14 August 2007).

16 'An indelicate delicacy', *Deseret Morning News* (Salt Lake City) (14 August 2007).

17 Martin Luther, *Table Talk* (San Francisco: Harper, 1995), p. 60.

18 Augustine, *Confessions*, trans. R. S. Pine-Coffin (London: Penguin Books, 1961), pp. 235–7.

19 Friedrich Nietzsche, *Ecce Homo*, trans. R. J. Hollingdale (London: Penguin, 1992), p. 16.

20 Henry Lindlahr, *Nature Cure* (Chicago: Published by the Nature Cure Publishing Co., 1914), p. iii.

21 Richard A. Gordon, 'Eating disorders east and west: A culture bound syndrome unbound', in Mervat Nasser, Melanie A. Katzman, and Richard A. Gordon, eds, *Eating Disorders and Cultures in Transition* (Hove: Brunner-Routledge, 2001), pp. 1–16, here p. 12.

Chapter 1 Epidemic Obesity

1 J. Eric Oliver, *Fat Politics: The Real Story Behind America's Obesity Epidemic* (Oxford: Oxford University Press, 2006), pp. 36–59. Oliver looks at the institutional impact of the CDC and public health institutions on the spread of the metaphoric use of obesity. Certainly these are one location for such concern, but they are part of a more diffuse anxiety about the meaning of bodily shape and weight in the twentieth century.

2 *The New York Times* (July 18, 2004).

3 http://www.newswise.com/articles/2002/2/OBESITY. URI.html. http://www.newswise.com/articles/2002/2/OBESITY.URI.html (accessed 1 March 2008).

4 Ali H. Mokdad, Mary K. Serdula, William H. Dietz, Barbara A. Bowman, James S. Marks, and Jeffrey P.

Koplan, 'The spread of the obesity epidemic in the United States, 1991–1998', *JAMA* 282 (1999): 1519–22.

5 Annabel Ferriman, 'The man who will try to persuade us to give up some of life's good things', *The Times* [London], (Friday, August 7, 1981), p. 12.

6 James Wallace, 'Province is set to wage war on obesity: Queen's Park: New health promotion minister aims to treat the overweight like smokers', *The Standard* (St Catharines, Ontario) (July 16, 2005), p. A6.

7 Marilynn Marchione, 'Too fat to fight? Obesity takes a heavy toll on the military', *The Associated Press State & Local Wire* (Sunday, July 3, 2005, BC cycle).

8 Thus C. M. A. LeBlanc, 'The growing epidemic of child and youth obesity: Another twist?' *Canadian Journal of Public Health* 94 (2003): 329–30.

9 Untitled Editorial, *The Times* [London], (Tuesday, September 5, 1865), p. 6.

10 Eric Moonmanm, 'Fighting the West's man-made epidemic', *The Times* [London] (Monday, June 14, 1976), p. 12.

11 Daniel Q. Haney, 'Study says childhood obesity increasing among out-of-shape kids', *The Associated Press* (Friday, May 1, 1987, PM cycle).

12 Jeremy Lawrence, 'Obesity epidemic raises risk of children developing diabetes' *Independent* [London] (June 21, 2004).

13 David Derbyshire, 'Warning of "Epidemic"', *Telegraph* [London] (June 10, 2004).

14 Dave Fusaro, 'Fear and opportunity in vending machines: Who is better suited to solve the obesity epidemic than the food industry?', *Food Processing* 65 (2004): 6.

15 'Public sees childhood obesity as serious health threat', *Fitness & Wellness Business* Week (June 30, 2004): 28.

16 'Size up options', *MX* [Melbourne, Australia] (Wednesday, June 30, 2004): 23.

17 Great Britain Department for Health, *The Government Response to the Health Select Committee's Report on Obesity* (London: Stationery Office, 2004).

18 Richard [Madeley] and Judy [Finnigan], 'I was so right to doubt the fat children report', *Express Newspapers* (June 12, 2004).

19 Mick Hume, 'Force feeding us junk facts is distorting the truth to suit the message, *The Times* [London] (June 14, 2004, Monday).

20 Richard and Judy, 'I was so right' (above, n18).

21 S. R. Johnson, D. J. Schonfeld, D. Siegel, F. M. Krasnovsky, J. C. Boyce, P. A. Saliba, W. T. Boyce, and E. C. Perrin, 'What do minority elementary students understand about the causes of acquired immunodeficiency syndrome, colds, and obesity?' *Journal of Developmental and Behavior Pediatrics* 15 (1994): 239–47.

22 JoAnn E. Manson, Patrick J. Skerrett, Philip Greenland, and Theodore B. VanItallie, 'The escalating pandemics of obesity and sedentary lifestyle: A call to action for clinicians', *Archives of Internal Medicine* 164 (2004): 249–58.

23 Marilynn Larkin, 'Combating the global obesity epidemic', *The Lancet* 360 (2002): 1181 – as well as N. Wald and W. Willett, 'Reversing the obesity epidemic', *The Lancet* 364 (2004): 140.

24 E. B. R. Desapriya, 'Letter: Obesity epidemic', *The Lancet* 364 (2004): 1488.

25 'Epidemic', in Colin Blakemore and Sheila Jannett, eds, *The Oxford Companion to the Body* (Oxford: Oxford University Press, 2001), pp. 249–50, here 249.

26 http://www.biology-online.org/dictionary/epidemic.

27 http://en.wikipedia.org/wiki/Epidemic.

28 Tobias Venner, *Via recta ad vitam longam: or, A plaine philosphicall demonstration of the nature, faculties, and effects of all such things as by way of nourishments make for the*

preseruation of health with diuers necessary dieticall obserua-tions; as also of the true vse and effects of sleepe, exercise, excre-tions and perturbations, with iust applications to euery age, constitution of body, and time of yeere: by To. Venner, Doctor of Physicke in Bathe. Whereunto is annexed a necessary and compendious treatise of the famous baths of Bathe, lately pub-lished by the same author (London: Imprinted by Felix Kyngston, for Richard Moore, and are to be sold at his shop in Saint Dunstans Church-yard in Fleetstreet, 1628), p. 196.

29 Thomas Lodge, *A Treatise of the Plague: containing the nature, signes, and accidents of the same, with the certaine and absolute cure of the fevers, botches, and carbuncles that raigne in these times: and above all things most singular experiments and preservatives in the same, gathered by the observation of divers worthy travailers, and selected out of the writings of the best learned phisitians in this age* (London: Edward White and N. L., 1603), p. Bijb.

30 James Spedding, Robert Leslie Ellis, and Douglas Denon Heath, eds, *The Works of Francis Bacon*, 10 vols (Stuttgart: Friedrich Frommann, 1963; original publication 1857–74), 6: 33–4.

31 *The Works of John Milton*, edited by John Mitford, 8 vols (London: W. Pickering, 1851), 2: 97.

32 Virginia W. Chang and Nicholas A. Christakis, 'Medical modeling of obesity: A transition from action to experi-ence in a 20th century American medical textbook', *Soci-ology of Health & Illness* (2002): 151–77.

33 William R. Miller, ed., *The Addictive Behaviours: Treatment of Alcoholism, Drug Abuse, Smoking and Obesity* (Oxford: Pergamon Press, 1980), and Jon D. Kassel and Saul Schiff-man, 'What can hunger teach us about drug craving? A comparative analysis of the two constructs', *Advanced Behavior Research Therapy* 14 (1992): 141–67.

34 Yiying Zhang et al., 'Positional cloning of the mouse obese gene and its human homologue', *Nature* 372 (1994): 425–31. This was the key paper for any further research in the field, because it specifies the exact code of this gene.

35 'The food jihad', *St Louis Post-Dispatch* (July 11, 2005), p. B6.

36 The recent proposal that there is a vaccine developed at the Scripps Laboratory in California that may prevent weight gain in animals is such a magic bullet. The antibodies developed against the ghrelin hormone supposedly reduce the accumulation of fat. 'Scripps research scientists successfully test new anti-obesity vaccine; Prototype slows weight gain, reduces fat in animal models', *Ascribe Newswire* (31 July 2006).

37 Don C. Des Jarlais, Sandro Galea, Melissa Tracy, Susan Tross, and David Vlahov, 'Stigmatization of newly emerging infectious diseases: AIDS and SARS', *American Journal of Public Health* 96 (2006): 561–7.

38 Nikhil V. Dhurandhar, 'Infectobesity: Obesity of infectious origin', *Journal of Nutrition* 131 (2001): 2794S–7S. See also his N. V. Dhurandhar and R. L. Atkinson, 'Development of obesity in chickens after infection with a human adenovirus', *Obesity Research* 4 (1996): 24S; and N. V. Dhurandhar, B. A. Israel, J. M. Kolesar, G. F. Mayhew, M. E. Cook, and R. L. Atkinson, 'Adiposity in animals due to a human virus', *International Journal of Obesity* 24 (2000): 989–96.

39 Deborah Jones, 'Vaccine may target obesity in the future', *Agence France Presse – English* (October 18, 2005, Tuesday, 4:36 pm GMT).

40 Liz Neporent, 'Can a virus make you fat?' *New York Daily News* (November 2, 2003). Michael Woods, 'Can obesity be caused by a virus?' *Scripps Howard News Service* (September 27, 2000).

41 Tabitha M. Powledge, 'Is obesity an infectious disease?' *The Lancet Infectious Diseases* 4 (2004): 599.

42 Marilynn Marchione, 'Virus is linked to weight problems in humans', *Seattle Post-Intelligencer* (April 8, 1997).

43 Marilynn Marchione, 'Too fat to fight? Obesity takes a heavy toll on the military', *The Associated Press State & Local Wire* (July 3, 2005, Sunday, BC cycle).

44 Ibid.

45 Compare the desire to have such a quick fix, which is already present in the market. Roger Dobson, ' "Fat War" scramble to develop wonder pill to fight obesity', *Independent on Sunday* [London] (May 2, 2004). It is estimated that such a pill would be worth £2 billion per year.

46 L. D. Whigham, B. A. Israel, and R. L. Atkinson, 'Adipogenic potential of multiple human adenoviruses in vivo and in vitro in animals', *American Journal of Physiology – Regulatory Integrative & Comparative Physiology* 290 (2006): R190–4.

47 Ibid.

48 Jonathan Leake, 'Wash your hands: Obesity could be contagious', *Ottawa Citizen* (January 29, 2006): A2.

49 Nicholas A. Christakis and James H. Fowler, 'The spread of obesity in a large social network over 32 years', *The New England Journal of Medicine* 357 (4), July 26, 2007, pp. 370–9, here p. 370.

50 Gina Kolata, 'Find yourself packing it on? Blame friends', *The New York Times* (July 26, 2007).

51 The authors quote the following papers: L. D. Whigham, B. A. Israel, and R. L. Atkinson, 'Adipogenic potential of multiple human adenoviruses in vivo and in vitro in animals', *American Journal of Physiology* 290 (2006): R190–R194; and P. J. Turnbaugh, R. E. Ley, M. A. Mahowald, V. Magrini, E. R. Mardis, and J. I. Gordon, 'An obesity-associated gut microbiome with

increased capacity for energy harvest', *Nature* 444 (2006):1027–31.

52 Desapriya, 'Letter' (above, n24).

53 P. Manson, 'The need for special training in tropical medicine', *British Medical Journal* 2 (1899): 922–6, here p. 924.

54 W. I. B. Beveridge, *Frontiers in Comparative Medicine* (Minneapolis: University of Minnesota Press, 1972), p. 86.

55 Angela McLean, Robert M. May, John Pattison, and Robert A. Weiss, eds, *SARS: A Case Study in Emerging Infections* (Oxford: Oxford University Press, 2005); Christine Loh and Civic Exchange, eds, *At the Epicentre: Hong Kong and the SARS Outbreak* (Hong Kong: Hong Kong University Press, 2004); Stacey Knobler et al., eds, *Learning from SARS: Preparing for the Next Disease Outbreak* (Washington, DC: National Academies Press, 2004).

56 Arthur Kleinman and James L. Watson, 'Introduction', in Arthur Kleinman and James L. Watson, eds, *SARS in China: Prelude of Pandemic?* (Stanford: Stanford University Press, 2006), p. 1.

57 T. Hugh Pennington, *When Food Kills: BSE, E. coli, and Disaster Science* (Oxford, New York: Oxford University Press, 2003); Elinor Levy and Mark Fischetti, *The New Killer Diseases* (New York: Crown, 2003), especially pp. 1–32.

58 See Harriet Ritvo, 'Mad cow mysteries', in James L. Watson and Melissa L. Caldwell, eds, *The Cultural Politics of Food and Eating: A Reader* (Oxford: Blackwell, 2005), pp. 299–306.

59 A. C. Colchester and N. T. Colchester, 'The origin of bovine spongiform encephalopathy: The human prion disease hypothesis', *The Lancet* 366 (2005): 856–61, here 856.

60 Susarla K. Shankar and P. Satishchandra, 'Did BSE in the UK originate from the Indian subcontinent?' *The Lancet* 366 (2005): 790–1.

61 *Meat Kills: Just Say No!: 850 Million Animals Slaughtered in the UK Every Year* (Tonbridge : Animal Aid, n.d. [2002].) This is a leaflet promoting vegetarianism, highlighting recent meat-related health scares (BSE, CJD, E.coli etc.), evidence that vegetarians have 'lower overall mortality' and the unpleasantness of factory farming and slaughtering.

62 I am indebted to Anne Hardy, 'Animals, disease, and man: Making connections', *Perspectives in Biology and Medicine* 46 (2003): 200–15.

63 Zhou Xun, 'Postcard: Countdown to chaos in Beijing', *Far Eastern Economic Review* (May 15, 2003), p. 49; Robert F. Breiman et al., 'Role of China in the quest to define and control SARS', in Knobler et al., eds, *Learning from SARS* (above, n54), pp. 56–62.

64 Elaine Showalter, *Hystories: Hysterical Epidemics and Modern Culture* (London: Picador, 1997).

65 Stephen L. Muzzatti, 'Bits of falling sky and global pandemics: Moral panic and severe acute respiratory syndrome (SARS)', *Illness, Crisis & Loss* 13 (2005): 117–28.

66 Private communication, April 23, 2003. See Zhou Xun, 'Postcard' (above, n63), p. 49.

67 Private Communication, April 21, 2003.

68 Diana J. Bell, Scott Robertson, and Paul R. Hunter, 'Animal origins of SARS Coronavirus: Possible links with the international trade in small carnivores', McLean et al., eds, *SARS* (above, n55), pp. 51–60.

69 Megan Murray, 'The epidemiology of SARS', in Kleinman and Watson, 'Introduction' (above, n56), pp. 17–30, here p. 17.

70 Pete Davies, *Catching Cold: 1918's Forgotten Tragedy and the Scientific Hunt for the Virus that Caused It* (London: Michael Joseph, 1999); as well as J. S. Malik Peiris and Yi

Guan, 'Confronting SARS: A view from Hong Kong', in McLean et al., eds, *SARS* (above, n55), pp. 35–40.

71 Hong Zhang, 'Making light of the dark side', in Arthur Kleinman and James L. Watson, eds, *SARS in China: Prelude of Pandemic?* (Stanford: Stanford University Press, 2006), pp. 148–70, here p. 152.

72 Dennis Normile and Martin Enserink , 'SARS in China: Tracking the roots of a killer', *Science* 301 (2003): 297–9; Dennis Normile, 'Viral DNA match spurs china's civet roundup', *Science* 303 (2004): 292; Linda J. Saif, 'Animal corona viruses: Lessons for SARS', in Knobler et al., eds, *Learning from SARS* (above, n54), pp. 138–48.

73 *Federal Document Clearing House Congressional Testimony* (Thursday, November 17, 2005).

74 Audra Ang, 'China confirms second human death from bird flu', *The Associated Press* (November 23, 2005).

75 'Test confirms H5N1 virus in Romania's Danube Delta poultry', *Xinhua General News Service* (November 21, 2005).

76 Text by official Chinese news agency Xinhua (New China News Agency), Global News Wire – Asia Africa Intelligence Wire, BBC Monitoring/BBC Source: Financial Times Information Limited, BBC Monitoring International Reports, 2006.

77 Jia-Rui Chong, 'Bird flu defies control efforts', *Los Angeles Times* (March 27, 2006): A1.

78 Louise Barnett and Tim Moynihan, 'Killer flu will come to UK; Outbreak could claim 50,000 in Britain, millions across the world', *The Liverpool Daily Post* (August 26, 2005), p. 20.

79 'Bush flies flu powers; Prez seeks military control in case of pandemic', *Calgary Sun* (Alberta) (October 5, 2005), p. 22.

80 Ron Hutcheson, 'Bush: Military may be used for quarantine', *San Gabriel Valley Tribune* (October 4, 2005).

81 'Bush cautions against avian flu', *Saudi Press Agency* (October 5, 2005).

82 Julie Gerberding, 'Avian flu – Are we prepared?' *Congressional Quarterly* (Federal Document Clearing House Congressional Testimony) (November 9, 2005).

83 Cassandra Braun, 'Myla Goldberg transforms hard historical data about the 1918 influenza epidemic into a warm, spirited tale', *Contra Costa Times* (Walnut Creek, CA) (November 23, 2005).

84 Marisa Guthrie, ''Flu hits at critical time: May sweeps', *Daily News* (New York) (3 May 2006): 88.

85 To note a few, in addition to Pete Davies' *Catching Cold* (above, n70): John M. Barry, *The Great Influenza: The Epic Story of the Deadliest Plague in History* (New York: Viking, 2004); Alfred Jay Bollet, *Plagues & Poxes: The Impact of Human History on Epidemic Disease* (New York: Demos, 2004); Kirsty Duncan, *Hunting the 1918 Flu: One Scientist's Search for a Killer Virus* (Toronto and London: University of Toronto Press, 2003); Alfred W. Crosby, *America's Forgotten Pandemic: The Influenza of 1918* (Cambridge: Cambridge University Press, 2003); Howard Phillips and David Killingray, eds, *The Spanish Influenza Pandemic of 1918–19: New Perspectives* (London and New York: Routledge, 2003).

86 http://www.channel4.com/science/microsites/S/science/medicine/plague.html.

87 'Researchers reconstruct 1918 pandemic influenza virus effort designed to advance preparedness', *US Newswire* (October 5, 2005, Wednesday, 2:09 PM EST).

88 '1918 flu's genetic code may help fight bird flu', *US Federal News* (October 5, 2005, Wednesday, 3:05 PM EST).

89 Laurel Glaser, James Stevens, Dmitriy Zamarin, Ian A. Wilson, Adolfo García-Sastre, Terrence M. Tumpey, Christopher F. Basler, Jeffery K. Taubenberger, and Peter

Palese, 'A single amino acid substitution in 1918 influenza virus hemagglutinin changes receptor binding specificity', *Journal of Virology*, 79 (2005): 11533–6; Edward C. Holmes, Jeffery K. Taubenberger, and Bryan T. Grenfell, 'Heading off an influenza pandemic', *Science*, 309 (2005): 989.

90 Richard E. Neustadt and Ernest R. May, *Thinking In Time: The Uses of History for Decision Makers* (New York: The Free Press, 1986), pp. 48–57. Based on the report by Richard Neustadt and H. V. Fineberg, *The Swine Flu Affair: Decision-Making on a Slippery Disease* (Washington: US Department of Health, Education and Welfare, 1978).

91 Richard M. Krause, 'The swine flu episode and the fog of epidemics', *Emerging Infectious Diseases* 12 (2006): 40–3.

92 David J. Sencer and J. Donald Millar, 'Reflections on the 1976 swine flu vaccination program', *Emerging Infectious Diseases* 12 (2006): 29–33, here p. 33.

Chapter 2 Childhood Obesity

1 Kate Kyriacou, 'Big girls do cry and this is why; Life full of humiliations', *Sunday Mail* (South Australia) (April 2, 2006): 10.

2 Randall Denley, 'Talkin' 'bout my generation: Fat, lazy, stupid and poor: If the heart and stroke folks are right, we may die before we get old after all'. *Ottawa Citizen* (February 19, 2006): A10.

3 Anon., 'When you're fat, people think you're stupid', *The Irish Times* (June 10, 2005): 15.

4 World Health Organization, *Obesity: Preventing and Managing a Global Epidemic. Report of a WHO Consultation on Obesity, 3–5 June 1997*. WHO Technical Report Series, no. 894 (Geneva: World Health Organization, 1998).

5 Steve Bloomfield, 'Obesity ops double as epidemic grows', *Independent on Sunday* (London) (September 4, 2005): 12.

6 Anon., 'Mind your body', *The Straits Times* (Singapore) (April 13, 2005).

7 See the wide-ranging studies collected in Richard K. Flammenbaum, ed., *Global Dimensions of Childhood Obesity* (New York: Nova Science, 2007).

8 *Frederick Douglass' Paper* Rochester, New York (October 16, 1851), p. 8.

9 William Wadd, *Comments on Corpulency* (London: John Ebers, 1829), p. 53.

10 H. R. Klieneberger, *The Novel in England and Germany: A Comparative Study Source* (London: Wolff, 1981).

11 V. S. Pritchett, 'The Comic World of Dickens', in George H. Ford and Lauriat Lane, Jr, eds, *The Dickens Critics* (Ithaca: Cornell University Press, 1966), pp. 309–24, here 313.

12 Cited by Graeme Tytler, *Physiognomy in the European Novel: Faces and Fortunes* (Princeton: Princeton University Press, 1982), pp. 253–4.

13 Sander L. Gilman, 'On the use and abuse of the history of psychiatry for literary studies: Reading a Dickens text on insanity', *Deutsche Vierteljahrsschrift für Literaturwissenschaft und Geistesgeschichte* 52 (1978): 381–99. More recently see Max Vega-Ritter, ed. (with introduction), *Charles Dickens and Madness. Cahiers Victoriens et Edouardiens* 56 (2003): 11–116.

14 Albert Johannsen, *Phiz: Illustrations from the Novels of Charles Dickens* (Chicago: University of Chicago Press, 1956).

15 Juliet McMaster, *Dickens the Designer* (Totowa, NJ: Barnes and Noble, 1987), pp. 25, 88. See also Joyce Louise Huff, 'Conspicuous consumptions: Representations of corpulence in the nineteenth-century British novel', (Diss., George Washington University, 2000).

16 Charles Dickens, *The Pickwick Papers*, edited by James Kinsley (Oxford: Clarendon Press, 1986), p. 61.

17 Natalie McKnight, *Idiots, Madmen, and Other Prisoners in Dickens* (New York: St Martin's Press, 1993). She argues (pp. 6–7) that social class and intelligence seem to be interchangeable categories in these texts. 'The profoundly uneducated and the illiterate [are presented] in a similar fashion to the more typical idiots.' See also James A. Davies, 'Negative similarity: The fat boy in *The Pickwick Papers*', *Durham University Journal* 39 (1977): 29–34.

18 *The Christian Recorder*, Philadelphia, Pennsylvania (February 27, 1864), p. 12.

19 See Gail Turley Houston, *Consuming Fictions: Gender, Class, and Hunger in Dickens' Novels* (Carbondale: Southern Illinois University press, 1994), pp. 21–3, here 21.

20 Maria del Occidente (i.e. Maria Gowen Brooks, 1794/5–1845), *Idomen; or, the Vale of Yumuri* (New York: S. Coleman, 1843), p. 25.

21 Charles Dickens, *Sketches by Boz* (London: Oxford University Press, 1957), p. 371.

22 Wilhelm Ebstein, *Die Fettleibigkeit (Corpulenz) und ihre Behandlung nach physiologischen Grundsätzen*, 6th edn (Wiesbaden: J. F. Bergmann, 1884). Cited from *Corpulence and Its Treatment on Physiological Principles*, trans. A. H. Keane (London: H. Grevel, 1884), p. 11.

23 James Joyce, *Ulysses*, edited by Hans Walter Gabler (New York: Random House, 1986), p. 154. See Zack Bowen, 'Joyce's endomorphic encomia', *James Joyce Quarterly* 34 (1997): 259–65.

24 See S. F. Wainapel, 'Dickens and disability', *Disability and Rehabilitation* 18 (1996): 629–32 and Jonathan Loesberg, 'Dickensian deformed children and the Hegelian sublime', *Victorian Studies* 40 (1997): 625–54, where obesity is not discussed.

25 W. G. Don, 'Remarkable case of obesity in a Hindoo boy aged twelve years', *The Lancet* 73 (April 9, 1859): 363.

26 Thomas Love Peacock, *Nightmare Abbey [and] Crochet Castle*, edited by Raymond Wright (1831; Harmondsworth: Penguin, 1986), p. 364. See Douglas Hewitt, 'Entertaining ideas: A critique of Peacock's "Crotchet Castle"', *Essays in Criticism* 20 (1971): 200–12; James Mulvihill, 'Peacock's *Crotchet Castle*: Reconciling the spirits of the age'. *Nineteenth-Century Fiction* 38 (1983): 253–70.

27 McMaster, *Dickens the Designer* (above, n15), p. 88.

28 Edward Jukes, *On Indigestion and Costiveness; A Series of Hints to Both Sexes. . .* (London: John Churchill, 1833), pp. 287.

29 John Neubauer, *The Fin-de-Siècle Culture of Adolescence* (New Haven: Yale University Press, 1992).

30 Goldie Morgentaler, *Dickens and Heredity: When Like Begets Like* (New York: St Martin's Press, 2000), p. 35.

31 Christopher William Hufeland, *The Art of Prolonging Life*, 2 vols (London: J. Bell, 1797), I: 169. This is a fairly accurate translation of his *Die Kunst das menschliche Leben zu verlängern* (Jena: Akademische Buchhandlung, 1797).

32 John Tosh, *A Man's Place: Masculinity and the Middle-Class Home in Victorian England* (New Haven: Yale University Press, 1999), p. 4.

33 Louis Robinson, 'Darwinism in the nursery', *Nineteenth Century* 30 (1891): 831.

34 'The evolution of fatness', *Punch* (March 25, 1903): 203.

35 Where this comes to be clearly rejected is in the discourse of childhood and race. Thus Rabbi W. M. Feldman in his book *The Jewish Child: Its History, Folklore, Biology and Sociology* (London: Baillière, Tindall, Cox, 1917) rejects any model of the inheritance of acquired characteristics in looking at the Jewish child.

36 William Thomas Moncrieff, 1794–1857, 'The fat boy', from *An Original Collection of Songs* (London: 1850).

37 Wadd, *Comments on Corpulency* (above, n9), 131–6.

38 Johannes Joachim Becher, *Medicinische Schatz-Kammer* (Leipzig: Christoff Hülsen, 1700).

39 H. Immermann, *Handbuch der allgemeinen Ernährungsstörungen* (Leipzig: F. C. W. Vogel, 1879), p. 445.

40 Stephen C. Massett, *'Drifting about', or, What 'Jeems Pipes, of Pipesville' Saw-and-Did* (New York: Carleton, 1863) pp. 172–3.

41 A. Stayt Dutton, *The National Physique* (London: Baillière, Tindall and Cox, 1908), pp. 64–5.

42 Alexandra Minna Stern, 'Beauty is not always better: Perfect babies and the tyranny of pediatric norms', *Patterns of Prejudice* 36 (2002): 68–78.

43 Carl von Noorden, *Die Fettsucht* (Vienna: Holder, 1900). He sees pathological metabolism as a very rare cause of obesity.

44 Alfred Froehlich, 'Ein Fall von Tumor der Hypophysis cerebri ohne Akromegalie', *Wiener klinischer Wochenschrift* 15 (1901): 883–906. Froehlich's claims were very much more limited than the use to which 'Froehlich's syndrome' was put in the following decades.

45 Thus Israel Bram, 'The fat youngster', *Archives of Pediatrics* 40 (1943): 239–49 advocated thyroid extract as a treatment for all cases of obesity.

46 See the anonymous verse paraphrase of passages from the novel with illustrations by Thomas Nast: *The Fat Boy / from Dickens* (New York: McLoughlin Bros., n.d. [1870]).

47 'A case of narcolepsy', *The Lancet* 142 (July 8, 1893): 100.

48 'The fat boy of Peckham', *The Lancet* 163 (January 9, 1904): 106.

49 William Ord, 'The BRADSHAW Lecture on myxoedema and allied disorders', *The Lancet* 152 (November 12, 1898): 1243–8, here 1246.

50 E. Watson-Williams, 'Obesity', *The Lancet* 143 (August 15, 1953): 343.

51 H. Letheby Tidy, 'An address on dyspituitarism, obesity, and infantilism', *The Lancet* 203 (September 16, 1922): 567–602, references here on 600.

52 M. H. Kryger, 'Fat, sleep and Charles Dickens: Literary and medical contributions to the understanding of sleep apnea', *Clinics in Chest Medicine* 6 (1985): 555–62; K. Tjoorstad, 'Pickwick-syndromet. Fra litteraere spekulasjoner til sovnforskning', *Tidsskr Nor Laegeforen* 115 (1995): 3768–72 and Uwe Henrik Peters, *Das Pickwick-Syndrom: Schlafänfalle und Periodenatmung bei Adiposen* (München: Urban und Schwarzenberg, 1976). This syndrome continues to be used in discussion of the various implications of obesity and health. See Toshiji Saibara, Yasuko Nozaki, Yoshihsa Nemoto, Masafumi Ono and Saburo Onishi, 'Low economic status and coronary artery disease', *The Lancet* 359 (March 16, 2002): 980.

53 C. Sidney Burwell, Eugene D. Robin, Robert D. Whaley, Albert G. Bickelman, 'Extreme obesity associated with alveolar hypoventilation – A Pickwickian syndrome', *American Journal of Medicine* 21 (1956): 811–18.

54 On naming in medicine, see Charles E. Rosenberg and Janet Golden, eds, *Framing Disease: Studies in Cultural History* (New Jersey: Rutgers University Press, 1992).

55 P. Potvliege, 'Le syndrome "de Pickwick". Priorité de sa description par le duc de Saint-Simon (1675–1755)', *Nouvelle Presse Médicale* 11 (1982): 2360.

56 As have subsequent studies. See John G. Sotos, 'Taft and Pickwick: Sleep apnea in the White House', *Chest* 124 (2003): 1133–42.

57 See the trajectory marked by the following papers by Hilde Bruch, 'Obesity in childhood: Physiologic and psychologic aspects of the food intake of obese children', *American Journal of the Diseases of Children* 58 (1940): 738–81; 'Psychiatric aspects of obesity in children', *American Journal of Psychiatry* (March, 1943): 752–57 and *Eating Disorders: Obesity, Anorexia Nervosa, and the Person Within* (London: Routledge and Kegan Paul, 1974), p. 137. On contemporary views, see Jeffery Sobal and Donna Maurer, eds, *Interpreting Weight: The Social Management of Fatness and Thinness* (New York: Aldine de Gruyter, 1999) and Jeffery Sobal and Donna Maurer, eds, *Weighty Issues: Fatness and Thinness as Social Problems* (New York: Aldine de Gruyter, 1999).

58 A. H. Crisp and Edward Stonehill, 'Treatment of obesity with special reference to seven severely obese patients', *Journal of Psychosomatic Research* 14 (September 1970): 327–45, here 342.

59 S. P. Kalra, M. Bagnasco et al., 'Rhythmic, reciprocal ghrelin and leptin signaling: New insight in the development of obesity', *Regulatory Peptides* 111 (2003): 1–11.

60 Claudio Rabec, 'Leptin, obesity and control of breathing: The new aventures of Mr Pickwick', *Revista Electrónica de Biomedicina / Electronic Journal of Biomedicine* 1 (2006): 3–7.

61 A. A. Conti, A. Conti, and G.F. Gensini, 'Fat snorers and sleepy-heads: Were many distinguished characters of the past affected by the obstructive sleep apnea syndrome?' *Medical Hypothesis* 67 (4) (2006): 975–9.

62 Ellen A. Schur, Mary Sanders, and Hans Steiner, 'Body dissatisfaction and dieting in young children', *International Journal of Eating Disorders* 27 (2000): 74–82, here 77.

63 Jennifer Utter et al., 'Reading magazine articles about dieting and associated weight control behaviors among

adolescents', *Journal of Adolescent Health* 32 (2003): 78–82, here 80–1.

64 Schur, Sanders, Steiner, 'Body dissatisfaction' (above, n62), here 78–9.

65 Utter et al., 'Reading magazine articles' (above, n63).

66 Ibid., p. 60.

67 Schur, Sanders, and Steiner, 'Body dissatisfaction' (above, n62), p. 79.

68 M. Kostanski and E. Gullone, 'Dieting and body image in the child's world: Conceptualization and behavior, *Journal of Genetic Psychology* 160 (4) (1999) 488–99, here 494.

69 Martin Kostanski and Eleonora Gullone, 'Dieting and body image in the child's world:conceptualization and behavior, *Journal of Genetic Psychology* 160.4 (1999): 488–9.

70 Schur, Sanders, and Steiner, 'Body dissatisfaction' (above, n62), p. 78.

71 Alison E. Field et al., 'Relation between dieting and weight change among preadolescents and adolescents', *Pediatrics* 112.4 (2003): 900–6, here 903.

72 'Children's dieting linked to overweight', *Healthy Weight Journal* July/August (2001): 50.

73 Jean A., Lakin and Eleanor McClellan, 'Binge eating and bulimic behaviors in a school-age population', *Journal of Community Health Nursing* 4.3 (1987): 153–64, here 153.

74 Amelia Rodríguez Martín et al., 'Unhealthy eating behavior in adolescents', *European Journal of Epidemiology* 15.7 (1999): 643–48, here 646.

75 Kayo Inoko et al., 'Effect of medical treatments on psychiatric symptoms in children with anorexia nervosa', *Pediatrics International* 47 (2005): 326–8.

76 L. Bingham, 'Never too young to start slimming'. *Hull Daily Mail* (December 30, 2005): 4.

77 Viola Everitt, 'Food habits and well-being of school children', *The Elementary School Journal* 52 (February, 1952): 344–50, here 345.

78 Lancet, Editorial. 'Jamie Oliver for chief medical officer?' *The Lancet* 365 (9 April 2005): 1282.

79 Lise Belkin, 'The school-lunch test', *The New York Times Magazine* (20 August 2006): 30–5; 48; 52–5.

Chapter 3 The Stigma of Obesity

1 Werner Cahnman, 'The stigma of obesity', originally published in 1968 in the *Sociological Quarterly* 9 (1968): 283–95 and reprinted in Judith T. Marcus and Zoltan Tarr, eds, *Social Issues, Geopolitics, and Judaica* (New Brunswick NJ: Transaction Publishers, 2007), pp. 89–106, here 101.

2 Laura Crimaldi, 'Americans living large: Seats, beds get bigger', *The Boston Herald* (January 1, 2006): 4.

3 Ibid.

4 Peter Fimrite, 'Fat acceptance group celebrates living large', *The San Francisco Chronicle* (August 11, 2005): B4.

5 Lloyd Grove, 'Vogue editor rouses the fat & the furious', *Daily News* (New York) (September 19, 2005): 19.

6 Rebecca M. Puhl, Marlene B. Schwartz, and Kelly D. Brownell, 'impact of perceived consensus on stereotypes about obese people: A new approach for reducing bias', *Health Psychology*. 24 (2005): 517–25.

7 On the psychological and social implications, see Kelly D. Brownell, Rebecca M Puhl, Marlene B. Schwartz, and Leslie Rudd, *Weight Bias: Nature, Consequences, and Remedies* (New York: Guilford Press, 2005).

8 William Banting, *Letter on Corpulence, Addressed to the Public* (1st edition, 1863; 3rd edn (= 1st commercial edition), London: Harrison, 1864). With one exception, my quotations here are from the third edition. On Banting,

see Joyce L. Huff, 'A "horror of corpulence": Interrogating Bantingism and mid-nineteenth-century fat-phobia', in Jana Evans Braziel and Kathleen LeBesco, eds, *Bodies out of Bounds: Fatness and Transgression* (Berkeley: University of California Press, 2001), pp. 39–59.

9   This quotation comes from p. 28 of the original edition; see note 8 above.

10   Banting, *Letter on Corpulence* (above, n8), p. 14.

11   William E. Aytoun, 'Banting on corpulence', *Blackwood's Edinburgh Magazine* 96 (November 1864): 607–17, here 609.

12   Jean Anthelme Brillat-Savarin, *The Physiology of Taste or, Meditations on Transcendental Gastronomy*, trans. M. F. K. Fisher (Washington: Counterpoint, 1999), p. 245.

13   Banting, *Letter on Corpulence* (above, n8), p. 13.

14   William Harvey, *On Corpulence in Relation to Disease: With Some Remarks on Diet* (London: Henry Renshaw, 1872), p. 69.

15   Banting, *Letter on Corpulence* (above, n8), pp. 22–3.

16   A. W. Moore, *Corpulency, i.e., Fat, or Emponpoint, in Excess* (London: For the Author by Frederick William Ruston, 1857), pp. 12–13.

17   Watson Bradshaw, *On Corpulence* (London: Philip & Son, 1864), p. iii.

18   'A London Physician', *How to Get Fat or the Means of Preserving the Medium Between Leanness and Obesity* (London: John Smith, 1865).

19   S. Weir Mitchell, *Fat and Blood and How to Make Them* (Philadelphia: Lippincott, 1877), p. 16.

20   Harvey, *On Corpulence* (above, n14), p. vi.

21   Ibid., p. viii.

22   Banting, *Letter on Corpulence* (above, n8), p. 7.

23   Harvey, *On Corpulence* (above, n14), p. ix.

24   Aytoun, 'Banting on corpulence' (above, n11), p. 609.

25 Harvey, *On Corpulence* (above, n14), pp. 129–48.

26 J. Nichols, 'SHAKSPEARE'S DOCTORS', *The Lancet*, 83 (May 7, 1864): 518.

27 Wilhelm Ebstein, *Die Fettleibigkeit (Corpulenz) und ihre Behandlung nach physiologischen Grundstätzen*, 6th edn (Wiesbaden: J. F. Bergmann, 1884), here p. 2. Cited from *Corpulence and Its Treatment on Physiological Principles*, trans. A. H. Keane (London: H. Grevel, 1884), p. 9.

28 Max von Gruber, *Hygiene of Sex* (Baltimore: Williams & Wilkins, 1926), p. 82.

29 H. Immermann, *Handbuch der allgemeinen Ernährungsstörungen* (Leipzig: F. C. W. Vogel, 1879), p. 445.

30 'Homburg: From our roaming correspondent', *The Lancet* 108 (September 2, 1878): 341–2.

31 Ian Skottowe, 'The management of the psychoses of middle life', *The Lancet* (July 27, 1929): 167–9, here 167.

32 W. S. Gilbert, *The Bab Ballads*, edited by James Ellis (Cambridge: Harvard/Belknap Press, 2003), pp. 133–4, here 134.

33 Francis Toye, *Giuseppe Verdi: His Life and Works* (New York: Horizon, 1983), p. 234.

34 Angelo Mosso, *La fatica* (Milano: Treves, 1891); it was widely translated. All quotations here are from Angelo Mosso, *Fatigue*, translated by Margaret Drummond and W. B. Drummond (London: Swan Sonnenschein; New York : G. P. Putnam's, 1906).

35 Cited in *'Falstaff', commedia lirica in tre atti di Arrigo Boito, musica di Guisppe Verdi* (Milan: Ricordi, [1893]), p. 48. See also James A. Hepokoski, *Guiseppe Verdi: 'Falstaff'* (Cambridge: Cambridge University Press, 1983), pp. 138–44, and Julian Budden, 'Falstaff: Verdi e Shakespeare', *Falstaff: Città di Parma, Teatro Regio (stagione lirica 1994–1995)* (Parma: Teatro Regio), pp. 41–7.

36 See here the recent discussion by Emanuele Senici, 'Verdi's *Falstaff* in Italy's *fin de siècle*', *The Musical Quarterly* 85 (2001): 274–311; on Wagner, see pp. 299–302.

37 All references are to the score Giuseppe Verdi, *Falstaff* (New York: Dover, 1980 (original publication 1893)), here pp. 47–50.

38 Patricia Parker, *Literary Fat Ladies: Rhetoric, Gender, Property* (Methuen: London and New York, 1987), p. 14.

39 V. S. Pritchett, 'The comic world of Dickens', in George H. Ford and Lauriat Lane, Jr, eds, *The Dickens Critics* (Ithaca: Cornell University Press, 1966), pp. 309–24, here 313.

Chapter 4 Obesity as an Ethnic Problem

1 Anon., 'Ministerin Renate Künast will Ernährungsbewegung gegen Übergewicht bei Kindern', *Frankfurter Allgemeine Zeitung* (June 11, 2004), p. 10.

2 Julius Preuss, *Biblical and Talmudic Medicine*, trans. Fred Rosner (New York: Sanhedrin press, 1978), p. 215. All biblical quotations other than those from secondary sources are from the King James' Bible; all quotations from the Talmud other than those from secondary sources (such as Preuss) are from Isidore Epstein, ed. and trans., *Hebrew-English Edition of the Babylonian Talmud* (London: Soncino Press, 1965–89).

3 Jon L. Berquist, *Controlling Corporeality: The Body and the Household in Ancient Israel* (New Brunswick: Rutgers University Press, 2002), pp. 34–5.

4 Cited from Daniel Boyarin, 'The great fat massacre: Sex, death, and the grotesque body in the Talmud', in Howard Eilberg-Schwartz, ed., *People of the Body: Jews and Judaism from an Embodied Perspective* (Albany: State University of New York Press, 1992), pp. 69–100, here 88. I am using Boyarin's rather contemporary translation. The Soncino

translation follows: '"Rejoice, my heart! If matters on which thou [*sc.* the heart] art doubtful are thus, how much more so those on which thou art certain! I am well assured that neither worms nor decay will have power over thee." Yet in spite of this, his conscience disquieted him. Thereupon he was given a sleeping draught, taken into a marble chamber, and had his abdomen opened, and a basketsful of fat removed from him and placed in the sun during Tammuz and Ab, and yet it did not putrefy. But no fat putrefies! – [True,] no fat putrefies; nevertheless, if it contains red streaks, it does. But here, though it contained red streaks, it did not. Thereupon he applied to himself the verse, My flesh too shall dwell in safety.'

5 Toby Gelfand, '"Mon Cher Docteur Freud": Charcot's unpublished correspondence to Freud, 1888–1893', *Bulletin of the History of Medicine* 62, 563–88, here 574.

6 George Henry Lane Fox Pitt-Rivers, *The Clash of Culture and the Contact of Races* (London: Routledge, 1927), p. 82.

7 Jean Frumusan, *The Cure of Obesity*, trans. Elaine A. Wood (London: John Bale, 1930), p. 9.

8 Robert Saundby, 'Diabetes mellitus', in Thomas Clifford Allbutt, ed., *A System of Medicine* (London: Macmillan, 1897), pp. 197–9.

9 W. F. Christie, *Obesity: A Practical Handbook for Physicians* (London: William Heinemann, 1937), p. 31.

10 M. J. Oertel, 'Obesity', in Thomas J. Stedman, ed., *Twentieth Century Practice*, 20 vols, 2: *Nutritive Disorders* (London: Sampson Low, Marston and Co., 1895–1900), pp. 626–725, here pp. 647–48.

11 All citations in this paragraph are taken from Martin S. Staum, *Labeling People: French Scholars on Society, Race, and Empire 1815–1848* (Montreal and Kingston: McGill-Queens University Press, 2003), pp. 129–30 (Edwards) and 59 (Lauvergne).

12 Carl von Noorden, *Die Fettsucht* (Wien: Alfred Hölder, 1910), p. 63.

13 Joseph Jacobs and Maurice Fishberg, 'Diabetes mellitus', in *The Jewish Encyclopedia*, 12 vols (New York: Funk & Wagnalls, 1905–26), 4: 553–6.

14 Houston Stewart Chamberlain, *Foundations of the Nineteenth Century*, trans. John Lees, 2 vols (London: John Lane/The Bodley Head, 1913), 1: 366.

15 Hans F. K. Günther, *Rassenkunde des jüdischen Volkes* (München: J. F. Lehmann, 1930), p. 134.

16 Charles Bouchard, *Leçons cliniques sur les maladies des vieillards et les maladies chroniques* (Paris: A. Delahaye, 1867), quoted by Jacobs and Fishberg, 'Diabetes mellitus' (above, n13), p. 556.

17 Joseph Jacobs and Maurice Fishberg, 'Diathesis', in *The Jewish Encyclopedia*, 12 vols (New York: Funk & Wagnalls, 1905–26), 4: 574.

18 Leonard Williams, *Obesity* (London: Humphrey Milford / Oxford University Press, 1926), p. 53.

19 See Jean Leray, *Embonpoint et Obésité* (Paris: Masson et cie, 1931), pp. 11–12; W. F. Christie, *Surplus Fat and How to Reduce It* (London: William Heinemann, 1927), which begins with a long discussion of racial predisposition to fat, pp. 1–8.

20 W. H. Sheldon, S. S. Stevens, and W. B. Tucker, *The Varieties of Human Physique* (New York: Harper & Brothers, 1940), p. 221.

21 Richard M. Goodman, *Genetic Disorders among the Jewish People* (Baltimore: Johns Hopkins, 1979), pp. 334–41, citing K. Schmidt-Nielsen et al., 'Diabetes mellitus in the sand rat induced by standard laboratory diets', *Science* 143 (1964): 689. See also A. E. Mourant, Ada C. Kopec, Kazimiera Domaniewska-Sobczak, *The Genetics of the Jews* (Oxford: Clarendon Press, 1978).

22 See Reinhard Heitkamp, *Hilde Bruch (1904–1984): Leben und Werke* (Diss. Köln, 1987); Hilde Bruch, 'Obesity in childhood and personality development. 1941', *Obesity Research* 5 (March, 1997): 157–61; Joanne Hatch Bruch, *Unlocking the Golden Cage: An Intimate Biography of Hilde Bruch* (New York: Gurze, 1996); Joan Jacobs Brumberg, *Fasting Girls: The Emergence of Anorexia Nervosa as a Modern Disease* (Cambridge MA: Harvard University Press, 1988).

23 Hilde Bruch, *The Importance of Overweight* (New York: Norton, 1957), p. 5.

24 Hilde Bruch, 'Gaswechseluntersuchungen über die Erholung nach Arbeit bei einigen gesunden und kranken Kindern' (Diss. Freiburg i. Br., 1928), p. 10. Simultaneously published in the *Jahrbuch für Kinderheilkunde* 121 (1928): 7–28.

25 Sander Gilman, *Freud, Race, and Gender* (Princeton: Princeton University Press, 1993).

26 Sigmund Freud, 'Psychical (or mental) treatment (1890)', in Sigmund Freud, *Standard Edition of the Complete Psychological Works*, edited and translated by J. Strachey, A. Freud, A. Strachey, and A. Tyson, 24 vols (London: Hogarth, 1955–74), 1: 283–284.

27 Felix Deutsch, 'Studies in pathogenesis: biological and psychological aspects', *Psychoanalytic Quarterly* 2 (1933): 225–43, here pp. 235–6.

28 Franz Wittels, 'Mona Lisa and feminine beauty: A study in bisexuality', *International Journal of Psycho-Analysis* 15 (1934): 25–40, here p. 28.

29 A. H. Vander (1944), Review of 'Hilde Bruch, *Obesity in Childhood*', *Psychoanalytic Quarterly* 13 (1944): 131.

30 A. H. Crisp and Edward Stonehill, 'Treatment of obesity with special reference to seven severely obese patients', *Journal of Psychosomatic Research*, 14 (September 1970): 327–45, here p. 342.

31 Henry B. Richardson, 'Obesity and neurosis', *Psychiatric Quarterly* 20 (1946): 400–24.

32 R.N. Aruffo, 'Lactation as a denial of separation', *Psychoanalytic Quarterly*, 40 (1971): 100–22.

33 S. Aronson, 'The bereavement process in children of parents with AIDS', *Psychoanalytic Study of the Child* 51 (1996): 422–35.

34 J.R. Bemporad, E. Beresin, J.J. Ratey, G. O'Driscoll, K. Lindem, and D.B. Herzog, 'A psychoanalytic study of eating disorders', *Journal of the American Academy of Psychoanalysis* 20 (1992): 509–31.

35 Daniel Patrick Moynihan, *The Negro Family: The Case for National Action* (Washington DC: Office of Policy Planning and Research United States Department of Labor, 1965): 'From the wild Irish slums of the 19th century Eastern seaboard, to the riot-torn suburbs of Los Angeles, there is one unmistakable lesson in American history; a community that allows a large number of men to grow up in broken families, dominated by women, never acquiring any stable relationship to male authority, never acquiring any set of rational expectations about the future – that community asks for and gets chaos. Crime, violence, unrest, disorder – most particularly the furious, unrestrained lashing out at the whole social structure – that is not only to be expected; it is very near to inevitable. And it is richly deserved' (p. 34).

36 Psyche A. Williams-Forson, *Building Houses out of Chicken Legs: Black Women, Food, and Power* (Chapel Hill NC: University of North Carolina Press, 2006).

37 Jane Wardle, Susan Carnell, Claire M. A. Haworth, and Robert Plomin, 'Evidence for a strong genetic influence on childhood adiposity despite the force of the obesogenic environment', *American Journal of Clinic Nutrition* 87 (2008): 398–404.

Chapter 5 Regions of Fat

1 Krista M. C. Cline and Kenneth F. Ferraro, 'Does religion increase the prevalence and incidence of obesity in adulthood?' *Journal for the Scientific Study of Religion* 45 (2006): 269–81.

2 Kenneth F. Ferraro, 'Firm believers? Religion, body weight, and well-being', *Review of Religious Research* 39 (1998): 224–44.

3 See the work of Noel Ignatiev, *How the Irish Became White* (New York: Routledge, 1995) and Eric L. Goldstein, *The Price of Whiteness: Jews, Race, and American Identity* (Princeton: Princeton University Press, 2006).

4 Susan Gubar, *Racechanges: White Skin, Black Face in American Culture* (New York: Oxford University Press, 1997).

5 For a very comprehensive overview of the case of African–American obesity, see Eric J. Bailey, *Food Choice and Obesity in Black America: Creating a New Cultural Diet* (Westport CN: Praeger, 2006), here p. ix.

6 James C. Cobb, *Away Down South: A History of Southern Identity* (New York: Oxford University Press, 2005).

7 All references to Margaret Mitchell's *Gone With the Wind* are to the New York Warner Books 1999 edition. See p. 589 (here) and p. 144 (further down).

8 M. M. Manring, *Slave in a Box: The Strange Career of Aunt Jemima* (Charlottesville VA: University Press of Virginia, 1998).

9 Mitchell, *Gone With the Wind* (above, n7), here p. 421 and further down p. 32. See also David O'Connell, *The Irish Roots of Margaret Mitchell's Gone With the Wind* (Decatur GA: Claves and Petry, 1996).

10 Neal Gabler, *An Empire of Their Own: How the Jews Invented Hollywood* (New York: Anchor, 1989), p. 290.

11 Jill Watts, *Hattie McDaniel: Black Ambition, White Hollywood* (New York: Amistad, 2005), p. 40.

12 All references are to W. J. Cash, *The Mind of the South* (New York: Vintage, 1991).

13 'Decline of emigration to the United States', *Charleston Mercury* (26 February 1856).

14 'An interview with Pius IX', *New-Orleans Commercial Bulletin* (8 June 1868).

15 'A laughable occurrence', *New-Orleans Commercial Bulletin* (14 September 1833).

16 A British disease', *Georgia Weekly Telegraph* (8 April 1879).

17 S. Weir Mitchell, *Fat and Blood and How to Make Them* (Philadelphia: Lippincott, 1877), p. 15.

18 See the report in the *New-Orleans Commercial Bulletin* (8 November 1844) on 'The restoration of the Jews'.

19 Major Noah, 'Moorish ladies', *South Carolina Temperance Advocate* (July 1, 1847).

20 'The fat mans' clam bake', *The Atlanta Constitution* (September 2, 1873).

21 'Health for the people', *Charleston Mercury* (May 12 , 1856).

22 'Mr. Banting's diatetics', *Charleston Courier* (July 13, 1869).

23 'Cure for obesity', *Georgia Weekly Telegraph* (July 26, 1870).

24 'The fat men's convention', *Georgia Weekly Telegraph* (October 22, 1878).

25 'A word to the corpulent', *Georgia Weekly Telegraph* (April 29, 1879).

26 Will N. Harben, *White Marie: A Story of Georgian Plantation Life* (New York: Cassell & Company, 1889), p. 188.

27 All references are to John Kennedy Toole, *A Confederacy of Dunces* (New York: Grove Press, 1980). See also Hugh Ruppersburg, 'The South and John Kennedy Toole's *A Confederacy of Dunces*', *Studies in American Humor* 5 (1986): 118–26; Kenneth Holditch, 'Another kind of confederacy: John Kennedy Toole', in Richard S. Kennedy, ed., *Literary*

New Orleans in the Modern World (Baton Rouge LA: Louisiana State University Press, 1998), pp. 102–22; Andrei Codrescu, '*A Confederacy of Dunces*, making the natives wince', *The Chronicle of Higher Education* 46 (April 14, 2000).

28 Richard Klein, *Jewelry Talks: A Novel Thesis* (New York: Vintage, 2001).

29 All references are to to Salman Rushdie, *Grimus* (London: Granada, 1977).

Chapter 6 Chinese Obesity

1 A. C. Colchester and N. T. Colchester, 'The origin of bovine spongiform encephalopathy: The human prion disease hypothesis', *The Lancet* 366 (2005): 856–61.

2 Kathryn Jean Edgerton, 'The semiotics of starvation in late-Qing China: Cultural responses to the 'incredible famine' of 1876–1879 (Diss., Indiana University, 2002). See also Walter H. Mallory, *China: Land of Famine* (New York: American Geographical Society, 1926) for an early twentieth-century representation of China and famine.

3 'Preliminary report of committee on infant and invalid diet', *China Medical Journal* 26 (1912): 133–44.

4 Mary Stone, 'Hospital dietary in China', *China Medical Journal* 26 (1912): 298–301, here 299.

5 B. E. Read, 'Some factors controlling the food supply in China', *China Medical Journal* 25 (1921): 1–7.

6 Hartley Embrey and Tsou Ch'ing Wang, 'Analysis of some Chinese foods', *China Medical Journal* 35 (1921): 247–57.

7 W. H. Adolph and P. C. Kiang, 'The nutritive value of soy bean products', *China Medical Journal* 34 (1920): 268–75; William H. Adolph, 'Diet studies in Shantung', *China Medical Journal* 37 (1923): 1013–19.

8 Thus the journal regularly reprints summaries of western medical essays, such as one taken from the *Berliner*

Klinische Wochenschrift of March 1914 advocating 'cream and bed rest': *China Medical Journal* 29 (1915): 419–20.

9 Jean I. Dow, 'Maternity famine relief', *China Medical Journal* 36 (1922): 59–67.

10 Letter to the editor by Sargent, 'The trade in Chinese children', *China Medical Journal* 34 (1920): 695.

11 Thus in an editorial 'Relation of oriental diet to disease', *China Medical Journal* 38 (1924): 834–36, the concern is about diseases ranging from appendicitis to gall stones and cancer.

12 I am grateful to my colleague Zhou Xun of the University of Hong Kong for supplying me with these materials from Chinese libraries and archives and to Professor Zhou Gang of the Louisiana State University for the translations. On the women's magazines, see Charlotte L. Beahan, 'Feminism and nationalism in the Chinese women's press: 1902–1911', *Modern China* 1 (1975): 379–416; Jacqueline Nivard, 'L'Évolution de la presse féminine chinoise de 1898 à 1949', *Études Chinoises* 5 (1986): 157–84.

13 Shigehisa Kuriyama, *The Expressiveness of the Body and the Divergence of Greek and Chinese Medicine* (New York: Zone Books, 1999), pp. 111–51. Of importance is the new study by Larissa Heinrich, *The Afterlife of Images: Translating the Pathological Body between China and the West* (Durham: Duke University Press, 2008), which builds on my early work on medical representation in China.

14 Quoted in Vivienne Lo and Penelope Barrett, 'Cooking up fine remedies: On the culinary aesthetic in a sixteenth-century *Materia Medica*', *Medical History* 49 (2005): 395–422, here 417.

15 James L. Watson, 'Food as a lens: The past, present, and future of family life in China', in Jun Jing, ed., *Feeding China's Little Emperors: Food, Children, and Social Change* (Stanford University Press, 2000), pp. 199–212, here 208.

16 Daniel Pick, *Faces of Degeneration: A European Disorder, c.1848–c.1918* (Cambridge: Cambridge University Press, 1989).

17 Wang Dungen, 'Reforming the human body' (*'Renti Gailiang'*), *Shenbao Ziyoutan* (29 August 1911: Tuesday), p. 3.

18 Mao Zedong, 'A study of physical education' (April, 1917), in *Mao's Road to Power: Revolutionary Writings 1912–1949*, edited by Stuart R. Schram, 5 vols (Armonk NY: M.E. Sharpe, 1992–9), vol. 1 (1992): 113–27. I am grateful to my colleague Zhou Xun for this reference. See also Andrew D. Morris, *Marrow the Nation: A History of Sport and Physical Culture in Republican China* (Berkeley/Los Angeles: University of California Press, 2004), pp. 17–46.

19 Watson, 'Food as a lens' (above, n15), p. 208.

20 Shuhui and Weiseng, 'On obesity' ('Lun Feipang Zhi Bing'), *Funu Shibao* [*Women's Newspaper*] 10 (April, 1913), pp. 26–8.

21 Wilhelm Ebstein, *Die Fettleibigkeit (Corpulenz) und ihre Behandlung nach physiologischen Grundsätzen*, 6th edn (Wiesbaden: J. F. Bergmann, 1884), p. 10.

22 Daizuo, 'Keep the body slim' ('Jianshou Ja'), *Jiating Zizhi* [*Family Magazine*] 3 (1922), pp. 1–4, here p. 1.

23 W. S. Hedley, *Therapeutic Electricity and Practical Muscle Testing* (Philadelphia: P. Blakiston's Son and Co., 1900), p. 209–10.

24 Zhou Zhenyu, 'The cause and danger of female obesity' ('Funu Feipang De Yuanyin He Haichu'), *Xin Nuxing* [*The New Woman*] 1 (1926), pp. 42–5. Published in Shanghai, this journal had a reputation for its views on sexuality and health.

25 'What causes obesity?' *JAMA* (September 27, 1924): 1003.

26 See my *Fat Boys: A Slim Book* (Lincoln: University of Nebraska Press, 2004).

27 Qihui, 'Tragedy at the dinner table' ('Canzhuoshang De Beiju'), *Liangyou* 167 (June 1941), pages unnumbered.

28 Watson, 'Food as a lens' (above, n15), p. 208.

29 Jasper Becker, *Hungry Ghosts: China's Secret Famine* (London: J. Murray, 1996).

30 Colin Campbell and Junshi Chen, 'Diet and chronic degenerative diseases: A summary of results from an eco-logical study in rural China', in Norman J. Temple and Denis P. Burkitt, eds, *Western Diseases: their Dietary Prevention and Reversibility* (Totowa NJ: Humana Press, 1994), pp. 67–118.

31 Longde Wang, Lingzhi Kong, Fan Wu, Yamin Bai, and Robert Burton, 'Preventing chronic diseases in China', 366 (19 November 2005–25 November 2005): 1821–4, here 1821; see also Dongfeng Gu, Kristi Reynolds, Xigui Wu, Jing Chen, Xiufang Duan, Robert F. Reynolds, Paul K. Whelton, and Jiang He, 'Prevalence of the metabolic syndrome and overweight among adults in China', *The Lancet*, 365 (16 April 2005–22 April 2005): 1398–1405.

32 Roddey Reid, *Globalizing Tobacco Control: Anti-Smoking Campaigns in California, France and Japan* (Bloomington IN.: Indiana University Press, 2006).

33 See Chunming Chen and William H. Dietz, eds, *Obesity in Childhood and Adolescence* (Philadelphia: Lippincott Williams & Wilkins, 2002).

34 G. S. Ma, Y. P. Li, Y. F. Wu, at al., '[The prevalence of body overweight and obesity and its changes among Chinese people during 1992 to 2002]', *Zhonghua Yu Fang Yi Xue Za Zhi* [*Chinese Journal of Preventive Medicine*] 39 (2005): 311–5.

35 Xiaoping Weng and Benjamin Caballero, *Obesity and Its Related Diseases in China: The Impact of the Nutrition Transition in Urban and Rural Adults* (Youngstown NY: Cambria Press, 2007), p. 1.

36 W. P. Jia, K. S. Xiang, L. Chen, J. X. Lu, and Y. M. Wu, 'Epidemiological study on obesity and its comorbidities in urban Chinese older than 20 years of age in Shanghai, China', *Obesity Reviews* 3 (2002): 157–65.

37 Robert Saundby, 'Diabetes mellitus', in Thomas Clifford Allbutt, ed., *A System of Medicine* (London: Macmillan, 1897), pp. 197–9.

38 Weng and Caballero, *Obesity* (above, n35), pp. 17–18.

39 See James L. Watson, 'China's big Mac attack', in James L. Watson and Melissa L. Caldwell, eds, *The Cultural Politics of Food and Eating: A Reader* (Oxford: Blackwell, 2005), pp. 70–9.

40 James L. Watson, ed., *Golden Arches East: McDonald's in East Asia* (Stanford CA: Stanford University Press, 2006), p. vii.

41 James L. Watson and Melissa L. Caldwell, eds, *The Cultural Politics of Food and Eating: A Reader* (Oxford: Blackwell, 2005), p. 78.

42 'Yunxiang Yan, 'McDonald's in Beijing: The localization of Americana', in Watson ed., *Golden Arches East* (above, n40), pp. 39–76, here 71 and 'McDonald's in Hong Kong: Consumerism, dietary change, and the rise of a children's culture', in idem, pp. 77–1009, here 89–90.

43 David Y. H. Wu, 'McDonald's in Taipei: Hamburgers, betel nuts, and national identity', in Watson ed., *Golden Arches East* (above, n40), pp. 110–35, here 133.

44 Tsung O. Cheng, 'Obesity in Chinese children', *Journal of the Royal Society of Medicine* 97 (May 2004): 254.

45 Zumin Shi, Nanna Lien, Bernadette Nirmal Kumar, Ingvild Dalen, and Gerd Holmboe-Ottesen, 'The sociodemographic correlates of nutritional status of school adolescents in Jiangsu province', *Journal of Adolescent Health* 37 (2005): 313–22.

46 J. X. Jiang, X. L. Xia, T. Greiner, G.L. Lian, and U. Rosenqvist, 'A two year family based behaviour treatment for obese children', *Archives of Disease In Childhood* 90(2005): 1235–8.

47 B. Xie, C.P. Chou, D. Spruijt-Metz, C. Liu, J. Xia, J. Gong, Y. Li, and C. A. Johnson, 'Effects of perceived peer isolation and social support availability on the relationship between body mass index and depressive symptoms', *International Journal of Obesity* 29 (2005): 1137–43.

48 Neeraj Kaushal, *Do Food Stamps Cause Obesity? Evidence from Immigrant Experiences* (Cambridge MA: NBER, [January] 2007).

49 Jyu-Lin Chen and Christine Kennedy, 'Factors associated with obesity in Chinese–American children', *Pediatric Nursing* 31 (2005): 110–15, here 111. The American context is here vital. It is very different from that of the health worries of the Chinese diaspora in today's urban Britain. See Ruby C. M. Chau and Sam W. K. Yu, 'Pragmatism, globalism and culturalism: Health pluralism of Chinese people in Britain', in Ian Shaw and Kaisa Kauppinen, eds, *Constructions of Health and Illness: European Perspectives* (Aldershot: Ashgate, 2004), pp. 65–79.

50 G. G. Harrison, M. Kagawa-Singer, S. B. Foerster, H. Lee et al., 'Seizing the moment: California's opportunity to prevent nutrition-related health disparities in low-income Asian American population', *Cancer* 104 (2005), Suppl: 2962–8.

51 Michael McCarthy, 'Stunted children are at high risk of later obesity', *The Lancet* 349/Issue 9044 (4 January 1997): 34.

52 Weili Yan, Xiaoyan Yang, Yujian Zheng et al., 'The metabolic syndrome in Uygur And Kazak populations', *Diabetes Care* 28 (2005): 2554–5.

53 Frank Dikotter, *The Discourse of Race in Modern China* (Stanford CA: Stanford University Press, 1992).

54 Jing Tsu, *Failure, Nationalism, And Literature: The Making of Modern Chinese Identity, 1895–1937* (Stanford: Stanford University Press, 2005).

55 Jean Eid, Henry G. Overman, Diego Puga, and Mathew A. Turner, *Fat City: Questioning the Relationship Between Urban Sprawl and Obesity* (London: CEPR, [March] 2007), p. 1.

56 Goeff Dickson and Grant Schofield, 'Globalisation and globesity: The impact of the 2008 Beijing Olympics on China', *International Journal of Sport Management and Marketing* 1 (1/2): 169–79, here 169.

57 W. P. T. James, 'Appropriate Asian body mass indices', *Obesity Reviews* 3 (2002): 139. This is still being debated in 2005: Tsung O. Cheng, 'Using WHO's body mass index cutoff points to classify as overweight and obese underestimates the prevalence of overweight and obese among the Chinese', *International Journal of Cardiology* 103 (2005): 343.

58 Y. Tahara, K. Moji, S. Muraki, S. Honda, K. Aoyagi, 'Comparison of body size and composition between young adult Japanese–Americans and Japanese nationals in the 1980s', *Annals of Human Biology* 30 (2003): 392–401.

59 Naomi Moriyama, *Japanese Women Don't Get Old or Fat: Secrets of My Mother's Tokyo Kitchen* (New York: Delacorte, 2005).

60 Theodore C. Bestor, 'How sushi went global', in Watson and Caldwell, eds, *Cultural Politics of Food and Eating* (above, n39), pp. 13–20.

61 Richard Parish, 'Health promotion: Rhetoric and reality', in Robin Bunton, Sarah Nettleton, and Roger Burrows, eds, *Sociology of Health Promotion Critical Analyses of Consumption, Lifestyle and Risk* (London: Routledge, 1995), pp. 13–23.

62 T. Colin Campbell and Thomas M. Campbell II, *The China Study: The Most Comprehensive Study of Nutrition*

Ever Conducted and the Startling Implications for Diet, Weight Loss and Long-Term Health (Dallas: Benbella Books, 2005), pp. 69–110.

63 Weng and Caballero *Obesity* (above, n35), p. xi.

64 G. Li, X. Chen, Y. Jang, J. Wang, X. Xing, W. Yang, and Y. Hu, 'Obesity, coronary heart disease risk factors and diabetes in Chinese: An approach to the criteria of obesity in the Chinese population', *Obesity Reviews* 3 (2002): 167–72, here 167.

65 K. Schmidt-Nielsen et al., 'Diabetes mellitus in the sand rat induced by standard laboratory diets', *Science* 143 (1964): 689.

66 'Malnutrition hits 30 percent of China's poverty-stricken children: Survey', *Agence France Presse* (8 October 2005).

67 Clay Chandler, 'LITTLE EMPERORS: China's only children – More than 100 million of them – Make up the largest Me Generation ever. And their appetites are big', *Fortune* (October 4, 2004): 138–42.

68 Ibid.

69 D. G. Chen, X. F. Cheng, and L. L. Wang, 'Clinical analysis of 200 cases of child anorexia', *Chinese Mental Health Journal* 7 (1993): 5–6 (in Chinese).

70 Jun Jing, 'Introduction', in Jun Jing, ed., *Feeding China's Little Emperors: Food, Children, and Social Change* (Stanford: Stanford University Press, 2000), pp. 1–26, here 5.

71 L. S. Adair and B. M. Popkin, 'Are child eating patterns being transformed globally?' *Obesity Research* 13 (2005): 1281–99.

72 http://ific.org/foodinsight/2001/jf/globesityfi101.cfm.

73 From a leaflet handed out outside McDonald's in Leicester Square, London, in April 2004, which criticized McDonald's as exploiting its workers, damaging the environment, farming animals under cruel conditions and promoting food which 'is linked with a greater risk of

heart disease, cancer, diabetes and other diseases': *What's wrong with McDonald's? / Anti-McDonald's Campaign* (Nottingham: Anti-McDonald's Campaign [2004]). Certainly the major book on this topic remains Eric Schlosser, *Fast Food Nation: The Dark Side of the All-American Meal* (New York: Perennial, 2002).

74 Yunxiang Yan, 'Of hamburger and social space: McDonald's in Beijing', in Watson and Caldwell, eds, *Cultural Politics of Food and Eating* (above, n39), pp. 80–103, here p. 82.

75 Jing, ed., *Feeding China's Little Emperors* (above, n70), pp. 213–17.

76 M. T. Cabioglu and N. Ergene, 'Electroacupuncture therapy for weight loss reduces serum total cholesterol, triglycerides, and LDL cholesterol levels in obese women', *The American Journal of Chinese Medicine* 33 (2005): 525–33.

Conclusion 'Globesity' and Its Odd History

1 Tom Kuntz, 'What we said and what we meant, A to Z', *The New York Times* (December 28, 2003), p. 2.

2 Donna Eberwine, 'Globesity: The crisis of growing proportions', *Perspectives in Health* 7 (3) (2002): 6–11, here p. 8.

3 T. Colin Campbell and Junshi Chen, 'Diet and chronic degenerative diseases: A summary of results from an ecological study in rural China', in Norman J. Temple and Denis P. Burkitt, eds, *Western Diseases: their Dietary Prevention and Reversibility* (Totowa NJ: Humana Press, 1994), pp. 67–118, here p. 68.

4 Jean Anthelme Brillat-Savarin, *The Physiology of Taste or, Meditations on Transcendental Gastronomy*, trans. M. F. K. Fisher (Washington: Counterpoint, 1999), pp. 239 and 241.

5 Immanuel Kant, *Immanuel Kant's Menschenkunde. Nach handschriftlichen Vorlesungen. Nach handschriftlichten Vorlesungen*, edited by Friedrich Christian Starke (Leipzig: Die Expedition des europäischen Aufsehers, 1832), p. 299.

6 Christopher William Hufeland, *The Art of Prolonging Life*, 2 vols (London: J. Bell, 1797), pp. 169.

7 Edmund Gayton, *The art of Longevity, or, A Diaeteticall Instition* (London: Printed for the author, 1659), pp. 25–6.

8 Georg Forster, *Voyage around the World*, edited by Nicolas Thomas and Oliver Berghof, 2 vols (Honolulu: University of Hawaii Press, 2000), pp. 164–5.

9 James Cook, *A Voyage towards the South Pole, and Round the World. Performed in His Majesty's Ships the Resolution and Adventure, in the Years 1772, 1773, 1774, and 1775* (London: printed for W. Strahan; and T. Cadell, 1777), p. 347.

10 Edwin James, 1905. *Early Western Travels, Vol. 15: Part II of James's Account of S. H. Long's Expedition, 1819–1820*, edited by Reuben Gold Thwaites (Cleveland: A.H. Clark Co., 1905), p. 68.

11 John B. Wyeth, *Early Western Travels, Vol. 21: Wyeth's Oregon, or a Short History of a Long Journey, 1832: Townsend's Narrative of a Journey Across the Rocky Mountains, 1834*, edited by Reuben Gold Thwaites (Cleveland: A.H. Clark Co., 1905), p. 307.

12 Chandler Robbins, *Remarks on the Disorders of Literary Men, or, An Inquiry into the Means of Preventing the Evils Usually Incident to Sedentary and Studious Habits* (Boston: Cummings, Hillard, 1825), pp. 56–7.

13 William Newnham, *Essay on the Disorders Incident to Literary Men: And on the Best Means of Preserving Their Health*, Read before The Royal Society of Literature, 5 Nov. 1834 (London: John Hatchard and Sons, 1836), p. 3.

14 Robbins (above, n12), pp. 31–2.

15 Sander L. Gilman, 'Black bodies, white bodies: Toward an iconography of female sexuality', *Critical Inquiry* 12 (1985): 203–42.

16 Frances Galton, *Narrative of an Explorer in Tropical South Africa* (London: Ward, Lock and Co, 1890), p. 97 (originally published in 1852).

17 Ibid., pp. 53–4. On the Hottentot and her body, see also Linda E. Merians, 'What they are, who we are: Representations of the Hottentot in eighteenth-century Britain', *Eighteenth-Century Life* 17 (1993): 14–39.

18 William Mavor, *An Historical Account of the Most Celebrated Voyages, Travels, and Discoveries, From the Time of Columbus to the Present Period* (Philadelphia: Samuel F. Bradford, 1802), p. 18.

19 Thus Aldo Casttellani and Albert J. Chalman, *Manual of Tropical Medicine*, 3rd edn (London: Baillière, Tindal and Cox, 1919) do not reflect on this as a problem at all.

20 Michael Gelfand, *The Sick African* (Cape Town: Stewart Printing, 1944): diseases of nutrition, pp. 153–170; obesity, p. 306.

21 Cyril Percy Donnison, *Civilization and Disease* (Baillière & Co.: London, 1937).

22 Julian Huxley, *African View* (London: Chatto and Windus, 1931), p. 162.

23 Hugh Trowell, 'Hypertension, obesity, diabetes mellitus and coronary heart disease', in H. C. Trowell and D. P. Burkett, eds, *Western Diseases: Their Emergence and Prevention* (London: Edward Arnold, 1981), pp. 3–32, here p. 14.

24 Weston Price, *Nutrition and Physical Degeneration. A Comparison of Primitive and Modern Diets and Their Effects, etc.* (Redlands CA: Published by the Author; New York, London: P. B. Hoeber, 1939), p. 5.

25 B. A. Morel, *Traité des Degenerescences Physiques, Intellectuelles et Morales de l'espece Humaine* (Paris: Masson, 1857).

26 S. B. Eaton, Majorie Shostak, and Melvin Konner, *The Paleolithic Prescription* (New York: Harper & Row, 1988).

FURTHER READING

Adam, Gerald R. and Sharyn M. Crossman. *Physically Attractive: A Cultural Imperative*. Roslyn Heights NY: Libra, 1978.

Anspaugh, Jean Renfro. *Fat Like Us*. Durham: Generation Books, 2001.

Banner, Lois W. *American Beauty*. Chicago: University of Chicago Press, 1983.

Beller, Anne Scott. *Fat & Thin: A Natural History of Obesity*. New York: Farrar, Straus, and Giroux, 1977.

Berg, Kathleen, Dermot J. Hurley, James A. McSherry and Nancy E. Strange, and 'Rose'. *Eating Disorders: A Patient Centered Approach*. Abingdon: Radcliffe Medical Press, 2002.

Berry, Venise T. *All of Me: A Voluptuous Tale*. New York: Dutton, 2000.

Bleich, Sara, David Cutler, Christopher Murray, Alyce Adams. *Why is the Developed World Obese?* Cambridge, MA: National Bureau of Economic Research, 2007.

Boia, Lucian. *Forever Young: A Cultural History of Longevity from Antiquity to the Present*. London: Reaktion Books, 2004.

Bordo, Susan. *Unbearable Weight: Feminism, Western Culture and the Body*. Berkeley and London: University of California Press, 1993.

Braziel, Jana Evans and Kathleen LeBesco, eds. *Bodies out of Bounds: Fatness and Transgression*. Berkeley: University of California Press, 2001.

Brown, P. J. and Melvin Konner. 'An anthropological perspective on obesity'. *Annals of the New York Academy of Sciences* 499 (1987): 129–46.

Brownell, Kelly D., Rebecca M. Puhl, Marlene B. Schwartz, Leslie Rudd. *Weight Bias: Nature, Consequences, and Remedies*, New York: Guilford Press, 2005.

Campos, Paul. *The Obesity Myth: Why Americans* [sic] *Obsession with Weight is Hazardous to your Health*. New York: Gotham, 2004.

Chapkis, Wendy. *Beauty Secrets: Women and the Politics of Appearance*. Boston: South End Press, 1986.

Chernin, Kim. *The Obsession: Reflections on Tyranny of Slenderness*. New York: Harper and Row, 1981.

Cooke, Kaz. *Real Gorgeous: The Truth about Body and Beauty*. London: Bloomsbury, 1995.

Counihan, Carol. *The Anthropology of Food and Body*. New York: Routledge, 1999.

Counihan, Carol, ed. *Food in the USA*. New York: Routledge, 2002.

Counihan, Carol and Penny Van Esterik, eds. *Food and Culture*. New York: Routledge, 1997.

Coveney, John. *Food, Morals and Meaning: The Pleasure and Anxiety of Eating*. New York: Routledge, 2000.

Crister, Greg. *Fat land: How Americans Became the Fattest People in the World*. Boston: Houghton Mifflin, 2003.

Donley, Carol and Sheryl Buckley, eds. *The Tyranny of the Normal: An Anthology*. Kent: Kent State University, 1995.

Douglas, Mary. *Purity and Danger* (revised edn). London: Routledge and Kegan Paul, 2002.

Ettlinger, Steve. *Twinkie, Deconstructed: My Journey to Discover How the Ingredients Found in Processed Foods are Grown, Mined (Yes, Mined), and Manipulated into What America Eats*. New York NY: Hudson Street Press, 2007.

Fairburn, Christopher G. and Kelly D. Brownell, eds. *Eating Disorders and Obesity: A Comprehensive Handbook*. New York: Guilford Press, 2005.

Finkelstein, Eric and Laurie Zuckerman. *The Fattening of America: How the Economy Makes Us Fat, If It Matters, and What To Do About It*. Hoboken NJ: Wiley, 2008.

Forth, Christopher E. and Ana Carden-Coyne, eds. *Cultures of the Abdomen*. New York: Palgrave, 2005.

Friday, Nancy. *The Power of Beauty*. New York: Harper Collins Publishers, 1996.

Frisch, Rose E. *Female Fertility and the Body Fat Connection*. Chicago: University of Chicago Press, 2002.

Frost, Liz. *Young Women and the Body: A Feminist Sociology*. New York: Palgrave Macmillan, 2001.

Furman, Frida Kurman. *Facing the Mirror: Older Women and Beauty Shop Culture*. New York: Routledge, 1997.

Gard, Michael and Jan Wright. *The Obesity Epidemic: Science, Morality, and Ideology*. London: Routledge, 2005.

Geissler, Catherine and Derek J. Oddy, eds. *Food, Diet and Economic Change Past and Present*. Leicester: Leicester University Press and New York: Distributed in the US and Canada by St Martin's Press, 1993.

Gianoulis, Tina. 'Dieting', in Tom Pendergast and Sara Pendergast, eds, *St. James Encyclopedia of Popular Culture*, 5 vols, Detroit: St James Press, 1999, I: 706–8.

Gilman, Sander L. *Fat Boys: A Slim Book*. Lincoln: University of Nebraska Press, 2004.

Gordon, Richard A. *Eating Disorders: Anatomy of a Social Epidemic*. Oxford: Blackwell Publishers, 2000.

Griffith, R. Marie. *Born again Bodies: Flesh and Spirit in American Christianity*. Berkeley: University of California Press, 2004.

Halprin, Sara. *Look at my Ugly Face: Myths and Musings on Beauty and Other Perilous Obsessions with Women's Appearance*. New York NY: Viking, 1995.

Harris, Neil. *Cultural Excursions: Marketing Appetites and Cultural Tastes in America*. Chicago: University of Chicago Press, 1990.

Heywood, Leslie. *Dedication to Hunger: The Anorexic Aesthetic in Modern Culture*. Berkeley: University of California, 1996.

Hesse-Biber, Sharlene. *Am I Thin Enough Yet: The Cult of Thinness and the Commercialization of Identity*. New York: Oxford University Press, 1996.

Hoek, Hans Wijbrand, Janet L. Treasure, and Melanie A. Katzman, eds. *Neurobiology in the Treatment of Eating Disorders*. Chicester: John Wiley, 1998.

Hrdy, Sarah Blaffer. *Mother Nature: A History of Mothers, Infants, and Natural Selection*. New York: Pantheon Books, 1999.

Huggett, Jane. *The Mirror of Health: Food, Diet and Medical Theory 1450–1660*. Bristol: Stuart Press, 1995.

Jerrell, Donna and Ira Sukrungruang, *What are you Looking At? The First Fat Fiction Anthology*. Orlando: Harcourt, 2003.

Jerrell, Donna and Iva Sukrungruang, eds. *Scoot Over, Skinny: The Fat Nonfiction Anthology*. Orlando: Harcourt, 2005.

Kawachi, Ichiro and Sarah P. Wamala. *Globalization and Health*. Oxford and New York: Oxford University Press, 2007.

Klein, Richard. *Eat Fat*. New York: Pantheon, 1996.

Kulick, Don and Anne Meneley. *Fat: The Anthropology of an Obsession*. New York: Jeremy P. Tarcher/Penguin, 2005.

Lakoff, Robin Tolmach and Raquel L. Scherr. *Face Value: The Politics of Beauty*. Routledge & Kegan Paul, 1984.

Lambrecht, Bill. *Dinner at the New Gene Café: How Genetic Engineering Is Changing What We Eat, How We Live, and the Global Politics of Food*. New York: St Martin's Press, 2001.

Lask, Bryan and Rachel Bryant-Waugh, eds. *Anorexia Nervosa and Related Eating Disorders in Childhood and Adolescence* (2nd edn). Hove, East Sussex: Psychology Press, 2000.

LeBesco, Kathleen. *Revolting Bodies: The Struggle to Redefine Fat Identity*. Amherst: University of Massachusetts Press, 2004.

Leith, William. *The Hungry Years: Confessions of a Food Addict*, London: Bloomsbury, 2005.

Levenstein, Harvey A. *Revolution at the Table: The Transformation of the American Diet*. New York: Oxford University Press, 1988.

Lichtenstein, A. H. 'Dietary fat: A history', *Nutrition Reviews* 57 (1999): 11–14.

Lyons, M., J. I. M. Faust, R. B. Hemmes, D. R. Buskirk, J. Hirsch, and J. B. Zabriskie, 'A virally induced obesity syndrome in mice', *Science* 216 (1982): 82–5.

Manton, Catherine. *Fed Up: Women and Food in America*. Westport CT: Bergin & Garvey, 1999.

Marwick, Arthur. *Beauty in History: Society, Politics, and Personal Appearance*. London: Thames and Hudson, 1988.

McIntosh, Elaine N. *American Food Habits in Historical Perspective*. Westport, CT: Praeger, 1995.

Milman, Marcia. *Such a Pretty Face: Being Fat in America*. New York: W.W. Norton & Company, 1980.

Mintz, Sidney W. *Tasting Food, Tasting Freedom: Excursions into Eating, Culture, and the Past*. Boston: Beacon Press, 1996.

Mitchell, James E. *The Outpatient Treatment of Eating Disorders*. Minneapolis: University of Minnesota Press, 2001.

Nasser, Mervant. *Cultural and Weight Consciousness*. London: Routledge, 1997.

Nasser, Mervant, Melanie Katzman, and Richard A. Gordon. *Eating Disorders and Cultural in Transition*. Hove, East Sussex: Brunner-Routledge, 2001.

Obesity and Disability: The Shape of Things to Come (2004), Santa Monica CA: Rand Health.

Oliver, J. Eric. *Fat Politics: The Real Story: Politics behind America's Obesity Epidemic*. New York: Oxford University Press, 2005.

Orbach, Susie. *Fat is a Feminist Issue: How to Lose Weight Permanently Without Dieting*. New York: Paddington Press, 1978.

Owen, John B., Janet L. Treasure and David A. Collier, eds. *Animal Models – Disorders of Eating Behaviour and Body Composition*. Dordrecht: Kluwer, 2001.

Paglia, Carmille. *Sexual Personae. Art and Decadence from Nefertiti to Emily Dickinson*. New Haven: Yale University Press, 1990.

Pool, Robert. *Fat: Fighting the Obesity Epidemic*. Oxford: Oxford Univesity Press, 2001.

Rotberg, Robert I. and Theodore K. Rabb, eds. *Hunger and Hunger: The Impact of Changing Food Production and Consumption Patterns on Society*. Cambridge: Cambridge University Press, 1985.

Sartore, Richard. *Body Shaping: Trends, Fashions, and Rebellions*. Commack NY: Nova Science Publishers, 1996.

Schwartz, Hillel. *Never Satisfied: A Cultural History of Diets, Fantasies, and Fat*. New York: The Free Press, 1986.

Seid, Roberta Pollack. *Never Too Thin: Why Women Are at War with Their Bodies*. New York: Prentice Hall, 1989.

Simoons, Frederick J. *Food in China: A Cultural and Historical Inquiry*. Boca Raton: CRC Press, 1991.

Sobal, Jeffrey and Donna Maurer, eds. *Interpreting Weight: The Social Management of Fatness and Thinness*. New York: Aldine de Gruyter, 1999.

Stearns, Peter N. *Fat History: Bodies and Beauty in the Modern West*. New York: New York University Press, 1997.

Thone, Ruth Raymond. *Fat – A Fate Worse than Death: Women, Weight, and Appearance*. New York: The Haworth Press, 1997.

Wahlqvist, Mark L. 'Critical nutrition events in human history'. *Asia Pacific Journal of Clinical Nutrition* 1 (1992): 101–5.

Waldfogel, Sabra. 'The body beautiful, the body hateful: Feminine body image and the culture of consumption in 20th-century America', Diss. University of Minnesota, 1986.

Watson, James L. and Melissa Caldwell, eds. *The Cultural Politics of Food and Eating*. Malden MA: Blackwell Publishing, 2005.

Weng, Xiaoping and Benjamin Caballero. *Obesity and Its Related Diseases in China: The Impact of the Nutrition Transition in Urban and Rural Adults*, Youngstown NY: Cambria Press, 2007.

Williams-Forson, Psyche A. *Building Houses out of Chicken Legs: Black Women, Food, and Power*. Chapel Hill NC: University of North Carolina Press, 2006.

Wolf, Naomi. *The Beauty Myth: How Images of Female Beauty are Used Against Women*. New York: W. Morrow, 1991.

Wylie, Diana. 'Disease, diet, gender: Late twentieth-century perspectives on empire', *Oxford History of the British Empire*. Oxford: Oxford University Press, 1999. 5: 277–89.

INDEX

New Cultural Movement, 141
Newnham, William, 168
New Orleans, 123, 131–6
New Orleans Commercial Bulletin,
    129
new woman, 113, 141, 207n24
Nicholas Nickleby (Dickens), 60
Nicolai, Otto, 93, 94
Niemeyer, Felix, 85
Nietzsche, Friedrich, 6, 12
Nineteenth Century, The (journal), 59
Noah, Mordecai, 129–30
noble savage, 165, 170
Noeggerath, Carl, 113
Noorden, Carl von, 64, 191n43
Norwalk (Connecticut), 130
'Numb3rs' (television series), 38
Nutrition and Physical Degeneration
    (Price), 172

obesity: among Africans, 171; in
    Asia versus the West, 155–6;
    Brillat-Savarin on cause of, 4–5;
    as cause of morbidity and
    mortality, 18; cheap, available
    food as cause of, 9–10; in China,
    137–63; Christian attitude
    toward, 104; diabetes associated
    with, 18, 108, 111; dietary fat
    seen as cause of, 33–4; diet
    culture dominates marketplace
    as 'cure' for, 4; as ethnic
    problem, 101–22; external versus
    internal causation of, 63–4, 112,
    122; as failure to adapt rapidly to
    changing surroundings, 112,
    159; genetics seen as cause of, 3,
    21, 70–1, 121; globalization of,
    7, 13; Jews seen as predisposed
    to, 106–8; leptin regulation seen
    as cause of, 70–1; as major public
    health issue of new millennium,
    15; Moleschott on creativity and,
    92; moral panic about, 9, 21–2,
    102, 121; moral panic about Jews
    and, 102–5; as national rather
    than individual problem, 3;

natural man seen as immune to,
    165–7; person-to-person spread
    of, 26–7; pill for fighting,
    182n45; plurality of causes of,
    20–1; poverty associated with,
    21; psychoanalytic approach to,
    69, 112–22; and race, 102, 114;
    reconceptualization of, 14;
    religious hierarchy of, 124; shift
    from concern with male to
    concern with female, 113; the
    South associated with, 123–36;
    stoutness distinguished from, 8,
    129; vaccine for, 23, 26, 181n36;
    Venner on, 19–20; 'war against',
    3, 15–16; Whitman on, 8–9. *See
    also* childhood obesity; fat
    people; globesity; morbid
    obesity; obesity as disease;
    obesity epidemic; stigma of
    obesity
obesity as disease: Bruch's
    psychological theory contrasted
    with, 118; Harvey on, 84–5; as
    infectious disease, 22–7, 43;
    *Journal of the American Medical
    Association* on, 144; Medicare
    accepts, 14–15; obesity as sin
    contrasted with, 104–5; obesity
    epidemic concept presupposes,
    18; Philadelphia *Christian
    Recorder* on, 49; and race, 102;
    and self-help, 82; Shuhui and
    Weiseng's 'On Obesity' on,
    141–2; Venner on, 20; viral
    cause alleged, 2, 22–7, 33
obesity epidemic, 16–22; and
    Bush's evocation avian 'flu
    epidemic, 2; in China, 8,
    148–51, 155, 159; in Germany,
    101–2; odd demographics of,
    25; person-to-person spread of
    obesity and, 26–7; as political
    issue, 17; as proof of our desire
    for absolute bodily control, 174;
    stigma of obesity associated
    with claims of, 79